LIFE STORIES OF
100 AMERICAN
HEROES

ony • Neil Armstrong • Crispus Attucks • James Baldwin • Clara E
ey • John Brown • Ralph Bunche • Richard Byrd • Kit Carson • Ra
Davy Crockett • Benjamin O. Davis Jr. • Thomas A. Dooley • Fred
nin Franklin • Varian Fry • Geronimo • John Glenn • Ulysses S. Gra
atrick Henry • Wild Bill Hickok • Samuel Houston • Anne Hutchin
ief Joseph • John F. Kennedy • Bob Kerrey • Billie Jean King • Ma
wis and William Clark • Abraham Lincoln • Charles Lindbergh • Do
all • John McCain • John Muir • Audie Murphy • Thomas Paine • R
n • Oliver Hazard Perry • John J. Pershing • Molly Pitcher • Pocah
y Ride • Matthew B. Ridgway • Jackie Robinson • Eleanor Roosev
n Shepard • Robert Smalls • Elizabeth Cady Stanton • Anne Sulli
rge Washington • Roger Williams • Chuck Yeager • Alvin York • Sa
Neil Armstrong • Crispus Attucks • James Baldwin • Clara Barton •
n Brown • Ralph Bunche • Richard Byrd • Kit Carson • Rachel Cars
kett • Benjamin O. Davis Jr. • Thomas A. Dooley • Frederick Doug
in • Varian Fry • Geronimo • John Glenn • Ulysses S. Grant • Woo
enry • Wild Bill Hickok • Samuel Houston • Anne Hutchinson • A
n • John F. Kennedy • Bob Kerrey • Billie Jean King • Martin Luthe
liam Clark • Abraham Lincoln • Charles Lindbergh • Douglas MacA
McCain • John Muir • Audie Murphy • Thomas Paine • Rosa Parks
er Hazard Perry • John J. Pershing • Molly Pitcher • Pocahontas •
Matthew B. Ridgway • Jackie Robinson • Eleanor Roosevelt • Fra
d • Robert Smalls • Elizabeth Cady Stanton • Anne Sullivan • Tecu
ngton • Roger Williams • Chuck Yeager • Alvin York • Samuel Ada
trong • Crispus Attucks • James Baldwin • Clara Barton • Daisy Ba
vn • Ralph Bunche • Richard Byrd • Kit Carson • Rachel Carson • Jo
tt • Benjamin O. Davis Jr. • Thomas A. Dooley • Frederick Douglas
in • Varian Fry • Geronimo • John Glenn • Ulysses S. Grant • Woo
enry • Wild Bill Hickok • Samuel Houston • Anne Hutchinson • A
n • John F. Kennedy • Bob Kerrey • Billie Jean King • Martin Luthe
liam Clark • Abraham Lincoln • Charles Lindbergh • Douglas Maca
McCain • John Muir • Audie Murphy • Thomas Paine • Rosa Parks

2001

★VALUES inACTION™
LIFE STORIES OF
100 AMERICAN HEROES

by
Joanne Mattern

kidsbooks
Incorporated

PHOTO CREDITS

AP/Wide World: pp. 23, 50, 81, 147, 153, 157, 177, 212, 308, 342, 344, 363, 373, 385, 390, 433, 467, 473, 497, 539, 569 • **Library of Congress, Prints and Photography Division:** pp. 92, 97, 121, 130, 135, 141, 201, 264, 330, 338, 439, 521 • **The Granger Collection:** pp. 102, 171, 207, 241, 286, 314, 369, 422, 427, 445, 451, 491, 545, 551 • **Rachel Carson History Project:** p. 108 • **The Kansas State Historical Society, Topeka, Kansas:** p. 125 • **The John F. Kennedy Presidential Library:** pp. 275, 276 • **The Franklin D. Roosevelt Presidential Library:** p. 479

On the cover, left to right:

Top row—Jackie Robinson (AP/Wide World) • Molly Pitcher (The Granger Collection) • Dwight D. Eisenhower

Center row—Sally Ride (AP/Wide World) • Martin Luther King Jr. (AP/Wide World) • Daniel Boone (The Granger Collection)

Bottom row—Matthew Henson (The Granger Collection) • Chief Joseph (The Granger Collection) • Franklin D. Roosevelt

Copyright © 2001 Kidsbooks, Inc.
230 Fifth Avenue
New York, NY 10001

Manufactured in China

Contents

A Library of Life's Lessons

If actions speak louder than words, role models speak volumes on values. In these short biographies, 100 American heroes put their determination, compassion, hard work, courage, imagination, and many other values into action. These inspiring figures faced challenges, overcame adversity, and often accomplished what no person ever had before.

Franklin Delano Roosevelt led the nation through the Great Depression and World War II. Confined to a wheelchair because of polio, a disease that damages the spinal cord, FDR pushed fear and despair aside to guide the nation through its most trying times.

Elizabeth Cady Stanton risked her family's welfare and her own well-being to fight for women's suffrage. Stanton and her partner Susan B. Anthony accepted nothing less than victory and fought hard to earn women the right to vote.

As the first African-American to play major-league baseball, Jackie Robinson showed the world that race does not determine a person's worth. His skill as a ball player and his quiet dignity as a man furthered the fight for civil rights and earned him the respect of a nation.

Role models inspire us to aim high, do our best, and try again and again when we fail. A library of life's lessons, this collection of biographies will introduce young readers to people from whom they can learn and whose values they can respect.

Samuel Adams
American Patriot
(born 1722 • died 1803)

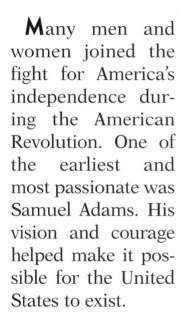

Many men and women joined the fight for America's independence during the American Revolution. One of the earliest and most passionate was Samuel Adams. His vision and courage helped make it possible for the United States to exist.

A Man of Strong Opinions

Samuel Adams was born in Boston, Massachusetts, on September 27, 1722. After graduating from Harvard College, he tried his hand at various professions. He briefly studied law; he worked as a merchant and a tax collector, and tried to publish a newspaper. All of his businesses failed, however—he was just too interested in other things to pay much attention to running them.

> "What a glorious morning for America."
> —Samuel Adams, on hearing gunfire at Lexington

It was the struggle against England that really mattered to Adams. By the mid-1700s, many people in the 13 colonies were tired of being ruled by England. Sam Adams, in particular, did not see why Americans should take orders from a king who lived 3,000 miles away. Adams spent a lot of time walking around Boston, talking to everyone he met. His favorite subject was how unfairly Britain treated the American colonies. He thought that America should be independent—allowed to make its own laws.

Adams especially resented the heavy taxes that Great Britain placed on the colonies. Americans had to pay money to Great Britain for just about everything they produced or purchased: sugar, tea, paint, glass, and many other products. More and more American colonists were upset by this, especially since no one in the British government represented their interests and needs. The phrase "No taxation without representation!" began to spread now, and

Sam Adams was one of the first to use it as a battle cry against British rule.

When Great Britain passed the Stamp Act in 1765, Adams really got angry. This law placed a tax on all printed matter, from marriage licenses to newspapers. Many other people in Boston considered the tax unfair, and elected Adams to be their representative in the Massachusetts legislature. He and the people of Boston protested so strongly against the Stamp Act that Great Britain eventually stopped charging the tax.

Adams was a member of the Massachusetts legislature from 1765 to 1774. During that time, he became the leader of the independence movement in the state. He protested angrily against the presence of British troops in the colonies. After the Boston Massacre, he demanded that they be removed. He

TOPICAL TIDBIT

A Rebels' Tea Party

The Boston Tea Party took place on the night of December 16, 1773. A group of about 60 men, dressed up in blankets and Indian headdresses, boarded three ships of the British-owned East India Company docked in Boston Harbor. On board was a large shipment of East India tea, which Adams and other patriots saw as a symbol of taxation and strict English rule. The American patriots did not want the tea sold in Boston, but the British governor had ordered that it be unloaded in the morning. The protesters unloaded it for him—right into the water.

also helped organize the Boston Tea Party, a tax protest in which colonists dumped tea from a British ship into Boston Harbor.

In 1774, Sam Adams was elected to represent Massachusetts at the First Continental Congress in Philadelphia. This Congress called for Americans to refuse to buy British goods, and recommended that the colonists fight against British taxes. The struggle to win independence from Great Britain had reached a new intensity.

In Danger

Adams's activities made him very unpopular with the British government. The British and their American supporters called him a traitor and tried to have him arrested. During the Battle of Lexington and Concord, on April 18, 1775, Adams and his friend and fellow rebel, John Hancock, were hiding from British soldiers in Lexington, Massachusetts. When they heard that the soldiers were headed their way, Adams and Hancock fled in a carriage to the safety of another town.

The United States Is Born

Sam Adams went back to Philadelphia in May 1775 to represent Massachusetts at the Second Continental Congress. In July 1776, he and 56 other delegates signed the Declaration of Independence, which insisted that the American colonies were now free of England's rule. Seven years later, in 1783, the American Revolution ended, and England finally recognized America as an independent nation.

During the Revolution, Sam Adams remained a member of the Continental Congress. He also helped write the Massachusetts State Constitution. From 1789 to 1793, he served as lieutenant governor of Massachusetts, and then as governor from 1794 to 1797. Sam Adams died in Boston at the age of 81, on October 2, 1803. Today, he is still remembered as a great patriot and a key leader in America's fight for independence. If not for his tireless work at convincing the colonists to insist on their freedom from Great Britain, the United States of America might never have been born. ◇

LIFE EVENTS

1722
Samuel Adams is born in Boston.

1764
England passes the Sugar Act. Adams is one of the first to protest against "taxation without representation." The Stamp Act is passed the following year.

1774
Adams is elected a delegate from Massachusetts to the Continental Congress. He is among the first to demand independence from England.

1776
Adams and others sign the Declaration of Independence.

1794
Adams becomes governor of the state of Massachusetts and serves until 1797. He dies in 1803.

Jane Addams
Making Life Better
(born 1860 • died 1935)

If you had been one of the immigrants who came to America in the early 1900s, your life would have been very different from what it is today. Your family might have been too poor to afford good food, and you would probably have had to live in a tiny apartment in a dirty, crowded tenement building. Most likely, you would have had to work instead of going to school.

That was the sort of struggle faced by many people who immigrated to America in the early 1900s. Jane

Addams believed that life should not be so hard for children and their families. She spent her life working to help the poor make their lives better.

A Rich Childhood

Jane Addams was born on September 6, 1860, in Cedarville, Illinois. The youngest of five children, she was a sickly child with a crooked back. Her mother died when Jane was only two years old. Yet, her father was one of the richest and most important people in town. He and his older daughters spoiled Jane, treating her like a princess.

Although Jane Addams lived a rich and comfortable life, she knew that other people were poor and had to live

> "She won an eminent place in the love and esteem of her people. She became the leading woman in the nation, one might almost say its leading citizen."
>
> —Halvandan Koht, member of Nobel committee, presenting the Nobel Peace Prize to Jane Addams on December 10, 1931

in dirty, crowded conditions. When she was a child, she told her father that one day she would have a big house and invite all the poor people to come over and play with her.

Addams did very well in school, attending Rockford Female Seminary and Women's Medical College. But when she graduated, she was not sure what she wanted to do next. She did know that she wanted to help the poor, but how?

Finding Her Way

When Addams was 27 years old, she and her friend Ellen Gates Starr took a trip to Europe. In London, England, they visited Toynbee Hall, which was a settlement house—a place that helped poor people live better lives. It offered activities for children and classes for adults. Nurses cared for sick people who could not afford a doctor.

Addams and Starr decided to start their own settlement house in the U.S. Addams's father had died several years earlier, leaving her an inheritance. She used that money to buy an abandoned mansion, the former Hull estate, in a poor neighborhood in Chicago, Illinois. In 1889, Hull House opened to help the needy families of the city.

Addams wanted Hull House to be a place where adults and children could feel safe, comfortable, and happy. It soon became the center of much activity. Addams built the first public playground in the U.S., so that children would not have to play in the street. She started a day-care center and a kindergarten. At that time, three out of four Chicago residents were immigrants who had come to America from many European countries. Hull House held classes to educate them, and offered programs to help them find jobs and places to live. It also presented plays, concerts, and art shows.

Eventually, Jane Addams's settlement house included 13 buildings, making it one of the largest centers of its kind. When people in other cities heard about Hull House, they were inspired by Addams's vision, and traveled there to learn how to run community centers in other places around the U.S.

Other Projects

Addams did not just work at Hull House. She tried to improve working conditions all over the country.

TOPICAL TIDBIT

Another Settlement House Pioneer

The settlement houses of the late 1800s were important models for modern social workers. One of the pioneers of the settlement movement was Samuel A. Barnett, an English minister who was determined to help the poor. In 1884, he purchased a building next to his church in London, which he called Toynbee Hall. Other concerned people were invited to move in and work to improve social conditions in the area. Toynbee Hall continues to serve the community to this day.

She fought to change laws so that children would not have to work. She also campaigned for women's right to vote.

Addams worked hard for world peace. From 1914 to 1918, she spoke out against World War I, urging negotiations instead of war. World War I devastated Europe, leaving many people poor, homeless, and hungry. After the war ended, Addams sent food and supplies to starving people in Europe. In 1931, she was awarded the Nobel Peace Prize for her life's work.

Jane Addams lived at Hull House until her death at age 74, on May 21, 1935. By then, her efforts to make the world a better place had made her one of the most famous and admired women in the nation. ◇

LIFE EVENTS

1860
Jane Addams is born in Cedarville, Illinois.

1887
Addams and a friend, Ellen Gates Starr, visit Toynbee Hall in London.

1889
Hull House opens in Chicago.

1920
Addams is one of the founders of the American Civil Liberties Union.

1931
Jane Addams is co-winner of the Nobel Peace Prize. However, she is too ill to attend the ceremony in Stockholm, Sweden. She dies in 1935.

Muhammad Ali
Outspoken Athlete
(born 1942)

Muhammad Ali is considered one of the greatest boxers in the history of the sport. He also is admired for having the courage to risk his career and title to stay true to his antiwar beliefs.

An Amazing Athlete

Muhammad Ali was born Cassius Marcellus Clay Jr. in Louisville, Kentucky, on January 17, 1942. A confident, outgoing child, he started boxing at age 12; by the time he was 18, he had a win-loss record of 108-8.

Clay was a member of the U.S. boxing team at the 1960 Olympic Games in Rome, Italy. He won a gold medal in the light-heavyweight competition. Back home, however, he found that his medal did not stop society from discriminating against him as a black man. After being refused service at a whites-only restaurant, Clay was so angry that he threw his medal into the Ohio River. The honor meant nothing, he said, if he was not treated with dignity as a human being.

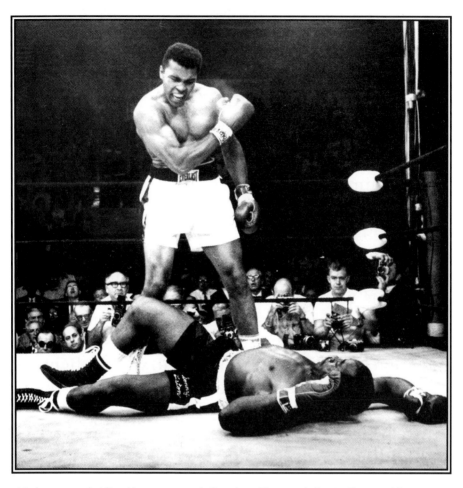

Muhammad Ali—then named Cassius Clay—defeats Sonny Liston on
May 25, 1965. The victory made Clay heavyweight champion
of the world.

Clay started boxing professionally on October 29,
1960. By 1964, he had won 19 professional fights and
become well-known for bragging about his ability.
While preparing for his fight against heavyweight

champion Sonny Liston, Clay boasted that he would defeat Liston—and he did. Clay became the new heavyweight champion of the world. He called himself "the Greatest."

> "I'm not the greatest; I'm the double greatest. Not only do I knock 'em out, I pick the round."
>
> —Cassius Clay (Muhammad Ali), 1962

Clay had an unusual way of boxing. He described it as "Float like a butterfly, sting like a bee." Instead of trying to overwhelm opponents with power, he danced around them and jabbed with his fists. His constant movements exhausted and confused his opponents. Then he moved in with a flurry of punches to win the fight. By 1967, he had successfully defended his title six times.

Muhammad Ali Speaks Out

In 1964, Cassius Clay joined the Nation of Islam, a religious group also known as the Black Muslims. He changed his name to Muhammad Ali.

During the 1960s and 1970s, the U.S. was fighting a war in Vietnam, a nation in Asia. Ali was drafted by the U.S. Army, but refused to go. He said that his religion made him a conscientious objector—someone who refuses to take part in war because he or she believes it to be morally wrong.

For refusing to join the army, Ali was stripped of his heavyweight title in 1967, and banned from boxing professionally in the U.S. Many Americans were angry at Ali for his stand on Vietnam. They also disliked the way he spoke out about civil rights and the lack of opportunities for African Americans.

In 1970, Ali was allowed to return to boxing. At that time, the heavyweight champion was Joe Frazier, who had won the title during Ali's absence from the sport. In March 1971, Frazier kept the title, defeating Ali in a match dubbed "the Fight of the Century."

In 1973, Frazier lost the heavyweight title to George Foreman. The next year, Ali fought a rematch with Frazier and won. Then he turned his attention to the reigning champion. Ali beat Foreman in Kinshasa, Zaire (now Congo), on October 29, 1974, in a fight known as "the Rumble in the Jungle." Once again, Ali was the heavyweight champion of the world.

TOPICAL TIDBIT

Protest at the Olympics

Muhammad Ali was not the only athlete of the 1960s to upset people with his political statements. At the 1968 Summer Olympics in Mexico City, U.S. track medalists Tommie Smith and John Carlos also sparked a national debate. During the playing of the U.S. national anthem, they raised their fists in the Black Power salute, a political gesture that was controversial at the time.

The End of a Career

Ali successfully defended his heavyweight title six more times before retiring in 1981. One of the most dramatic matches came in 1975, when he defeated Frazier in a fight called "the Thrilla in Manila." Ali ended his career with a record of 56 wins (37 of them by knockouts) and 5 losses.

After his retirement, Ali developed Parkinson's disease, a condition of the nervous system that causes shakiness and slurred speech. Many people think that the Parkinson's is a result of brain injuries that Ali suffered in the boxing ring.

Despite his illness, Ali continues to appear in public, especially at charity events. He has been called the greatest and most famous athlete in the world. He is admired for his bold style, his refusal to back down from controversy, and his courage to stand up for what he believes in. ◇

LIFE EVENTS

1942
Cassius Marcellus Clay Jr. is born in Lexington, Kentucky.

1964
Clay defeats Sonny Liston to win the heavyweight boxing championship.

1974
Muhammad Ali regains the heavyweight championship by defeating George Foreman in Kinshasa, Zaire.

1978
Ali loses the title to Leon Spinks, then regains it in a rematch seven months later, becoming the first fighter to win the championship three times.

1996
Ali lights the Flame at the Olympic Games in Atlanta, Georgia.

Ethan Allen
Soldier for Freedom
(born 1738 • died 1789)

Ethan Allen was never afraid to back down from a fight. Whether defending his country or his state, Allen was a fearless freedom fighter.

A Fight for Land

Ethan Allen was born in Litchfield, Connecticut, on January 21, 1738. Thirty-one years later, he moved to the town of Bennington in an area called the New Hampshire Grants. Today, that area is part of Vermont. In the 1750s and 1760s, however, no one was sure whether it belonged to New Hampshire or to New York. When the government of New York tried to take land from farmers who lived there, the people rebelled.

> "I act in the name of the great Jehovah and the Continental Congress!"
>
> —Ethan Allen to British Captain Delaplace

One of the leaders of this rebellion was Ethan Allen. Together with his brothers and a cousin, Allen owned 60,000 acres of wilderness in the New Hampshire Grants. Allen was a big, powerful man who had a lot of experience surviving in the woods. Some stories said that he was so tough, he could strangle a bear with his bare hands. Allen was not afraid to battle the New York government, or the courts that said that his land did not belong to him. He organized a group of soldiers into a volunteer militia that came to be known as the Green Mountain Boys, after the mountains where they lived.

Ethan Allen and the Green Mountain Boys knew that they could

not defeat the well-trained and well-supplied New York army head-on. Instead, they struck at the New York settlers at night, pulling down fences, driving cattle into the fields, and destroying crops. They also threatened violence to any New Yorkers they caught on their land. In return, New York called Ethan Allen an outlaw and put up a reward for his capture.

War Breaks Out

Before the conflict between New York and the Green Mountain Boys could be settled, revolution broke out between the American colonies and Great Britain. Allen and his army quickly joined the American forces to fight against the British.

Ethan Allen and the Green Mountain Boys won their greatest victory when they captured Fort Ticon-

TOPICAL TIDBIT

Benedict Arnold

Another notable figure present at the siege of Fort Ticonderoga was Benedict Arnold. Arnold was a brilliant American commander, but he grew bitter at being denied promotion. Finally, in 1780, he attempted to betray West Point to the British. The plot was exposed, and Benedict Arnold became known as his country's first traitor. The nickname "Benedict Arnold" is still used today for anyone considered a traitor.

deroga from the British on May 10, 1775. Allen and 83 soldiers slipped into the fort very early in the morning while most of the enemy soldiers were asleep. Allen ran up the stairs, waving his sword and yelling for the British captain to come out. When the British leader saw his men surrounded by the American militia, he surrendered without a single shot being fired.

Later, Allen and his Green Mountain Boys went to Canada to fight against British troops there. Allen was captured near Montreal on September 25, 1775, and he spent nearly three years in prison. Meanwhile, the Green Mountain Boys continued to fight against the British.

The Birth of Vermont

In 1777, while Ethan Allen was still in prison, the people who lived in the New Hampshire Grants asked the American government to name their area a separate state. In July 1777, their request was granted and the Republic of Vermont was created.

In 1778, Allen was freed in an exchange of prisoners between the Americans and the British, and he returned to Bennington. He was named a lieutenant colonel in the Continental Army and major general of the militia.

When Allen returned to Bennington in May 1778, he joined the fight to admit Vermont to the United States. New York, determined to keep it out, managed to block Vermont's statehood many times. New York's government even threatened to withdraw its forces and money from the Revolution. Allen became so frustrated and angry at these delays that he began secret talks with the British to make Vermont a British province. As a result, the American government charged Allen with treason— the crime of acting to give aid and comfort to the country's enemies. However, the charges were dropped when it became obvious that Allen was talking to the British only to force action on Vermont's statehood.

Ethan Allen died at his home in Burlington, Vermont, on February 12, 1789. Two years later, Vermont finally became the 14th state in the Union. Although Allen did not live to see Vermont's triumph, it was a battle that might not have been won without his hard work and dedication. ◇

LIFE EVENTS

1738
Ethan Allen is born in Litchfield, Connecticut.

1754
Allen fights in the French and Indian War.

1770
Allen raises a militia called the Green Mountain Boys.

1775
The Green Mountain Boys seize Fort Ticonderoga from the British in May. Allen is captured during an unsuccessful attack on the city of Montreal in September.

1778
Allen is released, then carries on the fight for Vermont statehood. Vermont finally becomes a state in 1791—two years after his death.

Susan B. Anthony
Pioneer of Women's Rights
(born 1820 • died 1906)

Today, we take for granted that men and women have equal rights. However, not that long ago, women had hardly any rights at all. They were not even allowed to vote. During the late 1800s, a group of women called suffragists fought hard to change that. One of the most important figures in the women's suffrage movement was Susan B. Anthony.

Not Created Equal

Susan Brownell Anthony was born on February 15, 1820, in Adams, Massachusetts. Later, her family moved to Rochester, New York. Susan saw many examples of unfair treatment of women as she was growing up. In the cotton factory owned by her father, all the foremen were men, even though the women who worked there knew just as much about running the machines. When Susan pointed out how unfair this was, her father told her that it would not be proper for a woman to be a foreman.

In those days, one of the few jobs available for women was teaching, which Anthony began doing at the age of 15. She only made $2.50 a week, while male teachers made $10 a week. This was yet another of many inequalities in society that made Anthony determined to make a difference.

An Important Friendship

In 1851, Susan B. Anthony met Elizabeth Cady Stanton. Like Anthony, Stanton was interested in equal rights for women. In 1848, she had helped organize the first women's rights convention, which was held in Seneca Falls, New York. She encouraged Anthony to fight for women's rights.

From 1854 to 1860, the two friends worked together to change New York State laws that were unfair to women. Anthony traveled all over the state, organizing women and giving speeches to educate the public. In those days, most people had never heard a woman speak in public. Anthony was shy about addressing an audience at first, but she became an energetic, entertaining, and exciting speaker. Her speeches—most of

TOPICAL TIDBIT

Learning to Fight for Justice

The women's suffrage movement grew out of two other social movements of the 19th century—for temperance (the banning of alcohol) and for the abolition of slavery. As a girl and young woman, Susan B. Anthony heard the passionate debates that were being waged over these issues, particularly in Northern cities. She met many people who were important in these movements, including abolitionists Frederick Douglass (a former slave) and William Lloyd Garrison. This helped Anthony develop her own dedication to battling all injustices in society.

which were written by Stanton—persuaded many Americans to support women's rights.

Anthony also thought that it was unfair that black Americans were not treated the same way as whites. From 1856 to 1861, she gave speeches and organized meetings of the American Anti-Slavery Society. In 1863, during the Civil War, Anthony founded the Women's Loyal League, which fought for the freedom of all slaves.

> "There never will be complete equality until women themselves help to make laws and elect lawmakers."
> —Susan B. Anthony

Anthony and Stanton knew that women had little chance of changing unfair laws if they did not have the right to vote for representatives in the government. So they devoted all their energy to winning suffrage—the right to vote—for women. In 1869, the two organized the National Woman Suffrage Association, whose goal was to change the U.S. Constitution to give women the right to vote.

Anthony wanted to get the public's attention in a dramatic way, so she registered and voted in the 1872 presidential election. She was arrested, found guilty of breaking the law, and fined $100, which she refused to pay. At her trial, the judge had not allowed Anthony to speak in her own defense. The trial received a tremendous amount of publicity, and many people were angered by the unfair way she was treated in court. After that, Anthony soon became the best-known figure in the women's-rights movement.

In 1883, Anthony went to Europe to meet women involved in suffrage movements on that continent. In 1888, she formed the International Council of Women, an organization that represented women in 48 countries around the world.

Susan B. Anthony continued to campaign and speak out for women's rights until her death at the age of 86 in Rochester, New York, on March 13, 1906. "Failure is impossible," she declared in a speech less than a month before her death. Although women still did not have the right to vote, Anthony knew that someday they would.

LIFE EVENTS

1820
Susan Brownell Anthony is born in Massachusetts.

1848
Elizabeth Cady Stanton organizes the first women's rights convention.

1868
Anthony and Stanton start a magazine called *Revolution*, dedicated to women's suffrage and other causes.

1872
Anthony is arrested for voting in the presidential election. Tried and convicted, she refuses to pay the fine.

1920
The Nineteenth Amendment to the U.S. Constitution grants women the vote—14 years after Anthony's death.

A Lasting Result

Women were finally granted the right to vote in the U.S. in 1920. Although Anthony did not live to see that day, she had played a key role in that victory. By bringing women's issues to the public, and uniting both men and women with her dynamic public speaking, Susan B. Anthony helped bring about one of the greatest social changes in American history.

To honor her work, in 1979 the U.S. Mint issued a dollar coin with her picture on it. She was the first American woman to appear on a U.S. coin. ◇

Neil Armstrong
First Man on the Moon
(born 1930)

During the 1960s, the U.S. space program set an incredibly ambitious goal: to put a man on the moon by the end of the decade. The man who achieved that feat was astronaut Neil Armstrong, the first person in history to walk on the moon.

Born to Fly

Neil Alden Armstrong was born on August 5, 1930, in Wapakoneta, Ohio. When he was six years old, Neil took his first flight in a small airplane. From that day on, all he wanted to do was fly.

He started learning to fly when he was 14 years old, working at a local drugstore for 40 cents an hour to pay for his lessons. At 16, Armstrong got his pilot's license. He did

> "Tranquility base here; the *Eagle* has landed."
>
> —Neil Armstrong to mission control as the lunar module touched down on the moon

not even have his driver's license yet, but he could fly a plane!

Armstrong went to college at Purdue University in Indiana, where he studied aeronautical engineering and joined the Naval Air Cadet program. Two years later, he was called into active duty in the Navy. Sent to fight in the Korean War, he saw action in several battles and was awarded three Air Medals for his bravery. After he finished his Navy service, Armstrong went back to college. When he graduated in 1955, he got a job as a test pilot for the U.S. government.

The Race for Space

In 1958, the U.S. government formed the National Aeronautics and Space Administration (NASA). NASA's goal was to send a man into outer space, and eventually put a man on the moon.

When Neil Armstrong heard about the new space program, he and 200 other hopefuls applied to join. In September 1962, Armstrong received the good news that he—along with just eight other men—had been chosen for NASA's Gemini program.

He spent hundreds of hours training to be an astronaut, learning to master the complicated instruments that made a spaceship fly. He studied physics, astronomy, and other sciences, and trained in machines that simulated what it was like to fly in space.

On March 16, 1966, Armstrong and another astronaut, David Scott, flew a spaceship named *Gemini 8* into orbit, where it was to dock with a satellite. The docking went fine, but afterward, *Gemini 8* began to tumble end-over-end. Nothing the two astronauts tried could stop the ship from spinning. Finally, Armstrong took the controls and, after a 30-minute struggle, gained control of the ship. After *Gemini 8* landed, experts discovered that an electrical problem had been responsible for the tumbling. Everyone at NASA was amazed that Armstrong had figured out how to save the ship and get back to Earth safely.

"One Giant Leap for Mankind"

Then as now, space travel was dangerous, and the goal of landing on the moon was especially so. In 1967, three astronauts training for the moon mission were killed while still on the launch pad: A fire had broken out aboard their *Apollo 1* spacecraft. Still, Armstrong and the other Apollo astronauts pressed on. Finally, on July 16, 1969, Neil Armstrong, Edwin

TOPICAL TIDBIT

The Father of Modern Rocketry

One of the hardest things about making the U.S. space program work was giving spacecraft enough power to fly thousands of miles from Earth. Robert H. Goddard figured out how to do it. In 1889, at age 17, he starting trying to build rockets whose dangerously explosive power could be controlled, making them safe enough to blast humans into space. He launched his first liquid-fuel rocket in 1926; by 1935, he had one that could travel faster than the speed of sound. Goddard died in 1945, but without his hard work, the *Apollo 11* crew could never have made the 1969 flight to the moon—about 239,000 miles from Earth.

"Buzz" Aldrin, and Michael Collins climbed into *Apollo 11* and blasted off toward the moon.

The journey to the moon took four days. On the morning of July 20, while Collins remained in orbit in *Columbia*, the command module of *Apollo 11*, Armstrong and Aldrin crawled into a smaller unit called *Eagle* and set out for the surface of the moon.

As Armstrong and Aldrin descended, they realized that the *Eagle* was about to crash into a large rock. Armstrong grabbed the controls and steered the *Eagle* to a safe landing.

A few hours later, Armstrong climbed out of the spaceship and became the first human being to set foot on the moon. As his feet touched the lunar surface, he said these now-famous words: "That's one small step for a man, one giant leap for mankind."

Armstrong and Aldrin spent less than a day on the moon, collecting rocks and other specimens for scientists to study back on Earth. They also planted a U.S. flag on the moon's surface, along with a plaque that said:

HERE MEN FROM THE PLANET EARTH
FIRST SET FOOT UPON THE MOON
JULY 1969 A.D.
WE CAME IN PEACE FOR ALL MANKIND

Armstrong and Aldrin climbed back into the *Eagle* for the flight back to their command module, the *Columbia*, which was still orbiting just overhead.

Then they turned their spacecraft back toward Earth.

Four days later, the three *Apollo 11* astronauts splashed down safely in the Pacific Ocean.

After the Moon

Neil Armstrong worked at NASA until 1971, when he retired from NASA. He went on to work as an aerospace engineering professor and a business executive. Today, he lives a quieter life with his family in Ohio, but he remains an inspiration to anyone who ever dreamed of reaching for the stars. ◇

LIFE EVENTS

1930
Neil Alden Armstrong is born in Wapakoneta, Ohio.

1955
Armstrong becomes a test pilot for the National Advisory Committee for Aeronautics, an agency that becomes NASA in 1958.

1962
Armstrong joins NASA's Gemini program.

1966
Armstrong commands the *Gemini-Titan 8* mission, performing the first docking of one spacecraft with another.

1969
Commanding the historic *Apollo 11* flight, Armstrong becomes the first person to walk on the moon.

Crispus Attucks
The Greatest Sacrifice
(born 1723? • died 1770)

During the 1770s, many Americans were caught up in the struggle to win independence from Great Britain. Crispus Attucks, an African American, became the first person to sacrifice his life in the American colonists' struggle for independence.

Runaway Slave

Very little is known about Crispus Attucks. He was born sometime around 1723. Historians believe that his father was African and his mother a Native American. Attucks, a slave, belonged to a farmer named William Brown. Attucks bought and sold cattle for his master's farm in Framingham, Massachusetts. In 1750, Attucks ran away. Brown put an ad in a Boston newspaper, offering a reward for his slave's return. He described Attucks as "a mulatto [mixed-race] fellow, about 27 years of age . . . 6 feet 2 inches high, short cur'l hair, his knees nearer together than common."

Crispus Attucks *(center)* was the first to fall in the
fight for American independence.

Despite Brown's advertisement, no one ever captured Attucks. Instead, he worked as a ropemaker and
a sailor on whaling ships. Eventually, he settled in
Boston, Massachusetts.

The Boston Massacre

Massachusetts, one of the original 13 American
colonies, was in the forefront of the movement to

separate from Great Britain. Smoldering resentment over British taxes and laws would, in a few short years, lead to the American Revolution. In 1770, however, war had not yet broken out between the American colonies and Great Britain. Tensions ran high, though, and fights often broke out between colonists and the British soldiers who had been sent to Boston to help keep the peace.

> "On that night the foundation of American independence was laid."
> —John Adams on the Boston Massacre

On a snowy afternoon on March 5, 1770, a group of about 30 colonists gathered in front of Boston's customhouse—the headquarters for the hated British tax collectors. One of the people in that crowd was Crispus Attucks. As a former slave, Attucks knew the importance of freedom, but that was not the only reason he and others in the crowd disliked the British. British soldiers often kidnapped American sailors and forced them to serve in the British navy. They also took part-time jobs for less pay than the colonists earned, making it hard for Boston laborers to find work.

The crowd began yelling at a British soldier standing guard in front of the customhouse. They mocked his red uniform and called him names. Then a group of teenagers began throwing snowballs at him. He called for help, and soon 20 British soldiers carrying rifles came marching down the street. No one is certain what happened next, but some eyewitnesses said that Attucks grabbed one of the soldiers and knocked him down. Some of the British soldiers fired on the crowd, and the first shot hit and killed Crispus Attucks. Four other colonists died in the clash.

Newspapers quickly named the incident "the Boston Massacre," and American patriots honored the five men killed that day as heroes. Even though it was against the law to bury blacks in the same cemetery as whites, Attucks was placed in the Park Street Cemetery along with the four white victims.

Eight British soldiers were tried for murder. John Adams—a lawyer who later became a key figure in the fight for American independence—defended them in court. They were found not guilty of all charges.

TOPICAL TIDBIT

The "Battle" of Golden Hill

The "Boston Massacre" was not the only pre-Revolution clash between American rebels and British troops. In early 1769, a patriot group called the Sons of Liberty protested British rule by raising a Liberty Pole in New York City, at a spot then called Golden Hill. British troops destroyed the pole. The next day, some 3,000 angry colonists gathered at the site. Fighting broke out between the protesters and the soldiers. Some people were wounded in the so-called Battle of Golden Hill, but no one was killed.

Hero or Troublemaker?

In 1888, a monument honoring Crispus Attucks and the other victims of the Boston Massacre was built on the Boston Common (now a city park). The Massachusetts Historical Society and the New England Historic Genealogical Society were opposed to honoring Attucks. They saw him as a troublemaker who had started the fight, and did not think that he should be considered a hero.

Was Crispus Attucks a hero or a troublemaker? No one will ever know for sure. However, the fact remains that he gave his life for the cause of freedom. His name will always be remembered as an important one in American history. ◇

LIFE EVENTS

About 1723
Crispus Attucks is born.

1750
Attucks, a slave, escapes from his master. He eventually settles in Boston.

1767
England passes the Townshend Acts, laws that set strict taxes on American colonists. They protest so furiously that British troops are sent to Boston the following year.

1770
British soldiers fire into a crowd of Boston citizens in what is called the Boston Massacre. Attucks is one of five citizens killed.

1888
A monument to the victims of the Boston Massacre is built on the Boston Common.

James Baldwin
Sharing the Black Experience
(born 1924 • died 1987)

It is always hard for people of one ethnic or cultural group to appreciate and understand the feelings and lives of people who belong to a different group. This was especially true of blacks and whites during the middle years of the 20th century. James Baldwin—an African American author of novels, essays, and short stories—tried to bridge the gap of understanding between the races. His writings helped show white Americans what it was like to be a black American during those difficult years.

> "I imagine one of the reasons people cling to their hates so stubbornly is because they sense, once hate is gone, [that] they will be forced to deal with pain."
>
> —James Baldwin, from *Notes of a Native Son*

A Difficult Childhood

James Arthur Baldwin was born in Harlem, New York, on August 2, 1924, the oldest of nine children in a very poor family. His mother, Emma Birdis Jones, later married David Baldwin, who adopted James. But the boy and his stepfather did not get along.

David Baldwin was a minister, and young James also felt the calling to a religious life. At age 14, he became a preacher at Fireside Pentecostal Church in Harlem.

Pentecostal ministers are known for their fiery sermons, and James was no exception. He soon became a well-known public speaker who expressed himself with great emotion and energy. Although he stopped preaching after just a few years, the experience was an important one. Later, his writing expressed his strong emotions about that time in his life.

There were few successful role models for James when he was growing up. His neighbors were poor and had little education, so James did not know that there was any other way for black people to live. Then he met Countee Cullen, a famous black poet and writer who had graduated from Harvard, one of the best colleges in America. Cullen, who was James's French teacher in junior high school, showed James that many opportunities were open to black men who worked hard to achieve them.

TOPICAL TIDBIT

A Place to Be Free

In the 20th century, it was not unusual for African American artists, writers, and musicians to leave the country to live in Europe. Paris was a city in which many blacks found a home. There, they felt free from the prejudice that they met everywhere in the U.S. They also enjoyed the friendship of many fellow artists. Richard Wright, author of *Native Son*, was another important black writer who lived in Paris at the same time as Baldwin.

Writing for Justice

Baldwin longed to go to college, but his family did not have the money to pay for his education. After he graduated from high school, he moved to a part of New York City called Greenwich Village, which was home to many artists and writers. He worked at odd jobs to make a living, but spent every free minute reading books to educate himself. Soon he began to write. It wasn't long before short stories, essays, and novels came pouring out of him.

Baldwin grew so angry at America's prejudice against African Americans, he found it hard to live in the U.S. In 1948, he moved to Paris, France, where he lived for the next eight years. He returned to New York in 1957 to work in the civil-rights movement, fighting to win equality for blacks. He spent the rest of his life moving back and forth between the U.S. and France.

Baldwin published his first novel, *Go Tell It on the Mountain,* in 1953. Based on his childhood experiences, the book became very successful and is still considered one of the finest works of black literature. That book, along with others that Baldwin wrote, helped many people, especially whites, recognize and understand racism at a time when the civil-rights movement was just beginning to grow. Baldwin's other books include the novels *Another Country* (1962) and *Nobody Knows My Name* (1961), the essays *The Fire Next Time* (1963) and *Notes of a Native*

Son (1955), the play *Blues for Mister Charlie* (1964), a short-story collection called *Going to Meet the Man*, a poetry collection called *Jimmy's Blues* (1985), and many other works.

Most of Baldwin's writing deals with racial tensions between blacks and whites. His works offer readers an unflinching look at the lives of black people living in America. Baldwin believed that racial discrimination was a disease that could be cured only when white America recognized its causes and worked to stop it. Throughout his life, he tried to educate people on the importance of living together under laws that treat everyone equally, no matter what the color of their skin.

At age 63, James Baldwin died of cancer on December 1, 1987, in Saint-Paul, France. His writings still provide a strong, clear voice that speaks to people of all races. ◇

LIFE EVENTS

1924
James Arthur Baldwin is born in New York, New York.

1953
Go Tell It On the Mountain, Baldwin's first novel, is published to great acclaim.

1955
Notes of a Native Son includes the title essay about Baldwin's youth, his angry stepfather, and being black in America.

1962
The New Yorker magazine devotes an entire issue to Baldwin's essay about the Black Muslims and the civil-rights movement. It becomes a best-selling book, *The Fire Next Time*.

1987
Baldwin dies in Saint-Paul, France.

Clara Barton
Angel of the Battlefield
(born 1821 • died 1912)

During the Civil War's first Battle of Bull Run, hundreds of soldiers lay injured and dying on the battlefield. No one seemed willing or able to help them. Suddenly, a woman appeared and calmly gave orders for workers to care for the wounded. She comforted injured soldiers, bandaged their wounds, and took them water to drink. That woman, Clara Barton, spent the rest of her life saving the lives of countless people, in war and in peace.

A Spoiled Child

Clarissa Harlowe Barton was born in Oxford, Massachusetts, in 1821. She had four brothers and sisters, all of whom were much older than she. In many ways, Clara benefited from the age difference, as her older siblings taught her so much: reading and mathematics; how to ride a horse, swim, and play ball; and how to use tools. Clara grew up believing that there was nothing she could not do.

Being so much younger than her brothers and sisters also had drawbacks. Clara grew spoiled and used to getting her own way. Even as an adult, she found it hard to compromise or take orders from other people.

> "You must never so much as think whether you like [your good deed] or not, whether it is bearable or not. You must never think of anything except the need, and how to meet it."
>
> —Clara Barton

Yet Clara Barton was always eager and willing to accept responsibility. She spent two years caring for an older brother who had been badly injured in an accident. Later, she became a teacher so well-liked that her students rarely missed a day of school.

Barton loved teaching and was very good at it. While in her thirties, she started a school in Bordentown, New Jersey, but the local school board chose a man to serve as principal over her. This made Barton furious. Refusing to take orders from someone else, she quit her job and decided to try something new.

In the Midst of Battle

For a while, she worked as a clerk in the U.S. Patent Office, becoming the first woman to hold a full-time job there. Then, in 1861, while Barton was living in Washington, D.C., the Civil War broke out. Deeply affected by the sight of the injured soldiers returning from battle, Barton wrote to local newspapers asking for donations of bandages, medicine, and food. She planned to personally deliver the supplies to the battlefields. To her amazement, the War Department said no. Barton refused to accept this decision, and persisted in her requests. Before long, the War Department gave in, and she was on her way.

Barton did whatever needed to be done, be it nursing wounded and sick soldiers, writing letters home for them, baking bread, or serving breakfast to the men. She cared for all the soldiers, whether they had been fighting for the Union army of the North or the Confederate army of the South. To Clara Barton, they were all "my boys," and to them she was known as "the Angel of the Battlefield."

The Civil War ended in 1865. At the request of President Abraham Lincoln, Barton took on the task of identifying bodies of the war dead and getting in touch with their families. The job took her four years.

The Red Cross

By 1869, Barton herself was sick and exhausted, so she went to Switzerland for a vacation. While there, she learned about the International Red Cross, an organization that had been founded 10 years earlier to help wounded soldiers all over the world. With this, Barton had discovered a new mission for her life. Soon she was hard at work as a nurse for the Red Cross in Germany and France during battles of the Franco-Prussian War.

TOPICAL TIDBIT

A Friend in Need

The institution that we know as the Red Cross began with the work of Henri Dunant, a Swiss humanitarian. In 1859, Dunant organized emergency aid services for wounded Austrian and French soldiers at the Battle of Solferino, in Italy. Through his efforts, the International Committee for the Relief of the Wounded was created in 1863. In time, the organization came to be known as the International Committee of the Red Cross. It now serves victims of natural disasters as well as of war throughout the world.

When Barton returned to the U.S. in 1873, she urged America to join the Red Cross. Barton made hundreds of speeches, passed out leaflets about the institution's work, and even spoke with President Ulysses S. Grant about it. Barton believed that the Red Cross should go beyond helping soldiers, to also provide aid to victims of floods, earthquakes, storms, fires, and other disasters.

In 1881, she finally was able to establish the American Red Cross. Barton served as its first president. In that role, she traveled all over the world to help victims of famines, floods, and wars. She retired in 1904.

Clara Barton died on April 12, 1912, at age 91. By the end of her life, she had received dozens of awards and honors, and had won the respect of people around the world for dedicating her life to helping others in times of trouble. ◇

LIFE EVENTS

1821
Clarissa Harlowe Barton is born in Massachusetts.

1861
When the Civil War breaks out, Barton tends wounded soldiers at the Battle of Bull Run. Her efforts throughout the war earn her the nickname "Angel of the Battlefield."

1865
Barton works to identify bodies of soldiers and notify their families.

1869
In Europe, Barton works with the International Red Cross, caring for the wounded during the Franco-Prussian War.

1881
Barton establishes the American Red Cross. She is its president until 1904.

Daisy Bates
Civil-rights Activist
(born 1914 • died 1999)

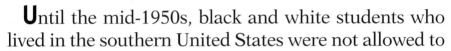

Until the mid-1950s, black and white students who lived in the southern United States were not allowed to

go to the same schools. Schools for whites usually had enough books and other supplies, well-trained teachers, and free bus transportation, but schools for blacks rarely had these things. Daisy Bates not only saw this as unfair, she worked hard to help bring about change. Her efforts in the civil-rights movement made it possible for all children in the United States to receive an equal education, regardless of the color of their skin.

Overcoming Hardships

Daisy Lee Gatson was born in the small town of Huttig, Arkansas, in 1914. She never knew her biological parents. When Daisy was very young, her mother was murdered by three white men, and her father, afraid to bring charges against the murderers, left town and never returned. Daisy was adopted by friends of her parents.

Like other black children in the South, Daisy attended a segregated school. The black school was in poor condition, and the students had to use old, outdated books that the white school had thrown away.

> "Events in history occur when the time has ripened for them, but they need a spark. Little Rock was that spark at that stage of the struggle of the American Negro for justice."
>
> —Daisy Bates

In 1941, Daisy married Lucius Bates and moved with him to Little Rock, the capital of Arkansas. Together, they started a newspaper called the *Arkansas*

State Press, which they dedicated to helping change conditions for black people. One of their most important victories was a series of articles that showed how white police officers abused local black residents. The articles helped sway public opinion, and black officers were soon hired to patrol black neighborhoods.

The Little Rock Nine

In 1954, the U.S. Supreme Court made a historic ruling in a case known as *Brown* v. *Board of Education of Topeka, Kansas*. The Court ruled that, under the U.S. Constitution, segregation (separating by race) in public schools was against the law. At that time, Daisy Bates was president of the state conference of the National Association for the Advancement of Colored People (NAACP). She and other NAACP members believed that Little Rock should integrate (mix races in) its schools right away, but the city put off making any changes.

Bates knew that it was up to people like her to take action. She began escorting black students to white schools, accompanied by newspaper photographers who would capture on film the black students being turned away. Meanwhile, the NAACP was in court, seeking to force white schools to obey the ruling to integrate. Finally, after a long legal battle, a judge said that Little Rock would have to start integrating its schools in September 1957.

Nine black students agreed to attend Little Rock's Central High School. The students and their families knew that many white people in Little Rock would fight any attempt to admit them. Daisy Bates promised to protect the students against any violence—but nobody really knew what would happen.

On August 22, a rock was thrown through the front window of Bates's home, but she did not let that stop her efforts. Instead, she asked several ministers to join her in accompanying the students into the school.

On September 23, Bates and eight of the nine students gathered outside Bates's home and headed for Central High. A crowd of whites was stirring angrily outside the school. While a group of white thugs was beating up four black journalists they had mistaken

TOPICAL TIDBIT

Breaking Past Barriers

The story of the Little Rock Nine was mirrored by other school-door dramas around the country. In 1962, James Meredith, a young black Air Force veteran, braved tear gas as well as an angry mob to enter the all-white University of Mississippi. In 1963, Alabama Governor George Wallace joined guardsmen he had ordered to block the first black students trying to enter the University of Alabama. In these and other such cases, federal troops had to be sent to finally enforce the law.

for students, Bates and the eight real students managed to slip into school.

Meanwhile, the ninth student, Elizabeth Eckford, was on her own. Eckford, who did not have a telephone, had not heard about the plan to meet at Daisy Bates's house. When Eckford arrived at Central High, she was screamed at and spat upon by the angry mob. The girl was not harmed: Two whites stepped forward and helped her escape. She made it home safely.

The crowd of whites outside Central High would not calm down and go home. Finally, the mayor of Little Rock had the eight black students removed from the school under police protection

Because of the threat of violence, President Dwight D. Eisenhower sent army troops to the school to enforce the integration law. On September 25, Bates successfully escorted the "Little Rock Nine" into Central High. She continued to help them throughout their time at the school—even though the Little Rock police arrested her on phony charges.

A Life's Work

Daisy Bates did not stop fighting segregation. After the Little Rock Nine succeeded in desegregating the Little Rock schools, Bates spent the rest of her life campaigning for equal treatment for African Americans, trying to improve their education, and helping them register to vote.

Daisy Bates died in 1999. A few days after her death, the Little Rock Nine received Congressional Gold Medals from President Bill Clinton. At the awards ceremony, the President said of Daisy Bates: "I ask you all to remember her today, her smiling self, for that gave a lot of confidence to those whom we honor." He and other speakers that day remembered and gave tribute to Daisy Bates for her courage and hard work in winning equal treatment for all. ◇

LIFE EVENTS

1914
Daisy Lee Gatson is born in Huttig, Arkansas.

1941
She marries Lucius Bates. In Little Rock, they start the *Arkansas State Press*, a newspaper that crusades for African American rights.

1954
The U.S. Supreme Court rules that segregated schools are unconstitutional.

1957
Daisy Bates leads nine black students integrating Little Rock's Central High School. A tense standoff with the governor gets nationwide attention.

1962
The Long Shadow of Little Rock, Bates's autobiography, is published.

Jim Beckwourth
A Brave Mountain Man
(born 1798 • died 1867?)

In the early 1800s, the frontier of the American West was a perilous place, full of unknown and unexpected hazards. Many courageous Americans set out to explore that wild, untamed world. Jim Beckwourth was one of the bravest.

Early Adventures

James Pierson Beckwourth was born on April 26, 1798, in Fredericksburg, Virginia. His father, who was white, had been a soldier in the American Revolution; his mother, who was black, had been born a slave. When Jim was seven years old, the family—his parents and their 13 children—moved west to Missouri. There, they started a village known

> "I now began to deem myself Indian-proof and to think I never should be killed by them."
>
> —Jim Beckwourth, after taking part in a battle against Blackfoot Indians

as Beckwourth's Settlement. Jim learned how to hunt, trap wild animals, ride horses, and live off the land. While at Beckwourth's Settlement, he also met many Native Americans who lived in the wilderness, and he learned to respect their customs. This knowledge, plus the skills he learned earlier, served Jim Beckwourth well during his years in the American West.

When Jim was ten, he moved to St. Louis to attend school. Four years later, he quit and went to work for a blacksmith. At night, he loved to be on St. Louis's Mississippi River waterfront, talking with traders, merchants, and sailors—listening to their thrilling tales of adventure. One evening, he stayed out so late that his boss got mad at him and the two got into a fight. The blacksmith fired Beckwourth, so the young man made up his mind to head west in search of his own adventures.

In 1823, Beckwourth joined a fur-trading company and traveled into Indian territory—lands in the western part of the United States that were claimed by Indian tribes. Beckwourth and his companions became known as the Mountain Men. Beckwourth and the other Mountain Men worked as trappers and

TOPICAL TIDBIT

Making Their Mark in the West

Many other African Americans played roles in the opening of the American West. Haitian-born Jean Baptiste Pointe du Sable made his way up the Mississippi River, establishing a settlement that later became the city of Chicago. York, a slave owned by explorer William Clark, took part in the Lewis and Clark expedition. Edward Rose was another great mountain man; Nat Love was a famous cowboy. Moses "Black" Harris and George Bonga were well-known fur traders and adventurers.

fur traders. They also guided U.S. Army troops through Indian territory and escorted settlers' wagon trains as they moved west.

Dealings With Native Americans

Beckwourth met many Native Americans during his travels in the west. Most of the encounters were friendly. Beckwourth spoke several Indian languages and enjoyed talking and trading with the Indians. He even attended their feasts and shared their customs. In 1828, he was adopted by a tribe of Crow Indians who thought that he was the long-lost son of one of the tribal chieftains. (People said that Beckwourth looked very much like an Indian, with his dark skin and high cheekbones.)

Beckwourth joined the Crow in battle against a Blackfoot tribe, and became well-known for his bravery, skill, and common sense. He later married the Crow chief's daughter, and even became chief of the tribe himself. After six years, however, Beckwourth grew restless again. He left the tribe to seek new adventures.

The Beckwourth Pass

In 1850, Beckwourth was traveling across the Sierra Nevada Mountains. Near the present-day site of Reno, Nevada, he discovered a pass—a relatively low and easy-to-reach way through a mountain range. That pass made it easier for travelers to reach California and the West Coast. Later, this pass and the valley on the other side were named Beckwourth Pass and Beckwourth Valley in his honor.

In 1852, Beckwourth and his wife settled in Beck-wourth Valley, where they trapped animals, farmed, and ran a hotel and trading post for settlers, trap-

This map shows where Beckwourth Pass is located. Jim Beckwourth found this useful route through the Sierra Nevada mountains in 1850.

pers, and traders. There, new settlers could buy supplies, food, and anything else they needed to start a new life in the West. Later, Beckwourth and his wife moved to a small ranch near Denver, Colorado.

Jim Beckwourth had not lost his taste for adventure, however. When the Civil War broke out in 1861, the 64-year-old former Mountain Man offered to work for the North's Union army. The government turned him down, saying that he was too old. In 1866, though, the U.S. asked him to lead a peacemaking mission to the Crow Indians. His death during that trip is shrouded in mystery. Some people have said that he was poisoned by a former wife, or by the Crow, to keep him from leaving again.

Whatever the cause of Jim Beckwourth's death, his name lives on—not only on maps, but in stories of true adventure in the American West. ◇

LIFE EVENTS

1798
James Pierson Beckwourth is born to a white father and black slave mother in Virginia.

1823
Beckwourth joins a fur-trading expedition and heads West.

1850
Beckwourth discovers a pass through the Sierra Nevada Mountains. Later, it is named for him.

1856
The Life and Adventures of James P. Beckwourth, an "autobiography" written by a journalist, is published.

1866
The U.S. Army hires Beckwourth for a peacemaking mission to the Crow. He dies soon afterward.

Daniel Boone
American Trailblazer
(born 1734 • died 1820)

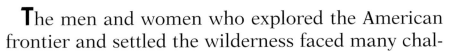

The men and women who explored the American frontier and settled the wilderness faced many challenges. They could rely on no one but themselves as they fought to survive everything from Indian attacks and harsh weather to lack of food. One of the most heroic and best-known of these early settlers was a man named Daniel Boone.

> "Brother, we have given you a fine land, but I believe you will have much trouble in settling it."
>
> —an old Indian to Daniel Boone, from *The Adventures of Col. Daniel Boone*

A Love of the Wilderness

From the very beginning of his life, Daniel Boone loved to be outside. The son of a blacksmith, Daniel was born on November 2, 1734, in what is now Pennsylvania. Every summer, Daniel and his mother

took the family's herd of cows to a distant pasture, where mother and son lived in a rough cabin. The boy loved to explore the woods around the cabin, and hunt and trap animals. Hunting was an important skill in those days, since it was the only way to put meat on the dinner table. By the time Daniel was 15, he was one of the best hunters in the county.

When he was 15, the Boones left Pennsylvania and settled in the Yadkin River valley of North Carolina. Young Boone loved his new home, where he found plenty of wild animals to hunt and lots of woods, streams, and fields to explore. He also met many Native Americans, who taught him other skills and ways to live in the wilderness.

A Path Through the Wilderness

When Boone was 20 years old, he joined the army of North Carolina, which was an English colony, to fight in the French and Indian War. During that war, he met a soldier who told him about a place called Kentucky, which lay on the far side of the Appalachian Mountains. Very few people lived in Kentucky,

TOPICAL TIDBIT

Growing by Leaps and Bounds

The push into Kentucky was the first important move west by white settlers from the colonies. Kentucky's origin as the home of many Native American tribes is reflected in its name, which comes from the Iroquois word meaning "prairie." Kentucky was admitted into the Union as the 15th state in 1792. Boonesborough was founded in 1775; less than 20 years later, it had nearly 75,000 settlers.

the soldier said, which made Boone eager to explore this exciting new territory.

In 1769, Boone and some of his friends headed west. To reach Kentucky, they crossed the mountains at the Cumberland Gap, where they saw beautiful fields filled with herds of buffalo. The group was soon attacked by a band of Native Americans who did not want white settlers on their land. One of Boone's friends was killed; Boone was captured. A week later, he managed to escape, but by then all his companions had gone home. Even though he had

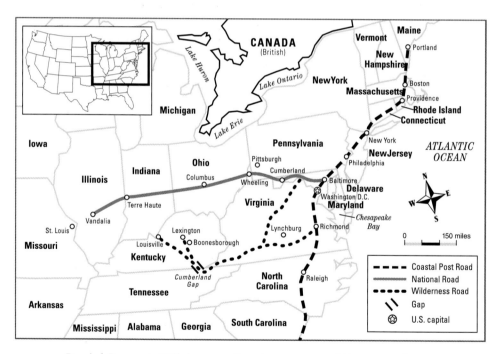

Daniel Boone's Wilderness Road was one of the most important routes of travel in early America.

lost all his supplies, Boone decided to stay in Kentucky by himself and explore the area. His travels took him as far as the Ohio River. It was two years before he returned home to North Carolina.

Boone did not stay there long. In 1773, he returned to Kentucky with his family and a few other settlers. The group ran into another group of unfriendly Indians, and Boone's oldest son, James, and several other members of the party were killed. Full of sorrow, Boone and his family turned back.

In 1775, Daniel Boone led a group of 30 men who carved a 250-mile-long road through the wilderness. It was called the Wilderness Road. It stretched from Tennessee, over the Cumberland Gap, and into the heart of Kentucky. The trailblazers also built a fort and cabins on the Kentucky River and named the settlement Boonesborough, after its founder. In June 1775, Boone returned to North Carolina for his wife and children, and took them to Kentucky for good.

Capture and Escape

In Kentucky, Boone and the other settlers continued to have trouble with hostile Native Americans. In early 1778, Boone was captured by a Shawnee Indian chief named Blackfish, who adopted him. In order to survive, Boone pretended to enjoy living with the Shawnee, but he really wanted to return to his family in Boonesborough. In June 1778, after four months in captivity, he finally escaped, walking for four days before reaching home.

Boone knew that the Shawnee would attack Boonesborough, so he and the other settlers prepared for battle. For nine days, the Shawnee laid siege to the fort, but they could not break through its walls. Finally, they gave up.

Boonesborough grew larger as more settlers headed west, and soon the town was too crowded for Boone. He and his wife and their youngest son moved a few miles away, where they lived in a log cabin in the woods for many years. The old explorer died at his son's house in Missouri on September 26, 1820, just a few weeks before his 86th birthday. Later, his body was reburied near Frankfort, Kentucky's capital, where he is still honored as an American legend—the man who opened the way into the wilderness. ◇

LIFE EVENTS

1734
Daniel Boone is born in Berks County, Pennsylvania.

1769
Boone and companions cross the Appalachian Mountains to reach the Kentucky wilderness. He is captured by Native Americans.

1775
Boone leads a group building the Wilderness Road. He founds Boonesborough on the Kentucky River.

1778
Shawnee Indians hold Boone captive for four months. Later, they make their last attack on Boonesborough.

1820
Already an American legend, Boone dies at age 85.

James Bowie
Hero of the Frontier
(born 1796 • died 1836)

In 1836, a group of brave Texans tried to defend the Alamo from an attack by Mexican soldiers. One of the heroes of that battle was a man named James Bowie. Even before the Alamo, Bowie was well-known as one of the West's bravest adventurers.

A Wild Past

James Bowie was born in Kentucky on April 10, 1796. In 1802, when Jim was six, his father, Rezin, decided that life in Tennessee had grown too settled and too crowded, so he moved the family to Louisiana. Jim and his brothers learned how to hunt, fish, trap, plant crops, and tend herds of cattle. They became known as "those wild Bowie boys" because they were always looking for an adventure.

The Bowie Knife

In 1827, Jim Bowie—involved in a street fight in Alexandria, Louisiana—used a large hunting knife to defend himself against three attackers. The fight was written up in newspapers, which described the knife's unusually long, thin blade. Jim became famous as the "inventor of the Bowie knife." (Historians now believe that Rezin Jr., Jim's brother, actually came up with the knife's design.) The Bowie knife soon became a popular weapon in the U.S. and England.

> "Keep under cover, boys, and reserve your fire; we haven't a man to spare."
>
> —Jim Bowie at the battle of Concepción in 1835

On to Texas

By 1828, Bowie had moved to San Antonio, Texas, which was then part of Mexico. He became a Mexican citizen and married the daughter of one of San Antonio's most important men.

He spent the next few years searching for lost Spanish silver mines and fighting Native Americans as a Texas Ranger. In 1833, his wife and children died of a disease called cholera. Bowie became even more restless and daring then. With his family gone, it seemed, he no longer cared what happened to him.

Remember the Alamo!

In 1835, Texans began a war to win independence from Mexico. Mexico's president, Antonio López de Santa Anna, was planning to attack San Antonio. When Bowie heard of the plan, he offered to lead a group of volunteers to defend a storehouse at the Alamo, a former mission that was being used as a fort. On January 19, 1836, Bowie and his 30 men joined Colonel James Neill and 100 soldiers at the Alamo. They soon found that most of the supplies were already gone. Bowie sent an urgent message to

TOPICAL TIDBIT

Before Texas Was Texas

The first residents of the area now called Texas were a group of Indian tribes who eventually formed an alliance called the Caddo confederacies. Europeans arrived in 1528. The modern history of Texas begins in 1821, when Stephen F. Austin received a grant from Mexico to start his first colony of settlers along the lower Brazos and Colorado rivers.

the Texas governor, asking for men, money, rifles, and cannon powder. "We will rather die in these ditches than give it [the Alamo] up," he wrote.

Before supplies could reach them, however, 5,000 Mexican soldiers arrived. Bowie was sick with pneumonia and had a broken hip, suffered in a fall while mounting a cannon on one of the Alamo's walls. Davy Crockett, also at the Alamo, wrote: "Colonel Bowie . . . manages to crawl from his bed every day that his comrades might see him. His presence alone is a tower of strength."

Bowie and his companions did their best to defend the fort, but they were hopelessly outnumbered. On March 6, 1836, the Mexican army stormed into the Alamo and killed all of the rebels. Only about 15 people were spared.

Never afraid to back down from a fight, James Bowie died as he had lived. He went down in history as one of America's bravest heroes and most colorful characters. ◇

LIFE EVENTS

1796
James Bowie is born in Logan County, Kentucky.

1827
The "Bowie knife"— a heavy knife with a long, thin blade— becomes famous after a street fight.

1828
Bowie moves to Texas, a province of Mexico.

1835
Texas starts a war of independence from Mexico. Bowie is a colonel in the Texas army.

1836
Bowie dies in defense of the Alamo.

Omar Bradley
Army Commander
(born 1893 • died 1981)

As a young soldier, Omar Bradley thought that he was a failure because he did not get the chance to fight in World War I. Little did he know that he would become one of the most important generals in

Omar Bradley *(front left)* stands with Dwight D. Eisenhower in 1944.

American history—someone who would help lead the U.S. and its allies to victory during World War II.

A Career in the Army

Omar Nelson Bradley was born in a log cabin near Clark, Missouri, on February 12, 1893. He was a good athlete, and starred on his high school's baseball team. He hoped to go to college, but one of the teachers at his Sunday school had another idea: He recommended that Omar apply for a position at the U.S. Military Academy at West Point. West Point is one of the most difficult schools to get into, but Omar did well on his admission tests. In July 1911, he entered the academy as a cadet. Four years later, in 1915, he graduated, 44th out of a class of 164.

A few months after his graduation, Lieutenant Omar Bradley was sent to protect U.S. citizens during a civil war in Mexico. Although he did not do any fighting there, he learned a lot about how soldiers lived and worked in the field.

Missed Opportunities

When the U.S. entered World War I in 1917, Bradley was promoted to the rank of captain. He expected to be sent to the battlefield in Europe, and was eager to take part in the fighting. Instead, the Army sent his unit to Montana to guard copper mines, leaving the young captain frustrated and disappointed. He spent the next few months trying to win an assignment to a different unit, so he could go to Europe. At last, in August 1918, he received orders to go to France, but the war ended that November—before he had a chance to make it overseas.

During the 1920s, Bradley worked as a college professor at South Dakota State College and at West Point. Later, he became a teacher at the infantry school at Fort Benning, Georgia, where he trained many men who later became important generals in World War II, Korea, and Vietnam. By February 1941, Bradley

> "In war there is no second prize for the runner-up."
> —Omar Bradley

had been promoted to brigadier general and was the commander of the infantry school at Fort Benning. Despite the honor, he still longed for a chance to put all his military training into action on the battlefield.

World War II

In December 1941, the U.S. entered World War II. Bradley spent the first few months of the war training new soldiers and getting infantry units ready for battle. Once again, it seemed as if he would not see action on the European battlefields.

After American troops suffered an embarrassing loss

to German troops in North Africa, Bradley was sent there in hopes that he could improve the soldiers' performance. The troops did well under his command, and fighting in North Africa was over by May 1943.

Next, Bradley took part in the successful U.S. invasion of Sicily, in Italy. That led to his being made commander of the U.S. army units that were getting ready to invade and liberate France. That invasion, known as D-Day, turned out to be the largest and most important operation of the war.

After the War

After World War II ended in August 1945, Bradley was named head of the Veterans Administration (VA). The VA had been created to help soldiers who had served during America's wars. However, it was unable

TOPICAL TIDBIT

A Big Victory

Of all the battles of World War II, the most decisive was the beach landing at Normandy, France, on June 7, 1944—D-Day. Some 156,000 U.S., Canadian, and British troops withstood withering fire from the German armies to take and hold the beach. Omar Bradley, commanding the U.S. 1st Army, pushed south to Paris. There, on August 25, the Germans surrendered to French forces and American troops entered the city in triumph.

to cope with the large number of men returning from World War II. Bradley completely reorganized the VA, making it more accessible and helpful to millions of Americans.

Bradley held many more important positions during the late 1940s and early 1950s, including Army Chief of Staff in 1948 and General of the Army in 1950. In 1946, Bradley was appointed chairman of the Joint Chiefs of Staff, the highest position in the U.S. military. He retired from a long, productive career in 1953.

Omar Bradley died on April 8, 1981, at the age of 88. He was buried with full military honors at Arlington National Cemetery, among soldiers and war heroes with whom he had worked so closely during his long career. ◇

LIFE EVENTS

1893
Omar Nelson Bradley is born near Clark, Missouri.

1915
Bradley graduates from West Point.

1917
The U.S. enters World War I. Captain Bradley does not get to see battle.

1941
The U.S. enters World War II. Brigadier General Bradley distinguishes himself in North Africa, in Sicily, and on D-Day.

1949
Bradley is named the first Chairman of the Joint Chiefs of Staff and serves until he retires in 1953.

1983
Bradley's memoir, *A Soldier's Story: A General's Life*, is published two years after his death.

John Brown
Fighting Against Slavery
(born 1800 • died 1859)

Few people were as violently opposed to slavery as a Connecticut-born American named John Brown. Throughout his life, John Brown fought against slavery any way he could. Eventually, he gave up his life for his beliefs.

The Fight to Free the Slaves

John Brown was born in 1800 in Torrington, Connecticut, into a very religious family. His parents, family, and friends all believed that slavery was evil. Following their example, young John agreed that it must be stopped. He became an ardent abolitionist—a person who is opposed to slavery.

> "This *is* a beautiful country."
>
> —John Brown, riding to the gallows, December 2, 1859

During his life, John Brown lived in many different places in the United States, including Ohio, Penn-

sylvania, Massachusetts, and New York, and he held many different jobs, including farmer, wool merchant, and tanner (someone who turns animal skins into leather). Brown, who had a wife and 20 children to support, was never successful at any of his jobs. His large family suffered many hardships because of their lack of money. What Brown really cared about was ending slavery and making life better for all African Americans.

Brown worked for the abolitionist movement in many different ways. In 1834, he started a project to educate young blacks. At that time, many states did not allow black people to go to school. Abolitionists believed that education would help slaves win their freedom and help free blacks make a living.

Despite his lack of income, Brown managed to pay for the publication of many pamphlets calling for freedom of the slaves. He and his wife also adopted a black child and raised him as their own. In addition, Brown took part in the Underground Railroad, a movement that helped slaves escape from the South to freedom in Northern states or Canada. In 1849, Brown and his family moved to the black community of North Elba, New York, to help newly freed residents adjust to life there.

John Brown Turns Violent

In 1855, John Brown followed five of his sons to Kansas territory. There, he joined the campaign to make Kansas a free state—one where slavery wasn't allowed. Bloody battles between proslavery and antislavery groups had broken out in Kansas. In 1856, a proslavery mob raided the town of Lawrence, an Underground Railroad stop, and killed five people. By then, Brown had become the leader of a group willing to use violence to achieve freedom for slaves. With a band of men, including four of his sons, he attacked a proslavery settlement. They killed five people there, in revenge for the Lawrence attack.

By 1857, Brown was planning his most daring and violent act yet. He decided to lead a band of abolitionists in a raid on the U.S. arsenal at Harpers Ferry, Virginia. (An *arsenal* is a place where weapons and ammunition are stored.) The plan was to steal guns and other weapons, then give them to runaway slaves to use to fight for their freedom. During the night of October 16, 1859, 21 men, including Brown, raided the arsenal at Harpers Ferry. U.S. Marines on guard there fought back. Ten men, including two of Brown's sons, were killed. Brown was wounded and captured, and was put on trial for treason and murder.

The Trial

John Brown's actions shocked many people, but during his trial, he won many supporters, especially among abolitionists living in the Northern states.

TOPICAL TIDBIT

Before and After the Raid

In the final days of his life, John Brown asked the great abolitionist Frederick Douglass to join in the raid on Harpers Ferry. Douglass refused. He knew that an attack on federal property would be sure to backfire. After the raid, Douglass fled to Canada for a time, to escape blame. Although Douglass condemned the attack, he still mourned John Brown as a "noble old hero."

They were impressed by his dignified manner, and by his firm belief that he had done nothing wrong. Brown was allowed to speak before the court. "I believe [that] to have interfered as I have done . . . in behalf of [God's] despised poor, was not wrong, but right," he said. He explained that he had been fighting to free people from "wicked, cruel, and unjust" slavery. If he had to die for doing that, said Brown, "so let it be done."

John Brown was found guilty of all charges and sentenced to death. He was hanged in Charlestown, Virginia, on December 2, 1859.

Today, people still debate whether it is right or wrong to use violence to stop injustice. Whichever way they decide, John Brown is still remembered for sacrificing his life to help end slavery and achieve his goal of freedom for all Americans. ◇

LIFE EVENTS

1800
John Brown is born in Torrington, Connecticut.

1849
Brown and his family settle in a black community in North Elba, New York.

1855
Brown moves to Kansas territory to aid the antislavery forces.

1856
Brown leads a bloody revenge attack on a pro-slavery settlement at Pottawatomie Creek, Kansas.

1859
On October 16, Brown and 20 other men raid the arsenal at Harpers Ferry, Virginia. Tried and convicted of murder and treason, he is executed on December 2.

Ralph Bunche
Working Toward Peace
(born 1904 • died 1971)

In the years following World War II, many men and women worked to make sure that there would never again be such a devastating war. One of the most important soldiers of peace was Ralph Bunche.

An Active Childhood

Ralph Johnson Bunche was born in Detroit, Michigan, on August 7, 1904. His father was a barber. Although the family worked hard, they never had much money. Ralph and his parents moved several times during his childhood. Sometimes, they had to move in with his grandmother, aunts, and uncles to save money.

> "Hearts are the strongest when they beat in response to noble ideals."
> —Ralph Bunche

In 1916, Ralph's parents died, so Ralph, his grandmother, and his aunts and uncles moved to Los Angeles to start a new life. At

first, they had trouble finding a house to rent because they were black. Soon, though, they managed to save enough money to buy a house of their own.

Education was very important to Ralph's grandmother. She insisted that he work hard in school and be given all the advantages that white students had. He also played football, baseball, and basketball during high school and, in 1922, he won a scholarship (part athletic and part academic) to the University of California at Los Angeles (UCLA). Later, he went to

Harvard University, also on scholarship. When he wasn't studying or attending school, Bunche worked selling newspapers, laying carpets, cleaning offices, and as a servant for a rich family in Hollywood.

Bunche was interested in governments and how they worked, so he studied political science in college. After graduating from Harvard, he became a political science teacher at Howard University, a leading college for black students in Washington, D.C. He also traveled around the world, studying how people of different cultures and races lived with each other.

Making a Difference All Over the World

Bunche went to work for the U.S. government in 1941. He became an expert on international treaties, which are agreements between countries. Because of his knowledge, he was asked to help plan a new organization called the United Nations (UN).

The UN is made up of representatives from many different countries around the world. Its goal is to resolve conflicts between nations before they turned into wars. Bunche helped write the UN charter, a document that describes an organization's goals and lays out the rules that its members will follow.

The UN faced its first challenge in 1948, when the Jewish state of Israel was created in the Middle East. Many Arab countries were angry at this action, and they quickly went to war against Israel. Bunche traveled to the area and held discussions with the governments on both sides of the conflict. When the chief mediator, Count Folke Bernadotte, was assassinated, Bunche took his place. In 1949, thanks to Bunche's hard work and patience, the fighting stopped. Bunche returned to the U.S. and received a hero's welcome. In 1950, he was awarded the Nobel Peace Prize for his efforts in ending the Arab-Israeli conflict.

Bunche worked for the UN for more than 25 years, until he retired in 1971. He directed several UN peacekeeping operations, and also led a program to find peaceful uses for atomic energy.

The equal treatment of blacks and whites was also an important goal in Bunche's life. He had experienced discrimination in his own life because of the color of his skin, and he was determined to change

TOPICAL TIDBIT

A Man of Peace

In his years as chief troubleshooter for the Secretary General of the United Nations, Ralph Bunche went all over the world, handling crises. He became an expert in supervising peacekeeping forces—neutral armies, directed by the UN, that try to stop countries from fighting each other. In 1956, UN forces were placed at Egypt's Suez Canal to prevent conflict between Egypt on one side and Britain, France, and Israel on the other. Peacekeeping forces under Bunche's direction also served in the Congo in 1960 and in Cyprus in 1964.

things for future generations. He was a long-time member of the National Association for the Advancement of Colored People (NAACP), and served on its board of directors for 22 years. In 1949, he received the Spingarn Medal, which is the NAACP's highest honor. In 1963, Bunche took part in the March on Washington, a huge demonstration at which black and white Americans called for equal rights. Later that year, Bunche received the Medal of Freedom from President John F. Kennedy.

Ralph Bunche died in New York City on December 9, 1971. At his funeral, he was praised as a man who had devoted his life to public service, and as someone who had longed for and worked hard for peace throughout the world. ◇

LIFE EVENTS

1904
Ralph Johnson Bunche is born in Detroit, Michigan.

1944
An American Dilemma, a groundbreaking study of race relations cowritten by Bunche, is published.

1945
Bunche helps develop the United Nations (UN). He joins it in 1947.

1950
Bunche is awarded the Nobel Peace Prize for his peacemaking role in the Arab-Israeli conflict.

1955
Bunche becomes special assistant to the UN's Secretary General. He goes on to mediate many conflicts and to work in the U.S. civil-rights struggle.

Richard E. Byrd
Brave Explorer
(born 1888 • died 1957)

Exploring Earth's North and South Poles has always been an adventure filled with danger. One of the bravest polar explorers was Admiral Richard E. Byrd, who devoted his life to solving the mysteries of the most remote and forbidding places on Earth.

A Life of Adventure

Richard Evelyn Byrd was born on October 25, 1888, in Winchester, Virginia. Richard's father loved to read, and the Byrd home was filled with books. By the time Richard was a teenager, he had read hundreds of books about history, mathematics, and science. His special interest was polar exploration. After reading one book about the subject, Richard wrote in his diary that one day he would reach the North Pole.

Books were not the only thing Richard was interested in. He was also very good at sports, enjoyed riding horses, and loved to travel. When he was just

13 years old, Richard traveled halfway around the world to visit a family friend in the Philippines.

Richard Byrd attended the Virginia Military Institute (VMI), then went to the U.S. Naval Academy in Annapolis, Maryland. Despite spending weeks in the hospital after breaking his ankle and foot in a gymnastics competition, he graduated with his class in 1912. Byrd served on several Navy ships and won a medal for saving two of his shipmates from drowning.

Taking to the Sky

Although Byrd enjoyed working on ships, what he really wanted to do was fly. In August 1917, he was transferred to a naval aeronautics station in Pensacola, Florida. He called his first solo flight "the greatest event in an aviator's life." Byrd quickly learned to fly every type of airplane. Later, he worked to prepare Navy airplanes for their first flights across the Atlantic Ocean.

> **"I'd like to see that land beyond the Pole. That area beyond the Pole is the center of the Great Unknown."**
>
> —Richard E. Byrd

Byrd retired from the Navy in February 1925, so that he could spend his time exploring unknown parts of the world. In June of that same year, he flew from Maine to Greenland with Donald B. MacMillan, a noted polar explorer. In Greenland, Byrd realized that aviation was the best way to explore and conquer the Arctic.

In April 1926, Byrd returned to the Arctic with his friend Floyd Bennett, an aviation mechanic. The two men became the first people to fly over the North Pole. It took them 15 and a half hours to fly to the Pole, then back to Spitsbergen, Norway, where they had started. When they returned to the U.S., they were given a hero's welcome and a ticker-tape parade down Broadway in New York City. They also received the Congressional Medal of Honor from President Calvin Coolidge. Byrd was honored by another ticker-tape parade in 1927, after he became one of the first men to fly across the Atlantic Ocean. (Byrd, flying with three other pilots, made the trip in May 1927, just one month after Charles Lindbergh's historic solo flight across the Atlantic.)

Antarctica

Despite Byrd's heroic flights to the North Pole and across the Atlantic, he was already looking for a new challenge. He decided to explore the continent of Antarctica. At that time, only a few people had ever set foot on Antarctica's deserted, frozen surface.

Byrd and his companions arrived in Antarctica by

TOPICAL TIDBIT

Another Hero of Both Poles

Richard Byrd's heroics at the poles were echoed by another American, Lincoln Ellsworth. Ellsworth made two flights to the North Pole with Norwegian explorer Roald Amundsen—one in a dirigible three days after Byrd's flight. In 1935, Ellsworth and Canadian pilot Herbert Hollick-Kenyon made the first flight across the Antarctic continent, from one end to the other—a journey that they completed on foot after running out of fuel.

boat in December 1928. His supplies—including airplanes, fuel, and food—were unloaded and taken by dogsled across the ice to their base camp, which he called Little America. From there, Byrd became the first person to fly over the South Pole in 1929. Along with that historic flight, he and the scientists who traveled with him made many short flights around Antarctica. During one of these trips, a fierce storm destroyed one of the planes and left three men

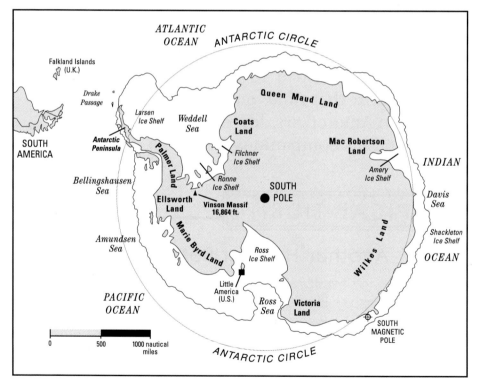

Little America was Richard Byrd's Antarctic base camp in 1928-1930. Byrd discovered nearby Marie Byrd Land and named it for his wife.

stranded in the ice and snow for two weeks. Finally, the weather improved and Byrd was able to fly in and rescue the men.

Between 1933 and 1947, Richard Byrd made three more trips to the Antarctic continent, where he discovered mountain ranges and explored and mapped more than a million square miles of territory. He also conducted weather experiments and performed other scientific research.

Byrd made several more flights over the South Pole. He also wrote several books describing his incredible experiences. When he died in 1957, he was honored as one of the most dedicated explorers in American history. Richard Byrd is buried at Arlington National Cemetery in Washington, D.C. A monument to his brave, adventurous spirit also stands in Antarctica. ◇

LIFE EVENTS

1888
Richard Evelyn Byrd is born in Winchester, Virginia.

1926
Byrd and Floyd Bennett are credited with being the first people to fly over the North Pole.

1928
Byrd makes his first expedition to Antarctica. In 1929, he is the first person to fly over the South Pole.

1946
Byrd begins "Operation High Jump," his fourth and most ambitious exploration of Antarctica. He and his party cover vast areas of unseen territory.

1956
Byrd makes his last flight over the South Pole. He dies the following year.

Kit Carson
King of the Mountain Men
(born 1809 • died 1868)

Kit Carson was a man of many talents. During his life, he worked as a trapper and hunter, a guide in the unmapped West, a soldier in the Civil War, and a government representative to Native American tribes. He was a true hero of the American West.

On the Trail

Christopher Houston Carson headed west at an early age. He was born in Madison County, Kentucky, on December 24, 1809, to a family that already included 10 children. Things were much too crowded in the Carson family's three-room cabin, so Kit's father sold the farm and moved his family to Missouri when Kit was not quite two years old.

When Kit was nine, his father was killed by a falling tree. Together with his older brothers and sister, young Kit helped run the family's farm. A few years later, when Kit was 13, his mother remarried. Kit became wild and angry. He went to live with an

older half-brother, and then with a local judge.

Young Kit went to work for a saddlemaker in Franklin, Missouri. He hated the job and would rather have been outdoors exploring the woods. What he did enjoy was listening to the stories told by travelers of their adventures in the American wilderness. Soon Kit was dreaming of going west himself.

While still in his teens, Kit talked his way into joining a group of trappers heading to Santa Fe by agreeing to take care of their horses and mules. The only problem was that he already had a job—with the saddlemaker. To solve the problem, Kit ran away.

Kit Carson had a number of jobs in New Mexico, including working as a cook, an interpreter for a group of traveling merchants, a miner, and a trapper.

> "Kit Carson fixed in my mind a pattern for heroes of quiet, steel-nerved courage; an ideal of what a real man should be."
>
> —Edgar L. Hewett, historian

By the time he was 21, he had become a respected scout, horseback rider, and hunter who had explored much of the western U.S.

In 1835, Carson married a Native American woman named Waanibe. Later, they moved to a New Mexico fort, where Carson's job was to hunt enough meat to feed the 25 people who lived there. Although he was a skilled hunter, he faced many dangers. These included not only animals, such as mountain lions and wolves, but also human enemies. The area was full of hostile Indians.

A Fateful Meeting

Around 1840, Carson's wife died and he took their young daughter back to Missouri to live with his sister. In Missouri, Carson met an explorer and mapmaker named Colonel John Charles Frémont. The

U.S. government had hired Frémont to map the land between Missouri and the Rocky Mountains. Frémont hired Kit Carson as his guide.

Carson made three trips west with Frémont. He also took letters and reports back to Washington, D.C., for Frémont and acted as a scout for General Stephen W. Kearny, who was part of an effort to take California from Mexico. All this activity, and the reports about it, stirred the imagination of Americans back East. Because Frémont's reports were filled with praise for and colorful stories about the man who delivered them, they made Kit Carson famous from coast to coast. He became known as "the King of the Mountain Men." Suddenly, he was an American hero.

TOPICAL TIDBIT

John C. Frémont

John C. Frémont is another important figure in the history of the American West. A skilled mapmaker, he mapped the upper Mississippi and Missouri rivers and much of the territory between the Mississippi valley and the Pacific Ocean. In 1846, he played a key role in the short-lived "Bear Flag Revolt" of Californians against Mexico, and was briefly proclaimed head of the "Republic of California." In 1856, he ran an unsuccessful campaign for president, as the first-ever candidate of the new Republican Party.

Hard Work—and War

After the job with Frémont, President James K. Polk asked Carson to be an Indian agent to several Native American tribes in New Mexico. Carson had a great love for the Indians and tried to be fair in all his dealings with them. Realizing that their way of life would soon vanish, he helped start programs to teach them farming and other new skills.

Then, in 1861, the Civil War broke out. Carson joined the Union army and was assigned to New Mexico, where he had to fight against certain Native American tribes. Carson took no pride in those battles, and his job made him miserable.

After the war, he was put in charge of a peacekeeping force in Colorado Territory. Kit Carson died there on May 23, 1868, at the age of 58. His name and accomplishments live on in stories of the American West. ◇

LIFE EVENTS

1809
Christopher Houston Carson is born in Madison County, Kentucky.

1826
Carson heads West, where he learns fur trapping and trading.

1842
John C. Frémont, charged with mapping the West, hires Carson as his guide. In the years following, Carson acquires his reputation as a mountain man.

1854
Carson is appointed an Indian agent at Taos, New Mexico.

1868
Carson is appointed superintendent of Indian affairs for Colorado Territory, a position he holds at his death.

Rachel Carson
Protecting the Earth
(born 1907 • died 1964)

People have long used chemicals called pesticides to kill harmful insects. But pesticides can also poison other animals, and even people. No one did more to open America's eyes to the dangers of pesticides than Rachel Carson. Her book *Silent Spring* changed the way people looked at the world.

> "To stand at the edge of the sea is to have knowledge of things that are as eternal as any earthly life can be."
> —Rachel Carson

A Lover of Nature

Rachel Louise Carson was born on May 27, 1907, in Springdale, Pennsylvania. The Carson family lived out in the country, and Rachel loved exploring the woods and fields near her home. Rachel's parents taught her to respect all life and love the natural world. She spent many hours watching birds and

other animals, and eating fresh fruits and vegetables from the family's garden.

Rachel's family also gave her a love of learning. Mrs. Carson had been a teacher, and she helped Rachel study and do research. If Rachel asked a question, her mother encouraged her to look up the answer for herself. Soon, Rachel was writing and drawing several "books" about the animals and plants she saw all around her. At age 11, Rachel published one of her stories in a children's magazine.

After graduating from high school, Rachel received a scholarship to the Pennsylvania College for Women in Pittsburgh, Pennsylvania. At first, she planned to be a writer. When she had to take a course in biology, however, she enjoyed it so much that she decided to be a biologist—a scientist who studies living things. She went on to study at the Marine Biological Laboratory at Woods Hole, Massachusetts. She also received a Master's degree in zoology from Johns Hopkins University in Baltimore, Maryland.

bio = life

An Uphill Climb

When Rachel Carson finished school in 1932, the United States was in the middle of the Great Depression. Many people had lost their jobs, and money was scarce. Carson faced a more particular problem: She had trouble finding a full-time job as a* biologist, because so few bosses were willing to hire a female scientist. In those days, many people believed that women were not smart enough or strong enough to do scientific work.

Finally, Carson got a job as a junior aquatic biologist for the U.S. Bureau of Fisheries. There, she wrote

* Most "biologist" positions require a doctorate (PhD).

scripts for a radio series called *Romance Under the Waters* and edited the bureau's publications. She also kept writing for herself, turning out articles for newspapers and magazines. In 1941, she published her first book, *Under the Sea-Wind*, which was about life in the ocean. Critics praised the beauty of Carson's writing as well as the strength of her scientific observations.

Rachel Carson Worries

After World War II, Carson began work on a series of booklets called "Conservation in Action," about the danger that civilization posed to many animals. At that time, Americans were taking more and more land to build houses, stores, factories, and highways. The more land people took, the less room animals had to live. Carson argued that forests,

TOPICAL TIDBIT

Powerful Words

For many people, it was Rachel Carson's vivid writing in *Silent Spring* that made them understand the dangers of pesticides for the first time. Describing a town where all the birds had died, she wrote: "It was a spring without voices. On the mornings that had once throbbed with the dawn chorus of scores of bird voices there was now no sound; only silence lay over the fields and woods and marsh."

swamps, and other wildlife habitats had to be preserved in order to save animals.

In 1950, she published her second book, *The Sea Around Us*. It won many awards and became a best-seller. Suddenly, Rachel Carson was famous. She quit her government job and began to write full-time. Her next book, *The Edge of the Sea*, also became a best-seller when it was published in 1955.

So far, all of her books had been about the ocean. Then Carson began finding out about the bad effects of a pesticide called DDT. Used to kill mosquitoes and other harmful insects, DDT killed butterflies and fish as well. It also damaged birds' eggs. Fewer birds hatched, and the bird population decreased. Furthermore, DDT poisoned people, because it polluted water supplies and got into the fruits and vegetables that people ate.

Carson wrote about the dan-

LIFE EVENTS

1907
Rachel Louise Carson is born in Springdale, Pennsylvania.

1929
Studying at the Marine Biological Laboratories, Carson becomes enchanted with the sea.

1936
Carson takes a job as an aquatic biologist with the U.S. Bureau of Fisheries.

1941
Carson's first book, *Under the Sea-Wind*, is published.

1951
The Sea Around Us, her second book, wins the National Book Award.

1962
Silent Spring, about the dangers of pesticides, is published. She dies two years later.

gers of pesticides in her next book, *Silent Spring*. Published in 1962, the book angered and upset many people. Newspaper articles claimed that Carson did not know what she was talking about, and that she was making a big deal about nothing. However, other people did pay attention to Carson's warnings—including President John F. Kennedy. He appointed a committee to study pesticides, and asked Carson to speak to Congress about the problem. More and more people began to realize that Carson was right. A few years later, Congress banned the use of DDT and other dangerous pesticides.

Rachel Carson died on April 14, 1964. After her death, *The New York Times* called her "one of the most influential women of our time." Her work truly changed the world for the better. ◇

John Chapman
Johnny Appleseed
(born 1774 • died 1845)

Can you be a hero just for planting apples? John Chapman is. His hard work and dedication changed the face of America, and turned him into a legend.

Mysterious Beginnings

Not much is known about John Chapman's early life. He was born on September 26, 1774, in Leominster, Massachusetts, where he lived with his parents and older sister. Johnny's father was a farmer and a carpenter. The family had little money.

> "He lived for others."
>
> —engraved on John Chapman's tombstone

In 1775, Johnny's father went off to fight in the American Revolution. The following year, his mother died. Johnny and his sister were probably cared for by relatives until his father returned from war a few years later.

When Mr. Chapman came home, he had a new

wife with him. The Chapman family moved to a tiny house in Longmeadow, Massachusetts, where Johnny's father and stepmother had 10 children over the next 20 years. Johnny probably found his only peace and quiet in the nearby woods, where he often went to be alone.

The boy went to school for only a few years. By the time he was a teenager, he had to find work.

Historians are not sure what he did during those first few years, but by the mid-1790s, he was in Pennsylvania working for a man who grew apples.

The Amazing Apple

Apples were an important food in America. They were easy to grow and could be stored for a long time. Apples were tasty and healthy, and could be used in many different ways: eaten raw, cooked into pies, or made into applesauce or apple butter. Apples could also be used to make vinegar or cider.

Moreover, John Chapman realized, an apple orchard was a thing of beauty—and a good business opportunity. He began by going to cider mills, pick-

TOPICAL TIDBIT

An Odd-looking Fellow

John Chapman's unique life and odd appearance made his transformation into the "Johnny Appleseed" of legend an easy one. The picture in popular stories was of a tall, thin fellow dressed in raggedy clothes, wearing a flour sack for a shirt and a pot for a hat. In fact, John Chapman was a short man, and the stew pot he carried to gather nuts, berries, and milk was probably never on his head. Otherwise, the picture was not much of an exaggeration.

ing out seeds that were usable, and planting them. In time, an apple orchard sprung up near the Big Brokenstraw River in Pennsylvania. Chapman's little orchard became a successful business. Settlers who were traveling west into the Ohio Valley stopped there to buy apple trees to plant.

Life on the Road

John Chapman enjoyed living in the wilderness, and did not mind being alone. He never married or had children, and he owned few possessions. He owned a lot of land, but never built a house or settled in one place. This allowed him to pick up and move on whenever he wanted to. When an area got too crowded, that is just what he did.

For the next five years, Chapman planted his seeds in western Pennsylvania and New York, along the banks of streams or rivers, where the land was good for growing things. When the young apple trees were big enough, he sold them for about six cents apiece. Chapman also traded his seedlings for food or clothes. If someone was too poor or had nothing to trade, he gave his trees away. The spreading of trees had started as a business, but it soon became a mission.

When Chapman was 25, he headed west into the new, unsettled territory west of the Ohio river, planting apple orchards along the way. His method was always the same: He would go into the wilderness with a bag of apple seeds on his shoulder, and look until he found fertile soil. Then he would plant his seeds in neat rows, build a little brush fence to keep out animals, then move on. By the time settlers arrived—in the area that later became the states of Ohio, Michigan, Indiana, and Illinois—they would find John Chapman's apple trees.

Chapman always worked by himself, living alone for weeks at a time. It was said that he talked to the animals, never carried a gun, and lived at peace with the Indians. He was a colorful figure, in his ragged, old clothes. He walked barefoot when the weather allowed, and wore shoes only in the winter. It was said that Chapman's feet were so tough, they looked like an elephant's.

Even as an old man, he could not stop moving. In 1843, a man in Indiana reported seeing him walk from Iowa

LIFE EVENTS

1774
John Chapman is born in Leominster, Massachusetts.

Late 1700s
Living in western Pennsylvania, Chapman collects apple seeds and starts his own orchard. He also plants apple trees in other places in Pennsylvania and New York.

Around 1801
Chapman heads west. For the next 40 years, he roams the Northwest Territory planting apple trees, and selling or giving away thousands of apple seedlings to settlers.

1845
John Chapman dies at age 70. Legends about him spring up across the country after his death.

(Elephants are said to have wonderful memories,)

to Pennsylvania. Chapman was 69 years old at the time! Still, everywhere he went, he planted apple seeds. In time, a legend of him spread and he became known as the Apple Tree Man, or Johnny Appleseed.

John Chapman died at a friend's house on March 18, 1845, after a short illness. He was 70. Soon stories about him began to appear in local magazines and newspapers. He went to become one of the most loved figures in American history. ◇

Cesar Chavez
The Worker's Friend
(born 1927 • died 1993)

Every year, thousands of people travel around the country, harvesting crops for little money. For decades, these people, known as migrant workers, had little hope or a chance at a better life. Then one man, Cesar Chavez, stepped forward to help them find fair treatment and respect.

A Poor Childhood

Cesar Estrada Chavez was born near Yuma, Arizona, on March 31, 1927. His grandfather had come to the U.S. from Mexico in 1889 and started a small farm. When the Great Depression hit, however, Cesar's father lost the farm because he could not afford to pay his taxes. The family got in their car and drove to California to start a new life.

> "Every time you go to the store and choose not to buy grapes, you cast a vote."
> —Cesar Chavez

Cesar, his parents, and his five brothers and sisters became migrant workers. They traveled all over California, picking crops for 12 hours a day, six days a week. It was a terribly difficult life. Migrant-worker families lived in tiny shacks made out of metal, with tar-paper roofs and no running water or bathrooms.

Workers were paid very little for their hard labor. They were afraid to complain, though, because then they would lose their jobs.

Because the family had to keep moving to find work, Cesar attended more than 30 schools by the time he finished eighth grade. Teachers did not pay much attention to him, and Cesar could barely read or write. Still, he managed to learn some English, a skill that became important later in his life.

"Don't Buy Grapes!"

Cesar quit school after eighth grade and found a job picking grapes in California's vineyards. In time, he became tired of the terrible working conditions. He tried to convince the other workers to ask the

TOPICAL TIDBIT

Giving Names to the Nameless

The plight of migrant farm workers first came to many Americans' attention in 1948, when a plane carrying 28 Mexicans crashed near Los Gatos, California. Songwriter Woody Guthrie was moved to compose a song, "Deportee (Plane Wreck at Los Gatos)." In it, he described the victims "all scattered like dry leaves" on the brown hills of Los Gatos Canyon. He also gave the workers names—such as Juan and Maria—to make the point that Americans didn't know about the struggles of the people who picked their food.

vineyard's owner for more money and a better place to live, but the men were afraid to complain.

When Cesar Chavez was in his early 20s, he met a man named Fred Ross. Ross worked for the Community Service Organization (CSO), a group trying to help migrant workers. Soon Chavez was doing volunteer work for the organization. When his farm boss found out, he thought that Chavez would cause trouble among the migrant workers, so he fired him.

Chavez got a full-time job with the Community Service Organization. He worked tirelessly, organizing meetings, registering workers to vote, and getting them in school. He also organized citizenship classes for Mexican workers.

In 1962, Chavez left the Community Service Organization to start his own organization, the National Farm Workers Association (NFWA). The NFWA was a huge success. Its members worked together to fight for the rights of migrant workers. The NFWA also provided other important services, such as selling goods cheaply to migrant families, lending them money, and hiring lawyers to help migrants who were treated unfairly by their employers.

In 1965, the NFWA decided to take drastic action to win better pay and working conditions: They went on strike. The farm owners fought back by hiring people from Mexico to come and work for little pay. It looked as if the strike would go on for a long time.

Then Chavez came up with a plan to force the farm

owners to settle. He and other NFWA members traveled all over America, asking people to boycott (refuse to buy) California grapes. They asked store owners not to sell them, truck drivers not to deliver them, and people everywhere not to buy or eat them. Chavez made many speeches and appeared in many newspapers. In time, people all over the country began to learn about the migrants' suffering, and began demanding fair treatment for the farm workers.

The grape boycott worked. Eventually, boycotts spread to other farm products, such as lettuce and tomatoes. In 1969, the strike finally ended with a victory for the farm workers.

Cesar Chavez continued to work with farm workers until his death on April 23, 1993. He helped end some of the worst conditions in the farm workers' existence, making life better for thousands of people. ◇

LIFE EVENTS

1927
Cesar Estrada Chavez is born near Yuma, Arizona, to a Mexican-American family.

1958
Chavez becomes general director of the Community Services Organization (CSO).

1962
Chavez starts the National Farm Workers Association (NFWA).

1965
The NFWA begins a historic strike against California grape farmers. It lasts for five years.

1971
The NFWA and the AFL-CIO join to form a new union—the United Farm Workers of America (UFW).

Crazy Horse
Native American Warrior
(born 1841 or 1842 • died 1877)

Many Native Americans suffered terribly at the hands of the United States Army. Many also fought bravely against the unfair and cruel treatment they received. One of the most legendary heroes of these conflicts was an Oglala Sioux named Crazy Horse.

A Strange Child

Crazy Horse was born in the Black Hills of Dakota Territory in 1841. His father was a medicine man, or holy man, in the Sioux tribe. From the beginning, there was something different about Crazy Horse. Unlike other Native American babies, he had light-colored skin and wavy, light-brown hair. He grew into a small, quiet child who usually stayed by himself. Because of his unusual hair, he was known as Curly. As he grew up, he became a skilled warrior and hunter. He also grew into a leader among other boys in the tribe.

— Sioux is pron. "Sue",

124

Trouble With White Men

When Curly was a child, more and more white settlers moved into the Black Hills to find gold. Many fights broke out between the settlers and the Native Americans. In 1854, a young Native stole a settler's cow. The settler went to the soldiers at Fort Laramie for help. A troop of 31 soldiers marched into the Sioux's camp and shot at them. When the Sioux fought back and killed all the soldiers, the U.S. government responded by sending 600 troops into Sioux country to keep the peace.

Curly was deeply troubled by the violence between the Sioux and the white men. He went off by himself and had a vision. Curly's father, hearing of this vision, thought that it had a special meaning—that his son would never be harmed in battle. The old medicine man gave Curly a new name. From now on, he would be known as Crazy Horse.

> "It is a good day to fight; it is a good day to die."
> —Crazy Horse's battle cry

During the 1860s, things became worse between the Sioux and the white soldiers. Several of Crazy Horse's friends were killed in battles. In 1866, Crazy Horse joined forces with an older chief named Red Cloud to stop the U.S. government from building forts along the Bozeman Trail, which led to Montana. For two years, Crazy Horse, Red Cloud, and their warriors burned forts and attacked any white person who tried to cross their land. Finally, the government abandoned the trail and made peace with the Native Americans there. The government promised that the Sioux would have all of present-day South Dakota, including the Black Hills— land that was sacred to the Sioux.

A War for Gold

In 1874, gold was discovered in the Black Hills. The U.S. government realized that it had been a mistake to give the Black Hills to the Sioux, and tried to buy the land. The Sioux refused. The government was forced to make up an excuse to claim the land. On December 6, 1875, the U.S. declared war on the tribe. All Sioux people were told to report to the U.S. government within six weeks.

By then, Crazy Horse was second-in-command of the Sioux nation under its chief, Sitting Bull. Crazy Horse and Sitting Bull refused to follow the government's instructions. Instead, they moved their people north. Six hundred U.S. soldiers under the command of General George Armstrong Custer went after them.

The two armies met on June 25, 1876, on the banks of the Little Bighorn River in eastern Montana. Crazy

TOPICAL TIDBIT

A Larger-Than-Life Hero

The memory of Crazy Horse lives on in a massive sculpture of the warrior that is being carved into 600-foot-high Thunderhead Mountain in the Black Hills. Started by Polish-American artist Korczak Ziolkowski in 1948, it will, when finished, show Crazy Horse in profile on his horse. It is expected to be the largest mountain sculpture in the world. (The head alone is 87 feet tall.) No one knows how long it will take to complete the sculpture.

Horse led 1,000 warriors into battle. Custer and all 225 men of his 7th Cavalry were wiped out. It was a rare victory for Native Americans in their fight against the white men. Crazy Horse was now known as one of the greatest Native American leaders of all time.

The triumph did not last long. By 1877, the chiefs were forced to give up their land. In the spring of 1877, after a long, hard winter, Crazy Horse surrendered at Camp Robinson in Nebraska. On September 4, the soldiers heard rumors that he was planning to cause trouble and decided to put him in jail. Crazy Horse resisted and was stabbed by a guard. A few hours later, he was dead. Crazy Horse's parents claimed the body and took it out of the camp. To this day, no one knows where the great warrior of the Sioux found his last resting place—but his name lives on in American history. ◇

LIFE EVENTS

1841 or 1842
Ta-sunko-witko, later known as Crazy Horse, is born to the Oglala Sioux tribe in the Black Hills, Dakota Territory.

1866
Crazy Horse leads his people in opposing U.S. Army plans to build forts in the Black Hills.

1874
Gold is found in the Black Hills. Whites stream to the area, ignoring Sioux treaty rights.

1876
Crazy Horse and the Sioux defeat General Custer's 7th Cavalry at the Little Bighorn River.

1877
Crazy Horse surrenders, but is killed in a scuffle with soldiers.

Davy Crockett
Hero of the Frontier
(born 1786 • died 1836)

Many American heroes come from humble beginnings, but few of them became as celebrated as Davy Crockett. Throughout his life, Davy always worked to help others stake their claim on the American frontier. In the process, he became an American legend.

Backwoods Beginnings

David Crockett was born in eastern Tennessee on August 17, 1786. His parents ran a mill along the Big Limestone River. When Davy was eight years old, a flood washed away the mill and the family's house. Davy's father then moved to Jefferson County, Tennessee, and opened a tavern. There young Davy met many travelers passing through, and listened with fascination to their tales of

> "I'll leave this rule for others when I'm dead: Be always sure you're right—then go ahead."
> —Davy Crockett

adventure on the frontier. He grew to admire people who could face challenges in the wilderness—and he longed to explore the wilderness himself.

Davy did not attend school until he was a teenager. After just a few days, he got into a fight with a bigger boy and hit him over the head with a rock. Knowing that his father would punish him for fighting, he got a job with a neighbor and left to drive a herd of cattle to Virginia. He was away for more than two years.

Young Davy grew to be a very good shot with a rifle, an important skill to have in the wilderness. He won many shooting contests. During this time, Davy also went back to school. Although he attended it for only six months, he learned to read and write and do simple math.

When Davy Crockett was 20, he got married and settled down to farm and hunt. He found it hard to make a living on the crowded land, though, so he and his family moved several times. Finally, they settled in Franklin County in eastern Tennessee, where Crockett began his frontier adventures.

Crockett Enters Politics

By 1813, there was a lot of trouble between Native Americans and the white settlers who were moving onto their lands. This trouble flared up into the Creek Indian War of 1813-1814. Crockett commanded troops against the Creek, an experience that won him the command of a local militia in 1818, and the rank of colonel.

In 1820, Crockett was elected to the Tennessee legislature. During his term, he worked to ease taxes on landholders and make it easier for settlers to keep their land in disputes. He later served three terms in the U.S. Congress, two terms from 1827 to 1831, and the third from 1833 to 1835. His motto was, "Be always sure you're right, then go ahead." As a member of Congress, he continued to fight for the rights of landholders and tried to make land more available to poor settlers. He saw himself as a poorly educated, simple man from the backwoods, and he wanted to help other people who had the same background.

When Crockett was not serving in the government, he returned home to live in the woods. By now, he was famous for his hunting skill and his fearlessness. He once reported that he had killed 58 bears in one season. Tales about his remarkable life were finally written down in an 1834 book called *A Narrative of the Life of David Crockett of the State of Tennessee*. The book became quite popular, and the fame of Davy Crockett grew.

TOPICAL TIDBIT

"King of the Wild Frontier"

The public image of Davy Crockett as a shrewd, rough-and-ready frontiersman began during his years in the Tennessee state legislature. Later, the Whig party publicized him as its "coonskin" candidate, referring to his love for hunting raccoons and wearing their fur. Many Americans still remember the wily Davy Crockett of the hugely popular Walt Disney movie of 1955. Children all over American imitated him by wearing his coonskin cap.

The War for Texas

During the 1830s, Texas was involved in a war for its independence from Mexico. Crockett wanted to explore the Texas wilderness and help fight for independence. Crockett volunteered for the Texas militia and soon found himself on his way to fight at a fort called the Alamo, which was under attack by the Mexican army. On March 6, 1836, the Mexican army broke through the walls of the fort and killed nearly everyone inside. Crockett survived the battle, but was taken prisoner along with five other survivors. The Mexican general executed Crockett and his companions on the spot.

After Davy Crockett's death, he became even more famous than he had been when alive. Songs, stories, and several movies have been based on his life. He had traveled from humble beginnings to become one of America's most legendary heroes. ◇

LIFE EVENTS

1786
David Crockett is born in eastern Tennessee.

1813
Crockett commands troops during the Creek Indian War.

1827
Crockett wins the first of his three terms in the U.S. House of Representatives.

1834
Crockett gives popular speeches for the Whig Party. His autobiography is published, spreading his fame.

1836
Crockett, a volunteer during the Texas war of independence, is killed at the Alamo.

Benjamin O. Davis Jr.
A Very Special Soldier
(born 1912)

Through much of the early 20th century, it was hard for African Americans to find opportunity in the U.S. military. During that time, Benjamin O. Davis Jr. defied the odds and became one of the most powerful and respected men in military service.

A Military Family

Benjamin Oliver Davis Jr. was born on December 18, 1912, in Washington, D.C. His father, Benjamin O. Davis Sr., was the first black brigadier (one-star) general in the U.S. Army. The Davis family moved many times as Benjamin Sr. took on military assignments around the country. For a while, young Benjamin and his siblings lived with their grandparents while their father was serving in the Philippines.

Benjamin Jr. did well in school. A popular student, he was elected president of his class at a mostly white high school in Cleveland. Afterward, he went on to attend Western Reserve University in Cleveland

and the University of Chicago. But his father wanted him to enter the U.S. Military Academy at West Point. Benjamin did not know if he wanted a military career—and West Point was not eager to have black students. Still, he took the entrance exam—and failed.

Benjamin was shocked when he failed the exam. Suddenly, he wanted to prove to himself and to his father that he could succeed at the academy. He studied hard and passed the test on his second try. He entered West Point on July 1, 1932.

The Silent Treatment

Davis was not welcome at West Point. The other cadets did not want a black man in their class. For four years, they subjected him to "silencing." No one ate with him or would room with him. No cadets spoke to him unless absolutely necessary. This made Davis even more determined to succeed. In 1936, he graduated in the top 15 percent of his class. He was the first black West Point graduate in the 20th century.

After graduating, Davis had to suffer through a series of unimportant jobs. He and his new wife had to live in segregated military housing. Then, World War II began, and everything changed.

Blacks and Whites in the Army

When the U.S. entered World War II in 1941, the army was segregated. Black soldiers and white soldiers fought in separate units, and were commanded only by officers of their own color.

Because the U.S. Army needed pilots for the war, it started an Advanced Army Flying School for blacks at Tuskegee Institute. Benjamin O. Davis Jr. was in its first class. In 1943, the Ninety-ninth Pursuit

Squadron headed to North Africa under Davis's command. The squadron, known as the Tuskegee Airmen, flew many missions in a short time. Still, they struggled against discrimination. One white commander said that the men of the Ninety-ninth did not have the same desire to fight as white pilots. A white general agreed, and it looked as if the Tuskegee Airmen were finished.

Davis returned to the U.S. to stick up for his men. He insisted to the War Department that the Ninety-Ninth fought just as hard, and in fact flew more missions than the white squadrons. The War Department was convinced by his arguments. In January 1944, it sent Davis and his Tuskegee Airmen to Europe to join the fight there.

TOPICAL TIDBIT

Like Father, Like Son

As a groundbreaking military man, Benjamin O. Davis Jr. followed in the footsteps of his father. Benjamin O. Davis Sr. was born in 1877. He served during the Spanish-American War (1898) before being commissioned a second lieutenant in the Army in 1901— the first African American officer in the U.S. military. He later became the U.S. Army's first black colonel, then its first black general. But Davis Sr.'s career was limited by discrimination. It took the bravery of his son to permanently open doors that had been closed to him and millions of other African Americans.

Now part of the 332nd Fighter Group, the Tuskegee Airmen escorted bombers over Italy. Right away, they proved themselves in a series of fierce battles. In one two-week period, they shot down seven German fighters for every one they lost. Davis led the 332nd on its most spectacular mission, a 1,600-mile trip to Berlin.

By the end of the war, the squadron had flown more than 200 escort missions, had shot down 111 enemy planes in the air—and had not lost a single bomber in their care. The Tuskegee Airmen had proven that they were just as brave and skilled as white pilots, and Benjamin O. Davis Jr. received the Distinguished Flying Cross.

The war ended in 1945, but Davis found a new battle to fight: arguing for an end to segregation in the U.S. armed forces. In 1948, President Harry S. Truman signed an order ending segregation in the military. The 332nd Fighter

"Suddenly the air was full of P-47s [jets], diving and whirling through our formations. They never left us. They showed no inclination to turn away from the flak rising up ahead. They flew through the clouds of bursting shells. . . . It was a grand gesture."
—a U.S. bomber pilot, describing the bravery of the Tuskegee Airmen, Italy 1943

Group became the first all-black unit to be integrated into the Air Force.

Away From the Spotlight

During the Korean War, Davis commanded an integrated flying unit. In 1959, he was promoted to major (two-star) general—the first black to achieve such a high rank in the Air Force. In 1965, he became the first black lieutenant (three-star) general. During the late 1960s, he commanded the 13th Air Force in Vietnam. In 1970, he retired.

After Davis left the military, he worked for the Department of Transportation to improve airport security and highway safety. By then, the U.S. armed forces—and the world—were very different places from what they had been during the 1940s. Benjamin O. Davis Jr. was one of the people who helped make that change. ◇

LIFE EVENTS

1912
Benjamin Oliver Davis Jr. is born in Washington, D.C.

1932
Davis enters West Point.

1943
Davis is placed in command of the Tuskegee Airmen, a black Air Force squadron, during World War II. He wins the Distinguished Flying Cross for missions over Europe.

1948
U.S. President Harry S. Truman orders the armed forces integrated.

1965
Davis becomes the first African American in any U.S. military branch to reach the rank of lieutenant general.

Thomas A. Dooley
The Jungle Doctor
(born 1927 • died 1961)

Some people become heroes because they act bravely in battle, explore dangerous places, or perform incredible feats. Another way some people become heroes is by helping others. Thomas A. Dooley was one of those heroes.

Musical Beginnings

Thomas Anthony Dooley was born in St. Louis, Missouri, on January 17, 1927. He was interested in music as a child. He took piano lessons for many years and performed with orchestras in St. Louis.

Tom's family wanted him to become a professional concert pianist. However, young Tom had decided that a career in music was not for him. He wanted to study medicine.

Dooley started college at the University of Notre Dame in Indiana in 1944. After his older half-brother was killed in World War II, Dooley decided that he owed his service to his country. He dropped out of

Thomas A. Dooley

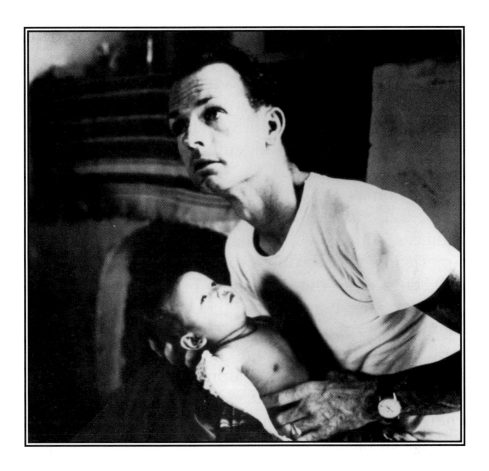

college to serve in the U.S. Navy from 1944 until 1946. Dooley returned to Notre Dame after the Navy, then went on to receive a Doctor of Medicine degree from St. Louis University in 1953.

A Life-changing Assignment

In May 1954, the country of Vietnam, in Southeast Asia, was ending a long war with the French. As part of an agreement the two countries made to stop the fighting, Vietnam was to be divided into two zones, North and South. Because North Vietnam was to be ruled by a Communist government, many Vietnamese chose to flee to the South, which had a more democratic government. Suddenly, this created many, many refugees.

Dr. Thomas Dooley volunteered for duty aboard the U.S.S. *Montague,* a Navy ship that transported refugees from North Vietnam to South Vietnam. The Americans called this evacuation of more than 600,000 people "the Passage to Freedom."

Dooley was horrified at the conditions that the Vietnamese refugees had to endure. They had little food, no clean water, and no medical care. As a medical officer in the city of Haiphong, Dooley's job was to prevent the spread of disease. Later, he was put in charge of building and maintaining Haiphong's refugee camps.

The Americans had to leave Haiphong in May 1955, when the Communist government took over the city. Dooley returned to the U.S. and wrote a book about his experiences in Vietnam. That book, *Deliver Us From Evil,* became a best-seller and was translated into 11 different languages. Dooley also became the youngest U.S. Navy Medical Corps officer to receive the Navy's Legion of Merit.

Dooley traveled around the U.S. giving lectures about the Navy's work in Vietnam. However, he could not stop thinking about the refugees and the terrible conditions they endured. He knew that he had to go back to Southeast Asia.

Jungle Hospitals

In 1956, Dooley quit the Navy and joined the International Rescue Committee. Taking some of the money he had earned from his book and lectures, he traveled to Nam Tha, a village in northern Laos, a country that borders Vietnam. Dooley chose Laos because the country had three million people and only one doctor.

Dooley and several of his friends started a hospital in Nam Tha. The hospital, which was located in the middle of the jungle, had no electricity, plumbing, air-conditioning, or modern medical equipment.

TOPICAL TIDBIT

Another Tom Dooley

By coincidence, two people named Tom Dooley were famous at the same time. In 1958, the Kingston Trio, a popular folk group, had a hit with a traditional American ballad called "Tom Dooley." The song told the true story of a man who killed a woman in 1866. The coincidence caused some confusion at the time—many people thought that the song was about the famous doctor!

Still, Dooley treated about 100 patients every day. He also trained local people to provide medical care, so that they could run the hospital after he left.

In November 1957, Dooley founded an organization called the Medical International Cooperation Organization, or MEDICO. MEDICO provided doctors and nurses, hospitals, and medical treatment to people in Southeast Asia.

> "My years in Asia have proved to me that the brotherhood of man exists as certainly as does the fatherhood of God."
> —Thomas A. Dooley

By 1958, Tom Dooley was widely admired in the U.S. Everyone from schoolchildren to secretaries raised money and sent supply packages to MEDICO. Dooley also made many radio and television appearances to raise money. Funds earned from two other books contributed to the organization that he had single-handedly started.

Soon after he founded MEDICO, Tom Dooley found out that he had cancer. In August 1959, he had surgery to remove a cancerous tumor. Despite his illness, he refused to stop working. By October, he had raised one million dollars for MEDICO; by Christmas, he was back in Laos.

In 1960, Dooley wrote *The Night They Burned the Mountain*, about the founding of MEDICO and his adventures in Southeast Asia. By June of that year, however, the cancer had spread through his body. Dooley returned to New York for treatment. He died on January 18, 1961—one day after his 34th birthday.

On June 7, 1962, President John F. Kennedy honored Dr. Thomas A. Dooley by presenting a gold medal to his mother. The President hailed the Jungle Doctor for "providing a model of American compassion before the rest of the world." ◇

LIFE EVENTS

1927
Thomas Anthony Dooley is born in St. Louis, Missouri.

1944
Dooley drops out of Notre Dame to join the Navy during World War II.

1954
Dooley volunteers to help evacuate 600,000 refugees from North to South Vietnam in the dramatic "Passage to Freedom."

1956
Deliver Us From Evil, Dooley's book about Vietnam, makes him a popular figure in America.

1957
Dooley forms MEDICO, dedicated to providing the people of Southeast Asia with medical care. He serves this cause until his death in 1961.

Frederick Douglass
A Voice Against Slavery
(born 1818 • died 1895)

Frederick Douglass endured cruel mistreatment as a slave. Later, he transformed himself into a powerful voice for freedom.

A Slave Child

Frederick Bailey was born in a slave cabin in Easton, Maryland, in February 1818. Like many slave children, he was taken away from his mother. Young Frederick was raised by his grandparents, who were also slaves.

When Frederick was six years old, his grandmother took him to the plantation where his master lived. The child had to do hard work for long hours. If he did not do what he was told, he was beaten. Frederick had little food, and had to sleep on a dirt floor with only an old flour sack for a blanket.

Things got better for Frederick when he was eight years old. He was sent to Baltimore, Maryland, to live with a man named Hugh Auld. There, he did house-

hold chores and ran errands for the Auld family. In this new household, Frederick had good food to eat and warm clothes to wear. He was allowed to play with the Aulds' young son, Thomas, and Mrs. Auld began teaching Frederick how to read.

It was, however, strictly against the law to teach a black person to read or write. When Mr. Auld found out what his wife was doing, he demanded that she stop her lessons. But young Frederick could not be denied: He convinced some of the white children in the neighborhood to share their books with him. His curious mind soaked up everything.

> "I am no coward. Liberty I will have, or die in the attempt to gain it."
> —Frederick Douglass

When Frederick was a teenager, Mr. Auld died and the youth was sent to work on a farm. Once again, he was given little food and had to live under harsh conditions. He was often whipped when he refused to obey his master. No matter what happened to him, though, no punishment could break Frederick Bailey's spirit.

A New Life

Frederick Bailey was determined to find a way to get to the North, where slavery was illegal. Luckily, he had a friend who was a free black man, and this man was willing to lend Bailey his identification papers. In 1838, using the friend's papers, 20-year-old Bailey took a train and made it all the way to New York City. He was free! He soon settled in New Bedford, Massachusetts, and changed his name to Frederick Douglass.

Although he was finally free, life was still hard. Because he was black, Douglass had trouble finding work. Finally, he got a job loading cargo onto ships.

While living in New Bedford, Douglass began attending meetings of abolitionists, people who were united in the cause of ending slavery. In 1841, Douglass spoke before the Massachusetts Anti-Slavery Society. The audience was spellbound by his stories of life as a slave. The Society asked Douglass to travel around New England, lecturing about the evils of slavery.

Audiences flocked to his speeches—but not everyone was there to listen to his message. Douglass was often laughed at and attacked by mobs of angry whites. However, just as he had during his slave days, Douglass refused to back down.

Douglass later wrote a book about his life, *Narrative of the Life of Frederick Douglass, an American Slave*. It made him famous all over the world. How-

TOPICAL TIDBIT

Words of Freedom

By 1848, Frederick Douglass had come a long way. A famous writer with a family, a home, and a busy, important life, he did something that few ex-slaves could ever do: He wrote a letter to his ex-master, Thomas Auld (Hugh Auld's brother). "I am your fellow-man, but not your slave," Douglass said in the letter, which was published in the press and read by many Americans.

ever, this fame was dangerous. Douglass was a runaway slave, which meant that—by law—he could be captured and sent back to his master at any time.

For his own safety, Douglass went to live in England for a time. After two years, he returned home and bought his freedom from his old master. The cost was $710.96.

Freedom for Everyone

In 1847, Douglass and his family moved to Rochester, New York. The Douglass house became a stop on the Underground Railroad, a secret network that smuggled runaway slaves to freedom in Canada. Douglass started an abolitionist newspaper called *The North Star*, which was praised by other abolitionists. His passionate writing and public speaking made him a leader in the antislavery movement. White people everywhere were surprised to learn that a black man, an ex-slave, could be capable of such brilliance.

During the Civil War, he became a trusted friend and adviser to President Abraham Lincoln. Douglass urged Lincoln to arm former slaves and allow them to fight for the Union. He also helped win better pay and better treatment for black soldiers.

In 1865, the Thirteenth Amendment to the Constitution finally outlawed slavery in the U.S. After the end of slavery, Douglass spoke out against segregation—the practice of keeping blacks and whites separated in public places. Douglass was also the first African American to hold important positions in the U.S. government including U.S. marshal and U.S. minister to Haiti.

Frederick Douglass believed in equal rights for everyone, not just blacks. He was active in the women's suffrage movement, which fought to win the right to vote for women. On February 20, 1895, Douglass gave a speech on women's rights. A few hours later, he died of a heart attack. His belief that anyone—black or white, woman or man—could use the power of the spoken and written word to change society is an example that still inspires us today. ◇

LIFE EVENTS

1818
Frederick Bailey is born to a slave mother in Maryland.

1838
Bailey escapes to freedom. He moves to Massachusetts and changes his last name to Douglass.

1841
Douglass becomes a popular speaker and a leader of the abolitionist movement.

1845
The Life and Times of Frederick Douglass, his autobiography, is published. He starts an antislavery publication, *The North Star*, in 1847.

1861
Douglass is a special adviser to President Lincoln. After the war, he becomes the first black citizen to hold high rank in the U.S. government.

Amelia Earhart
A Woman With Wings
(born 1897 • died 1937)

Today, we take airplane travel for granted. During the 1920s and 1930s, however, long-distance flying was a dangerous adventure that only a few people were willing to try. Amelia Earhart was one of the bravest and most inspiring of those daring few. As a woman, she also was the inspiration for many other women to follow their dreams.

> "Courage is the price that Life exacts for granting peace."
> —Amelia Earhart

An Adventurous Childhood

Amelia Mary Earhart was born in Atchison, Kansas, on July 24, 1897. She and her younger sister, Muriel, came from a wealthy family and enjoyed a comfortable childhood.

In those days, girls were not supposed to play the rough games that boys enjoyed. Unlike other par-

Amelia Earhart sits at the controls of her plane on March 6, 1937,
a few days before leaving on her around-the-world flight.

ents, however, the Earharts let their daughters play
whatever games they liked. The sisters enjoyed baseball, football, and other sports. Amelia became
known around the neighborhood as a daring girl
who was not afraid of anything. Once, she even
steered her sled underneath a passing horse!

In 1908, the Earharts moved to Des Moines, Iowa. Soon afterward, Amelia saw her first airplane at the Iowa State Fair. She was not very impressed. "It was a thing of rusty wire and wood and not at all interesting," she later wrote.

Taking to the Sky

When Earhart finished school, she became a nurse; a few years later, she moved to California. One day, she went to an airplane show where pilots were doing dives and tricks in the air. This was quite different! Suddenly, she was very excited about aviation. Earhart got into one of the planes and took a 10-minute ride over Los Angeles. From that day on, all Amelia Earhart wanted to do was fly.

TOPICAL TIDBIT

Daredevil in the Air

Many women were inspired by Amelia Earhart's feats. Among the most colorful was Pancho Barnes. Born Florence Lowe into a wealthy family, Barnes used her money not for leisure but for a life of adventure. She was an expert daredevil pilot. In 1930, she won the second Women's Air Derby, beating Amelia Earhart's record from the previous year. In 1929, Barnes performed air stunts for the movie *Hell's Angels*, becoming the first female stunt pilot in film history.

Earhart took flying lessons—much to her family's displeasure. At age 25, she earned her pilot's license. In 1922, she bought her own plane, a Kinner Canary, and that October, she set a women's altitude record by flying at 14,000 feet. It was only the first of several important records that she set in her brief lifetime.

By 1926, Earhart was known as the most daring female pilot in America. She was offered the chance to be the first female to fly across the Atlantic Ocean, as a passenger. Because she had no experience flying a multiengine plane or using instruments, two male pilots did the actual flying. Still, on June 18, 1928, she made the air trip across the Atlantic, a journey that made her famous all over the world.

On May 20-21, 1932, Earhart once again flew across the Atlantic, this time by herself. She broke several records during that journey. Not only was she the first woman to fly solo across the Atlantic, and only the second person to do it—the first was Charles Lindbergh—Earhart had also flown the longest non-stop distance for a woman ever. She also had crossed the ocean in record time.

A Flight Into Mystery

In January 1935, Earhart made history again, by flying from Hawaii to California. Before that flight, ten pilots had been killed attempting this trip; she was the first to succeed.

Her next trip was the biggest challenge she had ever faced. She announced that she was going to fly around the world. The only person to go with her would be a navigator named Frederick Noonan.

Earhart and Noonan took off from Miami, Florida, on June 1, 1937. At first, everything went smoothly. The two flew from Miami to Puerto Rico, then across the Caribbean Sea. Next, they flew along the northern edge of South America, then across the Atlantic Ocean to several points in Africa. India was their next stop, followed by Australia. On June 29,

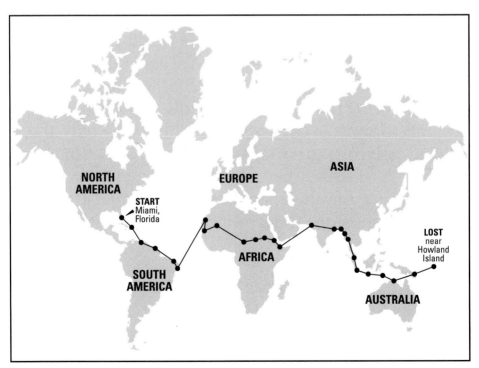

Amelia Earhart's historic around-the-world flight included these stops.

Amelia Earhart stands in the cockpit of the Lockheed Vega plane
that she flew across the Atlantic Ocean in May 1932.

they reached the Pacific island of New Guinea. They
had flown 22,000 miles and had just 7,000 more to
go. The last leg of the flight would take the two
adventurers over the Pacific Ocean.

Their plane left New Guinea on July 2. Over the next
20 hours, a U.S. Coast Guard ship received several

messages from the plane. Then the radio went dead.

Most people believed that Earhart's plane had crashed into the ocean near Howland Island, but a huge search failed to turn up any wreckage or bodies. No trace of Earhart, Noonan, or their plane has ever been found.

We may never know what happened to Amelia Earhart. However, she remains one of America's most compelling heroes. During her around-the-world trip, she wrote to her husband, publisher George P. Putnam: "Please know I am quite aware of the hazards. . . . Women must try to do things as men have tried. When they fail, their failure must be but a challenge to others." ◇

LIFE EVENTS

1897
Amelia Mary Earhart is born in Atchison, Kansas.

1922
Earhart sets a record for women of flying at 14,000 feet.

1927
Charles Lindbergh becomes the first person to fly across the Atlantic Ocean alone.

1932
Earhart becomes the first woman to match Lindbergh's feat, and does so in record time.

1937
Attempting to set another record by flying around the world, Earhart, her navigator, and their plane are lost over the Pacific Ocean.

Dwight D. Eisenhower
A Leader in War and Peace
(born 1890 • died 1969)

Some heroes are leaders in wars and battles; others lead nations in times of peace. Dwight D. Eisenhower did both during his days as the most powerful U.S. military leader during World War II and as the 34th president of the United States.

A Military Career

Dwight David Eisenhower was born in Denison, Texas, on October 14, 1890. Soon afterward, the family moved to Abilene, Kansas, where his father worked at a dairy. The Eisenhower family was a large one: Dwight was the third of seven sons.

Dwight was an average student, but an above-average athlete. He played on many teams throughout grade school and high school. After graduation, he won a place at the U.S. Military Academy at West Point. Dwight was mostly interested in attending the Academy because it was a free education—and a chance to play on West Point's football team.

Eisenhower was a star halfback on the U.S. Army team. During one season, however, he twisted his knee so badly that he had to give up football. He was so depressed, his roommate said, that he seemed to have lost all interest in life.

Eisenhower graduated from West Point in 1915. Several weeks later, he was assigned to the infantry at Fort Sam Houston in San Antonio, Texas, where he trained new soldiers. He was such a good instructor that the Army refused to send him to Europe to fight during World War I.

For most of his early military career, Eisenhower worked as a teacher and a football coach. The young officer, whose friends knew him as Ike, was also an enthusiastic student of military history. Learning how battles were conducted in the past helped him understand how to fight them. This knowledge turned out to be very useful to Eisenhower during World War II.

Eisenhower's hard work and knowledge won him the attention of George Marshall, the Army's Chief of Staff. In June 1942, Marshall sent him to London, England, to take command of the U.S. forces in Europe during World War II. Eisenhower's knowl-

TOPICAL TIDBIT

One Tough Job After Another

America, like most countries, has a tradition of electing some of its most popular generals as president. These include George Washington, Andrew Jackson, William Henry Harrison, Zachary Taylor, and Ulysses S. Grant. Unfortunately, being a good general and a good president require different skills. Other than George Washington, no ex-general was as successful in the role of president as Dwight D. Eisenhower.

edge of military strategy and his skill with men and officers of all backgrounds won him the admiration of many. People began to use a phrase that later became one of the best-known presidential campaign slogans in history: "I like Ike."

Eisenhower in Command

Under Eisenhower's command, U.S. troops fought in North Africa in 1942, the first major campaign of the war. Later, Eisenhower led the invasion of Sicily and Italy. By 1944, he was a four-star general. His next command was to take charge of a huge number of troops, ships, and planes that were about to invade France to drive out the German army. This invasion was the largest single military undertaking ever attempted. No other officer had ever had so many men and supplies under his command.

The invasion of France, code-named "Operation Overlord," came to be known as D-Day. On June 6, 1944, U.S., British, and Canadian troops landed on the beaches of Normandy, France. Although many men were killed during the landing, the allied forces were able to

> "I call upon all who love freedom to stand with us now. Together, we shall achieve victory."
>
> —General Eisenhower, announcing D-Day to the people of Europe

take control of France. In time, they reached Germany and helped win the war for the Allies in 1945.

After the war, Eisenhower—by then a five-star general—became the Army's Chief of Staff. In 1949, he became president of Columbia University in New York, but he soon left that job to become supreme commander of the North Atlantic Treaty Organization (NATO).

"I Like Ike!"

By the 1952 presidential race, Eisenhower was one of the most admired and popular men in the U.S. Both the Democratic Party and the Republican Party asked him to run for president as their candidate. Eisenhower chose to run as a Republican. People all over the country supported him, wearing campaign buttons that proclaimed "I LIKE IKE!" He was elected easily in November 1952. Four years later, he was elected to a second term.

Eisenhower was president during a fairly quiet time in U.S. history. His biggest accomplishments were ending the Korean War (1950-1953) and working toward friendlier relations with the Soviet Union. After commanding so many soldiers during World War II, Eisenhower's most important goal now was world peace. He once said, "I hate war as only a soldier who has lived it can, only as one who has seen its brutality, its futility, its stupidity."

After Eisenhower left office in 1960, he served as an adviser to presidents John F. Kennedy and Lyndon B. Johnson. However, he suffered a serious heart attack in 1965 and was unable to take part in public affairs after that. Dwight D. Eisenhower died on March 28, 1969. He is still remembered as one of the most popular presidents and most important military leaders in U.S. history. ◇

LIFE EVENTS

1890
Dwight David Eisenhower is born in Denison, Texas.

1941
The U.S. enters World War II. Eisenhower is promoted to brigadier general and begins planning strategy for an invasion of Europe.

1944
Allied forces strike at German forces in France in the D-Day invasion. It is led by Eisenhower, now the supreme commander of the Allied Expeditionary Forces (AEF).

1953-1961
Eisenhower serves two terms as the 34th president of the United States.

1969
Eisenhower dies.

David Farragut
Fearless Commander
(born 1801 • died 1870)

David Farragut's bravery and intelligence during the Civil War made him a national hero. His cry of "Damn the torpedoes! Full speed ahead!" is still remembered today.

A Life at Sea

David Glasgow Farragut was born on July 5, 1801, near Knoxville, Tennessee. His father was a sea captain. When David was very young, his father accepted a job as a sailing master in the Navy, and the family moved to New Orleans, Louisiana.

David's parents both died when he was young, and he was adopted and raised by a family friend named David Porter. Porter was a master commandant in the

> "I mean to be whipped or to whip my enemy, and not be scared to death."
>
> —David Farragut

Navy. Through his influence and encouragement, David was soon at sea himself.

During the early 1800s, young boys often served on board ships. David was only nine years old when he joined the U.S. Navy as a midshipman—someone who is studying to be a naval officer. David fought in the War of 1812 and even captured a British ship, despite his young age.

After the War of 1812, Farragut served in the Mediterranean Sea and the West Indies. He also took part in a blockade of Mexican ports on the Gulf of Mexico and established the Mare Island Navy Yard in San Francisco. By 1855, he had been promoted to the rank of captain in the Navy.

The Civil War

Farragut had been born in the South, and he was living in the southern state of Virginia in 1861, when the Civil War broke out between the northern and southern states. However, he immediately left his home and declared that he would fight for the Union Army of the north. The Navy was impressed with Farragut's loyalty. He was put in command of a ship called the *Hartford* and told to capture the city of New Orleans.

New Orleans was well-prepared for Farragut's attack. A large log boom had been placed in the harbor to block the passage of northern ships, and the shores were lined with forts. In addition, the Confederacy had several warships waiting outside the harbor.

None of these preparations could stop Farragut. During the night, two Union boats slipped up to the log boom and cut it free. On April 25, 1862, Farragut's fleet of ships arrived in New Orleans and captured the city. His victory opened the Mississippi River to the Union forces. Farragut became a national hero. In recognition of his accomplishment, he was promoted to rear admiral.

"Damn the Torpedoes!"

For the next two years, Farragut patrolled the Mississippi River. Then, in 1864, he was told to capture Mobile Bay, in Alabama. To reach the bay, Farragut and his ships had to pass through a three-mile-wide channel that was protected by three forts. Once inside the bay, Farragut would face several Confederate gunboats.

On August 5, he sailed into the channel outside Mobile Bay. There was so much smoke from the guns that it was impossible to see what was going on. So Farragut climbed to the top of the rigging and tied himself to the mast with a rope. Northern newspapers later described how Farragut had gone into battle "lashed to the mast."

At first, things did not go well for Farragut's forces. One of his ships struck a mine and sank. Another ship was stopped by a row of torpedoes in the water.

TOPICAL TIDBIT

Turning the Tide

The importance of naval power in the Civil War is sometimes overlooked. One of the decisive factors in the North's victory was the successful blockade of about 3,500 miles of Confederate coastline by Union ships. The blockade prevented escape and kept the South from importing supplies, which helped turn the tide for the North in the end.

Farragut realized that his fleet was right beneath the firing guns of one of the Confederate forts. There were only two choices: retreat or go ahead. Farragut chose to go ahead, sailing the *Hartford* past the stopped ships. When another ship's captain called out a warning about the torpedoes, Farragut shouted back, "Damn the torpedoes! Full speed ahead!" His fleet sailed into Mobile Bay. After a fierce three-hour battle, Farragut was able to sink the Confederate ships and gain control of the harbor.

After the Battle of Mobile Bay, Farragut became an even bigger hero than he had been before. In 1864, Congress created the rank of vice admiral for him. In 1866, he was promoted to the newly created rank of admiral. Farragut died on August 14, 1870, while visiting the Portsmouth Navy Yard in New Hampshire. After his death, he was hailed as the Navy's greatest hero. ◇

LIFE EVENTS

1801
David Glasgow Farragut is born near Knoxville, Tennessee.

1824
Farragut, an officer in the Navy, is given his first command.

1861
The Civil War breaks out. Farragut's first command is a successful attack on New Orleans.

1864
Farragut leads his forces in the successful attack on Mobile Bay.

1866
Farragut becomes the first full admiral of the U.S. Navy.

Benjamin Franklin
A Man of Great Ideas
(born 1706 • died 1790)

Benjamin Franklin was a man of enormous talent, energy, intelligence, and courage. He was a leader of the American Revolution, a scientist, an inventor, a writer, and a statesman who helped shape the nation in many ways.

Starting Out

Benjamin Franklin was born on January 17, 1706, in Boston, Massachusetts. There were a lot of mouths to feed in the family: There were 17 children, 10 boys and 7 girls. Ben was the youngest boy.

Like many children in those days, Ben went to school for only a couple of years—just long enough to learn to read, write, and do simple math. When he was 10, his father took him out of school to work in his candlemaking and soapmaking business. For the next two years, Ben ran errands, delivered soap, and made candles. However, he did not like working with candles and soaps, because the harsh chemicals

Benjamin Franklin's 1792 experiment with a kite and a metal key is one of the most famous scientific experiments in history.

smelled so bad. So when Ben was 12 years old, his father sent him to work at the printing shop of Ben's brother James.

Ben was good at the printing trade and he learned

fast. However, he did not get along very well with his brother. When Ben was 17, he ran away from Boston and went to Philadelphia, Pennsylvania, where he got a job in a printing shop. By the time he was 24, he had his own printing business and his own newspaper, the *Pennsylvania Gazette*. He wrote most of the newspaper himself. People loved his clever stories, wise advice, and funny jokes. The newspaper was very popular.

New Ideas

Franklin was always looking for ways to make life better. He started the first circulating library in the U.S. He also organized Philadelphia's first fire department, and came up with better ways to light

TOPICAL TIDBIT

Franklin the Inventor

The list of Benjamin Franklin's inventions and ideas is awesome. He is credited with starting the first fire department, for inventing bifocal eyeglasses, and for creating the school that later became the University of Pennsylvania. His drawing of a snake cut into pieces to urge the colonies to "Live Free or Die" is said to be the first political cartoon. Today, people are still rediscovering the wisdom of his advice on eating foods that are good for our health: "An apple a day keeps the doctor away."

the streets and dispose of garbage. Soon Franklin was one of the most popular and important people in the city.

Franklin liked to invent things. Some of his inventions were silly, such as a rocking chair with a fan that turned as one rocked. Others were more important. For instance, he invented a special kind of iron stove that produced more heat and less smoke than a fireplace. This invention, known as a Franklin stove, is still used today.

Franklin was also a noted scientist. He proved that lightning is electricity by flying a kite in a thunderstorm and feeling an electric shock come down a wire tied to a metal key at the bottom of the kite. Soon afterward, he invented the lightning rod, which protects buildings from lightning strikes by directing the energy into the ground.

> "We must indeed all hang together or, most assuredly, we shall all hang separately."
>
> —Benjamin Franklin, signing the Declaration of Independence

In 1732, Franklin wrote and published the first *Poor Richard's Almanack*. This book contained a calendar, weather forecasts, advice on when to plant crops, and other important information. Franklin also filled the book with jokes, advice, and interesting facts. The almanac, published every year until 1757, became popular throughout the American colonies, and was even printed in England and France. Soon, people everywhere were quoting Franklin's clever sayings, such as "A penny saved is a penny earned" and "Early to bed, early to rise, makes a man healthy, wealthy, and wise."

Life in Politics

In 1757, when Franklin was 51 years old, the Pennsylvania legislature sent him to London, England, to represent the colony. He loved London, and lived there for periods of time over the next 18 years. Franklin did his best to argue against the unfair taxes and rules that the English king had imposed on the colonies. Finally, in 1775, when he saw that war between Great Britain and the colonies could not be avoided any longer, he returned to Philadelphia and became active in the American Revolution.

LIFE EVENTS

1706
Benjamin Franklin is born in Boston, Massachusetts.

1729
Franklin begins publishing the *Pennsylvania Gazette*.

1732
Franklin publishes his first *Poor Richard's Almanack*.

1751
Franklin publishes his first paper on his experiments with electricity.

1776
Franklin is a signer of the Declaration of Independence.

1787
Franklin is a member of the Constitutional Convention.

1790
Franklin dies. Philadelphia gives him the biggest funeral in its history.

During the Revolution, Franklin was an important member of the Continental Congress. He helped Thomas Jefferson write the Declaration of Independence, and was one of the Founding Fathers who signed it. In 1776, Franklin went to France and convinced the French government to join America in its fight against the British. At the end of the war, he helped write the peace treaty between Great Britain and the U.S. Later, as a member of the Constitutional Convention, he helped draw up the new nation's Constitution.

Benjamin Franklin died in Philadelphia on April 17, 1790, at the age of 84. He had made life better for everyone through his clever inventions, practical advice, and service to the American people. ◇

Varian Fry
A Forgotten Hero
(born 1907 • died 1967)

Many heroes are honored and celebrated by people all over the world. Others do their work quietly and receive little recognition. Varian Fry was one of those quiet heroes. His efforts saved thousands of lives during World War II, but few people ever knew his name.

A Lonely Childhood

Varian Mackey Fry was born in New York, New York, on October 15, 1907, and grew up in nearby Ridgewood, New Jersey. He was an only child, and was often lonely. Classmates teased Varian because his first name sounded like a girl's, he wore glasses, and was not very good at sports. All these things kept him from fitting in with his classmates.

When he was a teenager, Varian attended Hotchkiss, an all-boys prep school in New England. Although he did well in school, Varian was horrified at the hazing, or tormenting, of underclassmen by

the seniors. During his third year, he was told to cross a room by hanging hand over hand from a hot steam pipe. Varian refused, then went to the school's headmaster and declared that he was so opposed to the school's hazing traditions, he no longer wished to attend. The next day, his father took him home.

Varian Fry attended another prep school, then went on to Harvard University, where he studied classical literature. After graduating from Harvard, he worked as a magazine writer in New York.

Working in Secret

In 1939, World War II broke out in Europe. In 1940, the German army invaded and occupied France, and French Jews and other citizens were being sent to concentration camps, where many were killed. Shortly after the German occupation began, Fry went to Marseilles, France, as a representative of a private U.S. relief committee. Besides the regular work he did for that organization, Fry often worked behind the scenes, doing many illegal things to help French refugees escape from the Nazis.

TOPICAL TIDBIT

Saved from the Nazis

The list of refugees whom Varian Fry helped rescue from the Nazis includes many famous names. The painter Marc Chagall and the writer Hannah Arendt are among them. Many other noted artists, writers, and scientists who later became U.S. citizens also fled from the Nazis during those years, including Igor Stravinsky, a famous composer, and Thomas Mann, a famous novelist.

Fry set up a secret network to rescue people who were in danger from the Nazis. He forged documents in order to get work permits that French citizens could use to escape to the U.S. Fry helped more than 2,000 people in this way. Some of the people he helped were famous, such as artist Marc Chagall; others were ordinary citizens.

When the U.S. government found out what Fry was doing, it ordered him to return home. Fry refused to go, however, and continued his work.

Fry no longer had a passport or legal right to stay in France. This made his work there even more dangerous. He was watched and often questioned by French authorities, who were under Nazi control. Fry later said, "I stayed because the refugees needed me. But it took courage, and courage is a quality that I hadn't previously been sure I possessed."

> "In all, we saved some two thousand human beings. We ought to have saved many times that number. But we did what we could."
>
> —Varian Fry

Finally, in September 1941, the French government forced Fry to leave the country because he was considered an "undesirable alien" who helped Jews and opposed the Nazis.

Punished for Good Deeds

After leaving France, Fry returned home to New York. He wanted to alert Americans to the terrible things the Nazis were doing to the Jews in Europe. He wrote an article for *The New Republic* magazine, entitled "The Massacre of the Jews." It was published in December 1942. Later, he wrote a book, called *Surrender on Demand*, about his experiences in France.

Instead of listening to Fry's information, however, U.S. officials became suspicious of him and considered him a dangerous troublemaker. The Federal Bureau of Investigation (FBI) opened a file on Fry and kept him under observation for many years.

Fry spent the rest of his life writing and editing books and magazines on foreign affairs. He also wrote for businesses and taught classical literature. Varian Fry died suddenly in his sleep on September 13, 1967, at the age of 59.

"We owe Varian Fry a promise . . . never to forget the horror that he struggled against so heroically, [and] to do whatever is necessary to ensure that such horrors never happen again."

—Warren Christopher, U.S. Secretary of State, on February 2, 1996

Shortly before Varian Fry's death, the French government realized how much good work he had done. It presented him with one of its highest awards, the Legion of Honor, for his work in Marseilles. In 1991, the U.S. finally honored this brave man by awarding him the Eisenhower Liberation Medal. In 1993-1994, his work was the subject of an exhibition at the United States Holocaust Memorial Museum in Washington, D.C. Varian Fry also was honored as a Commemorative Citizen of the State of Israel in 1996, almost 30 years after his death. It was a fitting tribute to a man who just wanted to save lives. ◇

LIFE EVENTS

1907
Varian Mackey Fry is born in New York.

1940
The German army occupies France at the start of World War II. Fry volunteers for the Emergency Rescue Committee.

1942
"Massacre of the Jews," an article written by Fry, is an early warning of the Holocaust.

1945
Fry's memoirs, *Surrender on Demand*, are published.

1991
Twenty-four years after his death, Varian Fry receives his first official recognition from the U.S. government.

Geronimo
Apache Warrior
(born 1829 • died 1909)

During his life, Geronimo struggled against enormous odds to win freedom for his Apache tribe. At first, the U.S. authorities thought of him as a savage. In time, however, they came to respect him as a brave warrior who would do anything to defend his people.

Quiet Beginnings

Geronimo's Native American name was Goyathlay, which means "One Who Yawns." He was born into the Chiricahua Apache *(chir-uh-KAH-wuh uh-PATCH-ee)* tribe in 1829, in what is now Clifton, Arizona. His father taught him how to hunt, make tools and weapons, care for horses, and survive in the wilderness. The boy also worked in the fields, helping to grow the tribe's crops of corn, melons, and beans.

When Goyathlay turned 17, he was considered a man and a warrior of the tribe. Soon afterward, he married another member of the tribe. The couple had three children.

Murder—and Revenge

Goyathlay's quiet life took a sudden change in 1858, when he was about 21 years old. Goyathlay, along with his wife, children, and mother, joined a band of Apaches traveling to Mexico to trade. Many Mexicans hated the Apache. One day, a band of Mexican soldiers led by General Juan Carrasco attacked the camp while the men were away. Goyathlay returned that evening to find that his entire family had been killed by the Mexican soldiers.

Goyathlay returned home and vowed revenge against the Mexicans. For the next few years, he and other Apache warriors took part in raids against Mexican settlers. They robbed and killed people and stole their horses and cattle. Goyathlay was such a fierce fighter that he became a hero to the Apache and feared by the Mexicans. The Mexicans called him *Geronimo*, which means "Jerome" in Spanish. The name stuck.

> "I was born on the prairies where the wind blew free and there was nothing to break the light of the sun. I was born where there were no enclosures."
>
> —Geronimo

Then the Apache began to have trouble with the Americans. From 1846 to 1848, the U.S. and Mexico fought a war over the territory that is now the southwestern U.S. When the U.S. finally won that war, it promised to prevent the Apache from raiding Mexican territory. White miners and settlers were moving onto Apache land in U.S. territory. The U.S. government broke its promise, and said that it was time for the Apache to go.

Geronimo and his warriors fought many battles to

keep their land but, in the end, they were no match for the powerful U.S. Army. In 1874, the U.S. government moved the Chiricahua Apache to the San Carlos Reservation in Arizona. Living conditions there were terrible, and the tribe was not allowed to practice its traditional rites. Finally, Geronimo and several other Apache warriors declared war on whites.

A Losing Battle

For the next few years, Geronimo and his fellow Apaches conducted many raids on American settlements. Newspapers around the country wrote stories about his daring deeds, clever strategies, and fierce style of fighting. Soon, the word *Geronimo* entered the English language as a war cry—an exclamation meaning "charge!" or "attack!"

The fighting could not go on forever. The Apache

TOPICAL TIDBIT

The Apache Wars

The wars between the U.S. Army and the Chiricahua Apache were among the fiercest on the frontier. Warriors such as Cochise, Mangas Coloradas, and Geronimo were known for their superior horsemanship, crafty use of the terrain, and courage. They contributed to the Apaches' reputation for fierceness.

warriors were outnumbered and outgunned. Geronimo returned to the reservation several times, but escaped again each time. Finally, in 1886, he surrendered for good. "Once I moved about like the wind," he said sadly. "Now I surrender to you, and that is all."

Geronimo spent the rest of his life as a prisoner. He and his tribe were sent to reservations in Florida, Alabama, and Oklahoma.

Even when Geronimo was an old man and had been in captivity for many years, his deeds still fascinated the American people. In 1904, he took part in the World's Fair in St. Louis, Missouri. Crowds of people gathered to meet the old warrior and buy his autograph and photo.

In 1905, President Theodore Roosevelt invited Geronimo to Washington, D.C., to ride in his inauguration parade. Thousands of people lined the

LIFE EVENTS

1829
Geronimo is born Goyathlay, or "One Who Yawns," to the Chiricahua Apache tribe, in what is now Arizona.

1846
Geronimo participates in raids against Mexico.

1858
Geronimo's mother, wife, and children are killed by Mexican soldiers.

1874
The U.S. Army forces thousands of Apaches onto a reservation. Geronimo leads the war against the Army.

1886
Geronimo finally surrenders. He dies in 1909.

parade route and cheered for the famous Apache.

The next day, Geronimo met with Roosevelt and begged him to let his people return to their home in Arizona. Roosevelt did not agree, because he was worried that allowing the Native Americans to return would lead to more fighting.

On February 17, 1909, four years after meeting President Roosevelt, Geronimo died on the reservation. He is still remembered as a brave warrior who was not afraid to fight for his people's freedom. ◇

John Glenn
First American to Orbit Earth
(born 1921)

John Glenn—who served his country as a war hero, an astronaut, and a U.S. senator—proved that there are many different ways one person can be a hero.

Taking to the Skies

John Herschel Glenn Jr. was born in Cambridge, Ohio, on July 18, 1921. As a boy, he spent many hours watching the sky for airplanes and pretending that he was flying. He also enjoyed building model airplanes out of wood.

While attending Muskingum College in Ohio, Glenn joined a government training program to learn how to fly. When the U.S. entered World War II in 1941, 20-year-old Glenn joined the Marine Corps. He flew 59 combat missions in the war, winning two Distinguished Flying Crosses and 10 Air Medals for his bravery.

During the Korean War, Glenn flew 90 more combat missions. He returned from one bombing mis-

sion with 203 holes in his plane. Another time, he ran out of fuel and had to glide more than 100 miles back to his base.

After the war, Glenn became a test pilot. His job was to fly new planes to make sure that they worked properly. In 1957, he became the first person to make a nonstop supersonic flight across the U.S., traveling from Los Angeles to New York in just 3 hours, 23 minutes, and 8.4 seconds. (*Supersonic* means faster than the speed of sound.)

Leaving Earth Behind

In 1959, Glenn was one of seven men picked for the U.S. space program's Project Mercury. At the time, America was engaged in what was called the "Space Race" with the Soviet Union. A lot was at stake. This was a period of Cold War between the U.S. and the Soviet Union—a time of high tension without actual warfare. Many people thought that outer space could be an important battleground between the two countries. The Soviets had already gotten a head start by sending *Sputnik*—the first artificial satellite—into space. They had also been the first to send a human into space. The U.S. had to catch up.

> "He is the kind of American of whom we are most proud."
> —President John F. Kennedy

The National Aeronautics and Space Administration (NASA) was the organization in charge of Project Mercury. NASA's first two Mercury flights were made to simply get a man into space, then back down alive. The third flight would be a crucial step: to completely orbit (circle) Earth. Of seven astronauts in the Mercury program, John Glenn was the one picked to make the historic flight.

On February 20, 1962, Glenn put on his spacesuit and climbed into *Friendship 7*, a tiny capsule perched on top of a huge rocket. With a roar, the rocket blasted into the sky. When it was 100 miles above Earth, the rocket dropped away and Glenn was alone in space, inside his tiny capsule. Just 90 minutes later, he had made one complete orbit. "The view is tremendous!" he reported.

Glenn's first orbit of Earth went perfectly. Then something went wrong with the control system. Glenn had to pilot the capsule himself during the second and third orbits.

As he was getting ready to return to Earth, ground control received a message that the heat shield on the

TOPICAL TIDBIT

A Hero to Millions

As the first American to orbit the globe, John Glenn was the most famous and celebrated of the Mercury astronauts. Millions of people around the world followed his 1962 flight on television and radio. Glenn was also one of the heroes of *The Right Stuff* by Tom Wolfe, a 1979 book about the Mercury Program. A movie based on the book was released in 1983.

capsule was loose. Without that shield's protection, Glenn's ship would burn up when it re-entered Earth's atmosphere. Glenn was told of the risks, but he remained steady and calm. The shield stayed on. Almost five hours after *Friendship 7* had blasted into orbit, it splashed down safely into the Atlantic Ocean.

Back Into Space

John Glenn was a national hero. He was given a ticker-tape parade in New York and he visited President John F. Kennedy at the White House. A few months later, inspired by Glenn's success, Kennedy pledged that the U.S. would get a rocket to the moon "and do it right, and do it first before this decade is out." That did happen, in 1969, but by then, Glenn had left the space program. He wanted to return to space, but he had become so popular that the government was afraid to risk his life by sending him back.

Glenn retired from NASA in 1964 and decided to run for the U.S. Senate. One day, however, he slipped on the bathroom rug and hit his head on the tub. The fall damaged his sense of balance. For months, he was so dizzy, he could barely walk. He had to drop out of the Senate race and stay home until he recovered.

In 1974, on his third try, Glenn was elected to the Senate. In 1984, he ran for president, but was not nominated by the Democratic Party. He served in the Senate until 1999.

By that time, NASA was regularly sending astronauts into space on space shuttles. These astronauts conducted many different experiments, including some that investigated how time in space affects the human body. They learned that many of the effects were the same as those of getting older.

When Glenn heard that, it gave him an idea. He volunteered to go on a shuttle mission to study those effects on his own body. To his delight, NASA agreed.

In October 1998, at age 77, Glenn returned to space on board the space shuttle *Discovery*. During the flight, he conducted experiments to monitor how his body worked in space. When John Glenn returned to Earth, he was a national hero once again. His determination and courage proved that you can achieve your dreams—not once, but twice. ◇

LIFE EVENTS

1921
John Herschel Glenn Jr. is born in Cambridge, Ohio.

1943
Glenn joins the Marine Corps as a pilot and flies 59 missions during World War II.

1959
Glenn is selected for NASA's Project Mercury.

1962
Glenn is the first American to orbit Earth.

1974
Glenn is elected for the first of his four terms as senator from Ohio.

1998
Former Mercury astronaut Glenn flies on space shuttle mission STS-95, the oldest person ever in space.

Ulysses S. Grant
Military Hero and President
(born 1822 • died 1885)

For most of his life, Ulysses S. Grant considered himself to be a failure. However, this "failure" went on to become one of America's greatest military heroes, as well as its 18th president.

"Useless" Grant

Hiram Ulysses Grant was born in a log cabin in Point Pleasant, Ohio, on April 27, 1822. His family always called him by his middle name. His father, Jesse Root Grant, was a tanner (someone who makes leather out of animal skins.) His mother, Hannah Simpson Grant, worked on the family's farm.

Ulysses loved animals, especially horses. By the time he was five, he could stand up on the back of a moving horse. As a teenager, he often earned money training horses for his neighbors.

Ulysses was good at schoolwork, but was very shy and awkward. Some people thought that he was not very smart, so he soon had a nickname: "Useless."

When Ulysses was 16 years old, his father got him an appointment to the U.S. Military Academy at West Point. Ulysses had no interest in being a soldier, but he did what his father said. When he arrived, he discovered that his name had been registered as Ulysses Simpson Grant by mistake. Grant thought that the initials U. S. G. were better than the initials H. U. G., so he kept the name.

The Civil War

Ulysses S. Grant did not make a very good impression at West Point. One of the other cadets said of him, "A more unpromising boy never entered the Military Academy." When Grant graduated from West Point in 1843, he was 21st in a class of 39. He was sent to fight along the Texas-Mexico border during the Mexican War, and took part in the capture of Mexico City on September 14, 1847.

Grant left the military in 1854. He planned to return to his wife and children in Missouri and spend the rest of his life farming. Despite working hard, however, Grant was unable to support his family. One year, he had to sell his gold watch for $22 to buy

TOPICAL TIDBIT

Commander of the Union Armies

President Lincoln was at his wits' end in 1864. He could not find a commander for the Union armies who could defeat the wily Confederate generals. Then he began studying the campaign of Ulysses Grant against Vicksburg, Mississippi, while it was happening. At first, Lincoln thought that Grant was making a big mistake in tactics. When Grant outflanked the Confederates and won the battle, however, Lincoln was overjoyed, and sent Grant a telegram saying so. At last he had found the man that he—and the country—needed.

Christmas presents. Finally, in 1860, He went to work in his father's store in Galena, Illinois.

When the Civil War broke out between the northern and southern U.S. states in 1861, Grant became a soldier again. At first, he trained volunteer troops. He was so good at this job that President Abraham Lincoln promoted him to brigadier general in August 1861.

> "The war is over— the rebels are our countrymen again."
>
> —General Ulysses S. Grant, in 1865

Soon afterward, Grant was in the thick of the fighting, attacking Confederate forts in Tennessee. He refused to accept anything less than surrender from Confederate commanders. That gave U. S. Grant a new nickname: "Unconditional Surrender" Grant.

On July 3, 1863, Grant captured the city of Vicksburg, Mississippi, one of the most important victories of the Civil War. A few months later, he turned defeat into victory at the Battle of Chattanooga. Wherever he fought, General Grant refused to accept defeat. He inspired his troops to fight hard—and to win. By March 1864, he was commander of the entire Union army. On April 9, 1865, he accepted the surrender of General Robert E. Lee, the Confederate Army's commander. The Civil War was over, and Ulysses S. Grant was a national hero.

President Grant

Grant was so popular, he was a natural choice to run for U.S. president. On November 3, 1868, he was elected the 18th president of the United States by a wide margin.

Grant served two terms as president. However, he was not as good a president as he was a soldier. He was inexperienced in politics and afraid to make decisions, so he surrounded himself with people he trusted. However, some of those people were dishonest, so Grant's administrations were troubled by scandal.

After Grant left the presidency in 1877, he set off on a popular world tour. Upon his return, he settled in New York, New York. He joined a Wall Street business, but it failed, and Grant lost all his money. Soon after, he found out that he had mouth cancer.

Grant was determined to provide for his wife, Julia,

LIFE EVENTS

1822
Hiram Ulysses Grant is born in Point Pleasant, Ohio.

1846
Grant serves in the Mexican War.

1861
The Civil War begins. Grant distinguishes himself in campaigns of the war.

1864
Grant is appointed commander of the U.S. Army.

1865
Grant accepts the surrender of Confederate General Robert E. Lee.

1868
Grant is elected to the first of two terms as president.

1885
Grant dies and is buried in a massive granite tomb in New York City.

after his death. He devoted the last few months of his life to writing his autobiography, which he hoped would earn an income for her. He wrote at a frantic pace, determined to finish it before he died. That was his last act of heroism. Ulysses S. Grant wrote the last words of his book just a few days before he died on July 23, 1885. His autobiography earned more than $400,000—enough money to provide for his wife for the rest of her life. ◇

Woody Guthrie
The Voice of America
(born 1912 • died 1967)

No one captured the lives of ordinary Americans in song the way Woody Guthrie did. During the middle of the 20th century, he traveled all over the U.S., writing songs that expressed the country's hopes and dreams.

A Sad Childhood

Woodrow Wilson Guthrie was born on July 14, 1912, in the small frontier town of Okemah, Oklahoma. When he was just six years old, his older sister died in a fire. Woody's mother, Nora Guthrie, could not cope with her child's death. She also suffered from Huntington's chorea, a disease that affects the nervous system. Eventually, she had to be confined to a mental hospital.

The family also had financial problems. Woody's father, Charles Guthrie, had once had a successful business selling land, but that business began to fail. The family had to move into a run-down, abandoned house. Mr. Guthrie also suffered from painful arthri-

tis. Woody and his older brother spent hours massaging their father's hands at night to ease the pain.

As a child, Woody enjoyed music. Before his sister's death, the Guthrie family often sang together after dinner. In time, Woody taught himself how to play the guitar and the harmonica. He also enjoyed observing people and finding out the stories of their lives. He was especially interested in hearing the stories of the migrant workers and drifters who passed through Okemah.

On the Road

With his mother in the hospital and his father in failing health, Woody was on his own by the age of 15. At first, he made a little money singing and playing harmonica on the streets. A few years later, he packed up his few belongings and headed to Texas. There, Woody made music with a few friends and worked at odd jobs.

"I hate a song that makes you think that you are not any good . . . that you are just born to lose. . . . I am out to fight those songs to my very last breath of air."
—Woody Guthrie

However, work was hard to find during the 1930s. The Great Depression had hit the country hard, and few jobs were available. To make matters worse, a severe lack of rain and poor farming methods had turned the Great Plains into a Dust Bowl. Huge dust storms filled the air, and farmers found it impossible to grow enough crops to survive.

By 1937, Woody Guthrie had traveled to California, along with thousands of other refugees from the Dust Bowl. He began to write folk songs about the workers and drifters who had fascinated him, and about the people who had escaped to California in search of a better life. Soon, he was performing on radio stations in California and Mexico.

Guthrie did not like to stay in one place for long. By 1939, he was in New York City, where he became popular among a group of musicians, writers, and artists who lived there. Guthrie also became involved in politics, and spoke out often against the unfair treatment of workers and poor people. He wrote songs quickly, commenting on events of the day. Guthrie's most famous song, "This Land Is Your Land," said to his audiences that America belonged

TOPICAL TIDBIT

The Dust Bowl

The area known as the Dust Bowl of the Great Plains extended over large parts of Colorado, Kansas, Texas, Oklahoma, and New Mexico. The dust storms that plagued the region were terrifying. High winds lifted dried-up topsoil into "black blizzards" that filled the air and blocked out the sun. People went down into basements to wait out the storms. During these long days, many people thought that the world was coming to an end.

to them, too—not just to the people who owned the land and the banks.

In 1943, Guthrie published his autobiography, *Bound for Glory*, which told the story of his Dust Bowl years. The book was very successful. By then, Guthrie was considered to be one of the most important folk singers in America.

For many years, Guthrie traveled around the country, singing and performing. It was impossible for him to stay in one place very long. He needed to be on the road, meeting people, and telling their stories. Over the years, he had three wives and eight children. (One of his sons, Arlo, later became a popular singer in his own right.)

In the end, the thing that stopped Woody Guthrie was illness. Beginning in the late 1940s, he began having symptoms of a puzzling disability. In time, it was found to be

LIFE EVENTS

1912
Woodrow Wilson Guthrie is born in Okemah, Oklahoma.

1937
Guthrie joins the mass migration of Dust Bowl refugees who head west to California.

1939
After achieving success on the radio in California, Guthrie leaves for New York, where he becomes part of a thriving music scene.

1943
Bound for Glory, Guthrie's auto-biography, is published.

1954
Guthrie first admits himself into Greystone Hospital in New Jersey. He is diagnosed with Huntington's chorea and dies in 1967.

Huntington's chorea, the same disease his mother had suffered from for so many years. Guthrie spent the last 13 years of his life in and out of hospitals as the disease gradually robbed him of his balance, speech, and ability to think clearly.

Woody Guthrie died of Huntington's chorea on October 3, 1967, but his music and his spirit live on. He has been inducted in the Songwriters' Hall of Fame and the Rock and Roll Hall of Fame, and has won many awards. Many of today's rock and country stars hail him as an inspiration, and schoolchildren all over America still sing "This Land Is Your Land." Guthrie's exciting and vivid songs truly capture the spirit of America. ◇

Nathan Hale
Only One Life to Give
(born 1755 • died 1776)

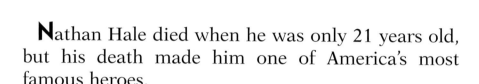

Nathan Hale died when he was only 21 years old, but his death made him one of America's most famous heroes.

An Ordinary Schoolteacher

Nathan Hale was born on June 6, 1755, in Coventry, Connecticut. His parents were Puritans who stressed the values of religion, hard work, and education. Nathan was a sickly child, but he grew into a strong, athletic young man.

Nathan was tutored by the local minister and soon developed a love of reading and learning. In 1769, 14-year-old Nathan and his older brother entered Yale College. At

> **"Let us march immediately, and never lay down our arms until we obtain our independence."**
>
> —Nathan Hale, after receiving news of the battle of Lexington and Concord

first, Nathan planned to become a minister, like many other students at Yale. However, after graduating in 1773 at age 18, he became a schoolteacher instead.

After teaching one year in East Haddam, Connecticut, Hale got a job at the Union School in New London, a busy seaport on the Connecticut coast. He taught Latin, writing, mathematics, and the classics to about 30 young men. He was a popular teacher with both the students and their parents.

America at War

By 1774, it was clear that the American colonies would soon go to war against Great Britain. Hale joined the Connecticut militia, a volunteer army. When war broke out in April 1775, he was hesitant to leave his teaching job. Then, in July, he received a letter from a friend, Benjamin Tallmadge, begging him to join the battle. "Was I in your condition," wrote Tallmadge, "I think the more extensive service would be my choice. Our holy religion, the honor of our God, a glorious country, and a happy constitution is what we have to defend." The letter made up Hale's mind.

The next day, he accepted a commission as a first lieutenant in a Connecticut regiment. Hale enjoyed military life and did his best to be a good leader.

In January 1776, he was promoted to captain and sent to New York City. He spent almost six months there, preparing forts for battle with the British. He also planned an attack on a British ship, an action that won him a personal thank you from General George Washington, commander of the American army.

The British had taken control of Long Island, New York, and planned to invade New York City. General Washington needed to find out when the British army planned to attack. Hale volunteered to go behind enemy lines on Long Island to gather information. One of his friends tried to talk him out of the dangerous mission, but Hale replied that the job was "necessary for the public good." To a young soldier who had not yet seen any fighting, it was also a good chance for adventure.

Captured!

Hale crossed the British lines on Long Island during the second week of September 1776. He pretended to be a schoolteacher looking for work, and managed to obtain important military information.

On the evening of September 21, Hale slipped

TOPICAL TIDBIT

Colonial Spies

General George Washington knew the value of using spies against an enemy. During the French and Indian War (1754-1763), he had served as an officer in the British Army. He noted how the French used small bands of Native Americans to creep through the woods to spy on his troops. This gave the French a good idea of how many men he had and which direction they were coming from. Later, commanding American forces during the Revolution, Washington used information from spies to help his men outfox and defeat the much larger British army.

away to Long Island Sound to wait for a boat that was scheduled to pick him up. Lights twinkled from a vessel on the sound and Hale signaled his position. Too late, he realized that the ship was British, not American. He tried to escape, but was quickly captured by British soldiers.

That very night, he was taken before General William Howe, the British commander. Hale admitted that he was a spy, and was held prisoner in a greenhouse. The next morning, he was marched to a park in northern New York City, where he was hanged as a spy. His last words were reported to be, "I only regret that I have but one life to lose for my country." This speech, and the dignity with which he faced death, impressed both British soldiers and American citizens. Today, Nathan Hale is still remembered as a dedicated, brave man who was willing to pay the highest price of all for his beliefs. ◇

LIFE EVENTS

1755
Nathan Hale is born in Coventry, Connecticut.

1773
Hale graduates from Yale and becomes a schoolteacher.

1775
Colonists clash with British soldiers at the battle of Lexington and Concord. Hale volunteers with the Seventh Connecticut militia.

1776
While stationed in New York, Hale volunteers for a spy mission. He is caught behind enemy lines and executed by the English.

Fannie Lou Hamer
Fighting for Freedom
(born 1917 • died 1977)

Many people fought to win equal rights for black Americans during the civil-rights movement. One of the most courageous of these freedom fighters was a poor, barely educated woman named Fannie Lou Hamer, who risked her life and livelihood to help ensure the right of every African American to vote.

A Sharecropper's Daughter

Fannie Lou Townsend was born in Montgomery County, Mississippi, on October 6, 1917. She was the youngest of 20 children. Fannie Lou's parents were sharecroppers on a plantation. Sharecropping was a hard existence. The family had to pay the plantation's owner for the house they lived in, the crops they grew, and the food they ate.

> "The only thing they could do was kill me."
>
> —Fannie Lou Hamer, on volunteering to register to vote

April 30, 1967: Fannie Lou Hamer testifies before a U.S. Senate committee about poverty in Mississippi.

Fannie Lou's earliest memories were of being hungry and tired. The house the family lived in was a run-down wooden shack with a tin roof. At night, Fannie Lou slept on a sack stuffed with dry grass.

While still a small child, Fannie Lou began working in the cotton fields with her parents and siblings. By the time she was six, she was picking 30 pounds of cotton a day. There was little time to go to school or play with other children.

Working Toward Equality

In 1945, Fannie Lou Townsend married Perry "Pap" Hamer. She and her husband worked on a plantation until 1962. Then, one otherwise ordinary day, Fannie Lou Hamer did an extraordinary and brave thing: She registered to vote.

Today, we take voting for granted. Until the 1960s, however, black Americans living in the South had to pass special tests and pay a "poll tax" if they wanted to vote. These tests and taxes were designed to keep blacks from voting. They were so unfair that many blacks did not even bother to try registering. Many of those who did register still could not vote, because if they tried to do so they were threatened—sometimes even killed—by whites.

After Hamer registered, she was fired from her job and forced to leave the plantation. She and her husband lost their house and all their possessions. Angry white men followed the Hamers everywhere, waving guns and cursing them. Still, Fannie Lou Hamer refused to take her name off the registration list. Instead of giving in to the threats, she fought back: She began organizing voter-registration campaigns all over Mississippi.

Paying the Price

In June 1963, Hamer and several other civil-rights workers took a bus to a voter-registration workshop. On the way home, the bus stopped in the small town of Winona, Mississippi. There, Hamer and the others were arrested, taken to jail, and severely beaten. The beating left Hamer blind in one eye and damaged her feet and her kidneys.

The group was held in jail for three days. Hamer and the other workers were finally allowed to leave after Martin Luther King Jr. sent his staff to the jail to demand that they be released. Later, Hamer went to Washington, D.C., to tell the government, the newspapers, and the American public about the terrible treatment that blacks faced in Mississippi.

"Is This America?"

In 1964, Hamer helped form the Mississippi Freedom Democratic Party (MFDP). A delegation of MFDP members (64 black, 4 white) traveled to the Democratic National Convention in Atlantic City, New Jersey. Hamer and other MFDP members demanded that they be seated as the official Mississippi delegation that would nominate the presidential candidate. At that time, the Mississippi delegation was all-white; blacks had been purposely excluded.

They were not allowed to participate fully, but Hamer gave a speech to a Democratic Party committee. It was televised. She told about the beating that she had received in Winona, as well as the threats and hardships that blacks faced every day, just for trying to vote. "Is this America?" she asked. "The land of the free and the home of the brave? Where we have to sleep with our telephones off the hook, because our lives be threatened daily?"

The MFDP did not win seats at the 1964 convention, but its members did participate in the 1968 convention in Chicago. When Hamer took her seat at the 1968 convention, she received a standing ovation.

The Freedom Farm Cooperative

Hamer also worked to help the poor people of Mississippi. In 1969, she organized the Freedom Farm

TOPICAL TIDBIT

Making Change, One Person at a Time

After the Civil War, Southern states began using many methods to keep blacks from voting, including literacy tests, poll taxes, and intimidation. Beginning in 1961, the Student Non-Violent Coordinating Committee (SNCC) started a major campaign to register blacks in the South. In a church in the tiny town of Ruleville, Mississippi, a small crowd heard a young preacher named James Bevel ask for volunteers to register. Fannie Lou Hamer raised her hand—and changed her life forever.

Cooperative, which provided land for poor families to grow their own food. She traveled all over the country, giving speeches to raise money and awareness of black poverty and hunger.

Hamer died of cancer on March 15, 1977, and was buried in her native Mississippi. Her tombstone is engraved with one of her favorite sayings: "I'm sick and tired of being sick and tired."

Fannie Lou Hamer rose from humble beginnings to change the lives of thousands of people through her courage and her refusal to give in. ◇

LIFE EVENTS

1917
Fannie Lou Townsend is born in Montgomery County, Mississippi.

1962
Hamer challenges discrimination by registering to vote.

1963
Hamer and a busload of civil-rights workers are jailed and severely beaten in Mississippi.

1964
Hamer leads the Mississippi Freedom Democratic Party (MFDP) during the Democratic National Convention.

1967
Hamer publishes *To Praise Our Bridges: An Autobiography.*

1968
Hamer formally participates at the Democratic National Convention.

Alexander Hamilton
Shaping the Nation
(born 1755 or 1757 • died 1804)

Alexander Hamilton came from simple beginnings, yet he rose to become one of the most powerful men in our history, as the creator of the U.S. economic system. However, his actions and attitude created many enemies—and led to his death.

A Humble Birth

Alexander Hamilton was born in Nevis, an island in the West Indies. Historians are not sure if he was born on January 11, 1755, or on January 11, 1757. They do know that his parents were not married, and that his father abandoned the family when Alexander was about eight years old. In 1768, Alexander's mother died and he was taken in by her family.

> "Real liberty is neither found in despotism or the extremes of democracy, but in moderate governments."
>
> —Alexander Hamilton

The boy got a job working in a shop. Later, he became a clerk for a rich merchant and explorer named Nicholas Cruger. Hamilton, who was good with numbers, was soon keeping all of Cruger's account books and running one of his stores. By the time he was 14, Alexander was running the business while the explorer traveled to New York.

Along with working, Alexander studied Latin, mathematics, and literature with Dr. Hugh Knox, a local minister. Knox was so impressed by the boy's ability that he paid for him to attend King's College (now Columbia University) in New York City. Young Hamilton left for America in 1773.

A Strict Commander

Hamilton was a bit of a show-off, and did not think that he had to follow rules if they got in his way. When he arrived at college, he announced that he wanted to finish school as quickly as possible, as he had a lot that he wanted to do with his life. School officials allowed him to attend advanced classes. He finished five years of work in only two years.

Hamilton also became active in the movement for American independence. He spoke in public and wrote pamphlets encouraging American colonists to break away from their British rulers. "Freedom is more important than tradition," he wrote.

In March 1776, Hamilton was made a captain and put in charge of a military unit. His job was to find young men to join the army, then train them to be good soldiers. He quickly signed up 30 men and drilled them mercilessly. Hamilton was such a harsh commander that many of his men ran away.

Although Hamilton was tough on his men, General George Washington considered him to be a good leader. Hamilton's unit joined Washington's army, and took part in the Battle of Trenton. That surprise attack on the British army on Christmas night, 1776, was an important victory for the American side.

In 1777, Hamilton became Washington's personal secretary. The two men worked closely together to plan the war against Great Britain.

Creating a New Nation

When the war ended in 1783, U.S. leaders set about writing a constitution for the new nation. Hamilton was a member of the New York Assembly, and was elected to represent the state at the first Constitutional Convention. At the time, there was a great debate on how strong the federal (national) government should be. Many people wanted greater independence for the 13 individual states. They attacked the draft of the Constitution as giving too much power to a single, central government.

Hamilton believed that a strong central government was important to make a real nation out of the 13 former colonies. Along with James Madison and John Jay, he wrote a series of influential essays defending that position. The 85 essays were published together as *The Federalist*. One of the most important documents in U.S. history, *The Federalist* helped convince

Americans to approve and accept the Constitution.

In 1789, Hamilton was named the first secretary of the U.S. Treasury. His job was to collect and distribute taxes and to create a stable currency (money). Establishing the first national bank, called the Bank of the United States, was a major step in this process. Hamilton also established a mint to make gold and silver coins, and he decided how much the coins would be worth.

Bitter Enemies

Hamilton was never afraid to let people know what he thought. His strong opinions on how the government should be run made him many enemies.

One of his bitterest enemies was Aaron Burr, vice

TOPICAL TIDBIT

Hamilton's Bank

The Bank of the United States (1791) was crucial to Alexander Hamilton's vision for the new country. The bank paid off debt from the Revolution and established a stable national currency. It also created uniform rules for all other banks. But the Bank was also the cause of much conflict. In the end, that conflict created America's first political parties: Hamilton's Federalist Party and Thomas Jefferson's Democratic-Republican Party. Today's Federal Reserve is the successor to the original Bank of the United States.

president to Thomas Jefferson. Burr and Hamilton had never gotten along. Several times, Hamilton used his influence to keep Burr from shaping policies or winning public office. In 1804, Burr lost the election for governor of New York—in part, because Hamilton had spoken out against him. The feud grew so heated that Burr challenged Hamilton to a gun duel.

The two men met at Weehawken, New Jersey, on July 11, 1804. Each man fired once. Hamilton's shot missed, but Burr's hit Hamilton in the right side. The next day, he died.

Alexander Hamilton was given a huge funeral in New York, and the nation observed six weeks of mourning after his death. Today, he is remembered as one of the founding fathers of the United States—a man whose integrity, determination, and courage helped shape our nation. ◇

LIFE EVENTS

1755 or 1757
Alexander Hamilton is born in Nevis, West Indies.

1774
Living in New York, Hamilton writes influential pamphlets attacking British taxation.

1777
Hamilton becomes the chief aide to General George Washington.

1787
Hamilton is a delegate to the Constitutional Convention. His *Federalist* essays begin appearing.

1789
Hamilton is the first secretary of the Treasury of the United States.

1804
Alexander Hamilton is killed in a duel with Aaron Burr.

Patrick Henry
"Give Me Liberty or Give Me Death!"
(born 1736 • died 1799)

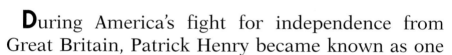

During America's fight for independence from Great Britain, Patrick Henry became known as one of the colonies' most fiery speakers. The energy and power of his words helped inspire our nation's people, and made him one of the most well-known figures of the American Revolution.

> "I am not a Virginian, but an American."
>
> —Patrick Henry, to the Virginia Convention, 1774

An Ordinary Childhood

Patrick Henry was born on May 29, 1736, in Hanover County, Virginia. His family was well-educated, but Patrick did not like going to school. He much preferred exploring the countryside, splashing barefoot through streams, or listening to birds sing.

Patrick had been named after his uncle. The elder Patrick Henry was a fine speaker, and young Patrick

loved to listen to him talk. Uncle Patrick seemed to know about everything, from history to politics. Patrick copied his uncle, and soon developed a powerful, clear speaking voice of his own.

Young Patrick also loved music. Once, when he had to stay inside because he had broken his collarbone, he passed the time by teaching himself to play the flute. He also was a very good fiddle player.

Earning a Living

When Patrick was 15 years old, his father sent him to work in a country store. Later, Patrick and his older brother ran a store of their own. However, neither of the brothers was very interested in the business, and it soon failed.

By then, Patrick Henry was married and had two children. He decided to earn a living as a lawyer. Being a lawyer would allow him to speak in public, and get paid for it. This seemed like a great idea for someone who was good at talking.

Talking Treason

Henry was a good lawyer. In 1765, he was elected to the Virginia House of Burgesses, which was part of the Virginia Assembly. Soon, he was criticizing the British king and the way Great Britain ruled the American colonies. During one speech, he declared that Virginia should oppose the Stamp Tax, which Great Britain had just placed on the colonies. When someone called out that Henry's words were treason (disloyalty to the king), Henry shouted back, "If this be treason, make the most of it!"

Henry became famous for his incredible speaking talent. In 1773, he gave such an exciting speech against a British tax on tea that the audience ran to the capitol building and ripped down the British flag.

On March 23, 1775, Henry gave his most famous

speech. Before a large audience in a church in Richmond, Virginia, he criticized Americans who did not want to fight back against Great Britain's unfair laws and taxes. "Gentlemen may cry peace," he shouted, "but there is no peace. Is life so dear or peace so sweet as to be purchased at the price of chains and slavery? . . . I know not what course others may take, but as for me, give me liberty or give me death!"

Patrick Henry's words inspired the people of Virginia to fight for their freedom. The American Revolution began just a month later, at Lexington and Concord, Massachusetts. When Virginia's militia joined the war, they went off to battle with "Liberty or Death" sewn on their shirts. The British were not

TOPICAL TIDBIT

The Bill of Rights

Patrick Henry was among the many Americans who were uneasy about the new country's Constitution. They were afraid that it did not do enough to guard the rights of individual citizens or of the states. The Bill of Rights, which is the first 10 amendments (changes) to the Constitution, was adopted in 1791 to correct this. Those 10 amendments include the rights to free speech and religion, and the right to bear arms. They forbid "double jeopardy" (being tried twice for the same crime) and "cruel and unusual punishment." They also guarantee a speedy trial and other legal safeguards that are crucial to democracy.

quite so thrilled with Henry's words. They called him an outlaw and threatened to arrest him for treason.

Patrick Henry was elected governor of Virginia in 1776. He served five terms, leading Virginia through the American Revolution and in the years following U.S. independence. In 1788, he helped add the Bill of Rights to the U.S. Constitution. Henry wanted to be sure to protect the freedoms the country had worked so hard to win.

President George Washington offered him a number of jobs in the new government, but he refused. In 1796, at the age of 60, Henry retired from public life until 1799, when he agreed to run for office once again. He was elected, but died on June 6, 1799. More than 200 years later, his brave words— "Give me liberty or give me death!"—still live on. ◇

LIFE EVENTS

1736
Patrick Henry is born in Studley, Virginia.

1765
Henry is elected to the colonial Virginia Assembly.

1775
Henry makes his famous "Give me liberty or give me death" speech at the Second Virginia Convention.

1776
Henry is elected governor of the state of Virginia.

1791
The Bill of Rights to the Constitution is adopted.

1799
Henry is again elected to the Virginia legislature, but dies before he can take his seat.

Wild Bill Hickok
Lawman of the Wild West
(born 1837 • died 1876)

During the 1800s, the western United States was a dangerous place filled with thieves and murderers. One man who was brave enough to battle such perils was Wild Bill Hickok, one of the most famous figures of the American West.

An Early Taste of Adventure

James Butler Hickok was born in Homer, Illinois, on May 27, 1837. The Hickoks' home was a stop on the Underground Railroad, a network of people and safe houses that helped runaway slaves make their way to freedom in Northern states or Canada. The Hickoks hid many slaves in their basement. At night, young James often led runaways to their next hiding place.

Hunting was an important part of life in those days. That was no problem for young James, who was an excellent shot. He often put meat on the family's dinner table by shooting deer, rabbits, and other wild animals.

In 1855, when he was 18 years old, James Hickok got a job driving mules along a canal path. One of the older drivers, Charles Hudson, started teasing the younger man, then pushed him into the canal. That made Hickok so angry that he began wrestling with Hudson. The two men fell into the canal. Hickok thought that Hudson had drowned, which scared him so much that he ran away.

Heading West

Hickok walked all the way to Kansas, where he joined the U.S. Army. His shooting was so good that he became the commander's bodyguard. Because he had run away from home, Hickok decided to hide his identity. He told everyone that his name was Bill.

After a few years in the army, Hickok became a stagecoach driver, riding a route from Kansas into the western territories. This was a dangerous job. Stagecoaches were often attacked by bandits or Native Americans. There was also danger from wild animals and buffalo stampedes. Hickok enjoyed his job, however, and always made sure that his wagon arrived safely.

On one trip through the Rocky Mountains, Hickok was attacked by a grizzly bear. He managed to kill the bear, but he was seriously injured. Everyone thought that he would die, but the tough young man survived.

The Army, and More Adventures

In 1861, the Civil War began. Hickok joined the North's Union Army. He was assigned to lead Army wagon trains. On one trip to Missouri, he saw an angry mob about to hang a young man. To stop them, Hickok drew his gun and pointed it at the mob's leaders. The mob quickly disappeared without a shot being fired. Hickok's bravery became the talk of the town. Someone yelled, "Good for you, Wild Bill!"—and Hickok had a new nickname.

Later, Hickok became a scout for the Union Army. He loved the dangerous job of slipping behind enemy lines to find out what the other side was doing. On one trip, Hickok was captured and ordered to be executed as a spy. The night before his execution, he broke free, killed his guard, and got away in the guard's clothes. Word of Hickok's daring escape made him a hero in the Northern states.

Laying Down the Law

After the Civil War ended in 1865, Hickok was asked to be the law officer at Fort Riley, Kansas. His job was to restore order and prevent soldiers from stealing horses and running away. This dangerous job paid $75 a month. With Hickok in charge, Fort Riley became a much safer, calmer place.

In 1867, some people from Hays City, Kansas asked Hickok to be their marshall. He was often shot at and threatened, but he won every gun battle and cleaned up the town.

Hickok later worked as the marshall in Abilene, Kansas, another rough

> "Leave town on the eastbound train, the westbound train, or go North [to Boot Hill, the cemetery] in the morning."
>
> —Marshall Bill Hickok of Abilene, Kansas, warning troublemakers that he would hunt them down

frontier town. One night, he killed one of his best friends by mistake during a shootout. That tragedy made him think seriously about quitting his job.

A Showman to the End

During the 1870s, Wild Bill Hickok was featured in many magazine articles and novels. He also joined Buffalo Bill's Wild West show for a couple of years. Those exciting shows starred well-known Western heroes. They toured the country staging mock battles as well as rodeos and buffalo roundups.

In 1876, Hickok went to Deadwood, a town in the Dakota Territory, to look for gold. By this time, he was tired of fighting, and his eyesight was failing. "My shooting days are over," he wrote to a friend.

Still, the outlaws there were afraid that he would be appointed marshall and clean up the town. Determined to stay, they looked for someone to kill the famous lawman. Several gunman were too afraid

TOPICAL TIDBIT

Dead Man's Hand

On August 2, 1876, Wild Bill Hickok joined a poker game in Carl Mann's Saloon in Deadwood. Carelessly, he took a seat with his back to the door—which he had always been careful not to do. When Jack McCall shot him, he fell backward and his "hand"— the group of cards he was holding—hit the floor. Hickok's fellow players looked at the cards: He'd had a pair of aces and a pair of eights. From then on, throughout the West, aces and eights was known as the Dead Man's Hand.

to try. Finally, a "local bum" named Jack McCall agreed to do it. On August 2, 1876, Jack McCall shot Wild Bill Hickok in the back of the head while Hickok was playing cards. Hickok was only 39 years old.

Wild Bill Hickok's reputation has long outlived him. Today, he is still remembered as a hero of the American West who was not afraid to fight for justice. ◇

LIFE EVENTS

1837
James Butler Hickok is born in Homer, Illinois.

1855
A fist fight causes Hickok to flee west to Kansas.

1861
The Civil War begins and Hickok joins the Union Army. Facing down an angry mob earns him the nickname Wild Bill.

1865
Hickok outdraws gunman Dave Tutt in Springfield, Missouri. A story in *Harper's New Monthly Magazine* begins to spread his legend.

1869
Hickok is elected marshall of Hays City, Kansas.

1876
Hickok is shot and killed in Deadwood, Dakota Territory.

Sam Houston
A Leader for Independence
(born 1793 • died 1863)

Texas declared its independence from Mexico in 1836. Sam Houston played an important role in helping Texas win that freedom. Without his further military and political leadership, Texas might not have become the 28th state in 1845.

A Farm Boy

Samuel Houston was born on March 2, 1793, in Rockbridge County, Virginia. His father had a large plantation, but did not manage it very well. As a result, the family had little money.

Sam did not go to school until he was eight years old. He learned to read, write, and do simple arithmetic, but probably spent only about six months in school over the next few years.

When Sam was 14, his father died. His mother and her nine children moved to Tennessee. Sam's mother sent him to work in a general store. He hated the job so much that he ran away and joined a tribe of

friendly Cherokee Indians, with whom he lived for almost three years.

Because Sam Houston often bought clothes and supplies for the Cherokee, he soon owed money to his family and friends back home. When he was 18 years old, he left the Cherokee and got a job as a schoolteacher. As soon as he earned enough money to pay off his debt, he quit teaching and joined the army to fight against the British in the War of 1812.

Houston's Political Career

That war ended in 1814. A few years later, in 1817, Houston was selected to represent the U.S. government in dealings with Tennessee's Native American tribes. Knowing that the treaty the government was offering to the Natives was unfair, Houston went to Washington, D.C., to complain. No one would listen to him.

Houston decided to join the government and work to win fair treatment for all of Tennessee's citizens. In 1823, he was elected to the U.S. House of Representatives. Four years later, he was elected governor of Tennessee. He also became a member of the Cherokee tribe, and met with President Andrew Jackson in an effort to help protect the Cherokee from dishonest government agents.

> "We must now act or abandon all hope! Be men, be free men, that your children may bless their father's name."
>
> —Sam Houston, before the Battle of San Jacinto

Freedom for Texas!

Despite his political success, Sam Houston was not happy. In 1832, he left Tennessee and moved to Texas, which was then part of Mexico. Many Texans wanted to break free from Mexico, and rule themselves as an independent country. Houston threw himself into the fight. In November 1835, he was named the commander of the Texas army.

Houston received an unusual present for his 43rd birthday. On that day—March 2, 1836—Texas declared its independence from Mexico. Four days later, 189 Texan defenders of a fort called the Alamo were killed by an army led by Antonio López de Santa Anna, a Mexican general. Houston had been on his way to rescue the soldiers, but was unable to get there in time.

Six weeks later, on April 21, Houston led his army against Santa Anna's at San Jacinto. Houston's battle cry, "Remember the Alamo!," inspired his outnumbered troops to win the battle and capture Santa Anna.

TOPICAL TIDBIT

The Battle of San Jacinto

The Battle of San Jacinto on April 21, 1836, is one of the most important events in Texas history. Sam Houston led an army of about 800 men against General Santa Anna's 1,500 troops. Attacking the Mexican position on the San Jacinto River—near where the city of Houston is now—the Texans shouted "Remember the Alamo!" as they charged. In less than half an hour, they had killed about 600 Mexican soldiers. Within 24 hours, they had captured Santa Anna and 700 of his men. The Mexican general was forced to surrender, and Texas had its independence.

In September 1836, Sam Houston was elected the first president of the independent Republic of Texas. He worked hard to win recognition of Texas by the U.S. He also protected his republic's borders from invasions by Mexicans and unfriendly Native Americans, and managed to pay off all of the Republic's debts. He served two terms as president.

The 28th State

Although Texas had fought hard to win its independence, it was too small to survive as a republic. Houston turned his efforts to getting the U.S. to grant statehood to Texas. On December 29, 1845, his work paid off: Texas became the 28th state in the Union.

Houston's political career was not over. He continued to work for Texas, serving three terms as a U.S. senator. In 1859, he was elected governor

LIFE EVENTS

1793
Samuel Houston is born in Rockbridge County, Virginia.

1823
Houston is elected U.S. representative from Tennessee.

1835
Texas declares independence from Mexico. Houston is made commander in chief of its army.

1836
Houston's men win the Battle of San Jacinto. He becomes president of the Republic of Texas.

1845
Texas becomes the 28th U.S. state.

1861
The Civil War breaks out. Houston, then Texas governor, refuses to pledge allegiance to the Confederacy and is forced from office. He dies in 1863.

of Texas. In 1861, however, Texas joined the Civil War on the side of the Confederate states of the South. Houston did not believe that the Confederacy could win the war, so he refused to swear allegiance (loyalty) to it. Because of this, he was forced to give up his position as governor.

Sam Houston died of pneumonia on July 26, 1863. When he died, the people of Texas were still angry at him for refusing to support the Confederacy. After the war ended in 1865, however, his achievements were recognized all over the U.S., including Texas. The city of Houston, Texas, was named after him, and he is still remembered as one of the most important American figures of the 1800s. ◇

Anne Hutchinson
Champion of Religious Freedom
(born 1591 • died 1643)

One of the founding principles of the United States was that everyone would be able to worship whatever religion they wanted. However, during colonial days, this was not always allowed. Anne Hutchinson was someone who suffered because of her beliefs. Her courage helped bring the idea of religious freedom to all Americans.

A Quiet Life

Anne Hutchinson did not seem like the type of person who would cause trouble. She was born Anne Marbury in England in 1591. In 1612, she married a merchant named William Hutchinson. In 1634, the Hutchinsons moved their family to Boston, which—at that time—was a small town in the Massachusetts Bay Colony. Most of the people who lived there were members of a strict religious movement called

In 1637, Anne Hutchinson was put on trial for her beliefs.

Puritanism. Puritans had many severe rules to follow. They strongly believed that the only true Christians were people who followed all of these rules to the letter.

William Hutchinson had been a rich landowner in England. When he, Anne, and their children moved to the American colonies, they soon became one of the most well-known and most popular families in Boston. Anne Hutchinson worked as a midwife, delivering babies, and she had many friends among the women of the town.

Trouble!

Anne Hutchinson was a very religious person. Her father had been a minister, and she had read the Bible and other religious works. She decided to share her views on religious questions with Boston's women, and so began holding meetings in her home. During those meetings, the women discussed what their minister had said in church on Sunday, and what they thought about it. They also talked about how they believed a person should worship God.

During the meetings, Hutchinson told her friends that she believed in a "covenant of grace" from God for each person. (A *covenant* is a formal, solemn, unbreakable promise.) She said that people had to talk to God themselves. They could not rely on what the minister said. Hutchinson also said that going to church was not important. She encouraged people to think for themselves and find their own way to worship God.

The leaders of the Massachusetts Bay Colony got very angry when they heard what Hutchinson was saying. They thought that she was encouraging people to make up their own rules and do whatever they felt was right. Church leaders worried that people would stop listening to them and stop attending services. Soon Hutchinson was in a lot of trouble.

At first, her friends stood by her. One of her strongest supporters was a well-known and respected minister named John Cotton. Later, however, Massachusetts got a new governor, John Winthrop, who hated Hutchinson's ideas. Under pressure from Winthrop, members of the community began to turn against Hutchinson. Finally, even John Cotton said that she was wrong.

Anne Hutchinson refused to change her beliefs so, in 1637, she was put on trial by Governor Winthrop. When Hutchinson said that Winthrop's rules were "against the word of God," she was convicted by the General Court. Winthrop banished Hutchinson—made her leave Massachusetts forever. However, since it was the middle of winter and Hutchinson was expecting a baby, she was allowed to stay in Boston until spring.

> "As I do understand it, laws, commands, rules, and edicts are for those who have not the light which makes plain the pathway. He who has God's grace in his heart cannot go astray."
>
> —Anne Hutchinson

Freedom—Then a Violent End

Early in 1638, Hutchinson and her family left Boston and moved to the neighboring colony of Rhode Island. Rhode Island had been founded by Roger Williams, who also had been banished from Massachusetts for his religious beliefs. In Rhode Island, Hutchinson was finally able to worship as she pleased.

Some of her friends and supporters joined the Hutchinsons in Rhode Island. Together, they founded the town of Portsmouth. The Hutchinsons lived there for the next four years, until William Hutchinson died in 1642. After that, Anne moved her family to Pelham Bay on Long Island, New York. They lived quietly there, in a small cabin in the wilderness. A few

TOPICAL TIDBIT

Mary Barrett Dyer

One of the people who followed Anne Hutchinson to Rhode Island was Mary Barrett Dyer. Like Hutchinson, Dyer strongly believed in religious freedom. Eventually, Dyer became a member of the Society of Friends, also called the Quakers, and returned to Massachusetts to be a Quaker missionary. When Massachusetts passed anti-Quaker laws, Dyer's life was in danger. She was banished twice and almost hanged for her beliefs—but kept going back. Finally, in 1660, she was hanged, but her death made more people see the importance of religious freedom.

months later, in 1643, Hutchinson and her family were attacked by Narragansett Indians, who burned their home, killing everyone except one of Hutchinson's daughters.

Although Anne Hutchinson had been banished from Massachusetts, she was not forgotten there. Today, a statue of her stands on Beacon Hill in Boston. It reminds everyone of his brave woman, who was not afraid to lose everything for what she believed in. ◇

LIFE EVENTS

1591
Anne Marbury is born in England.

1634
Anne and William Hutchinson move their family to the Massachusetts Bay Colony.

1636
Anne Hutchinson comes into conflict with John Winthrop, the governor of Massachusetts.

1637
Winthrop puts Hutchinson on trial for opposing the Puritan ministers. Convicted and banished, Hutchinson moves to the colony of Rhode Island in 1638.

1643
Hutchinson and her family, living on Long Island, are killed by Narragansett Indians.

Andrew Jackson
President of the
Common People

(born 1767 • died 1845)

Until Andrew Jackson, all U.S. presidents had started life in wealthy, well-educated families. Jackson was a rough, tough soldier with humble origins. However, his courage, energy, and intelligence made him one of the most popular and important presidents.

Backwoods Beginnings

Andrew Jackson was born on March 15, 1767, in South Carolina. His family had moved to America from Ireland two years earlier, and lived in a log cabin in the wilderness. Andy's father died just six days before Andy was born. His mother moved in with her sister, and Andy grew up in a large household full of cousins.

From the start, he was tough. If anyone pushed him around, the little boy was quick to fight back. He soon had a reputation as a hot-tempered, brave fighter.

Andy learned many things during his childhood. He learned to hunt, fish, and trap wild animals—skills important for people living in the wilderness. He was also very intelligent, and studied Latin, Greek, and science, along with reading, writing, and arithmetic.

Andy was nine years old when the American Revolution began in 1776. When he was 13, he joined the army and took part in several battles. He also was captured by the British and put to work for them. When he refused to clean the boots of a British officer, the man slashed him across the hand and head with his sword. Andrew Jackson proudly carried the scars from those wounds for the rest of his life.

The Battle of New Orleans

After the war ended, Jackson became a teacher, then a lawyer. In 1788, he and some friends traveled to Nashville, Tennessee, to practice law. They believed that the large number of settlers moving into Tennessee would need legal help.

Soon Jackson was a rich, successful frontier lawyer. His abilities helped him win election as Tennessee's representative to the U.S. Congress in 1796. Later, he became a judge on Tennessee's superior court. He held this post for six years. He quickly earned a reputation as an honest, fair, and dignified justice.

> "One man with courage makes a majority."
> —a favorite saying of Andrew Jackson

When the War of 1812 began, 45-year-old Jackson took command of 2,000 Tennessee volunteers. His men called him "Old Hickory" in honor of his courage, because hickory is the toughest wood in the wilderness. He won important battles against Native American tribes fighting on the British side. However, his greatest battle was against the British in New Orleans.

Jackson and his 2,000 soldiers arrived in New Orleans on December 2, 1814. Three weeks later, 6,000 British troops invaded the city. For two weeks, Jackson's outnumbered men fought the British in small battles. Then, on January 8, 1815, the final battle took place. It ended with a tremendous American victory. Only 31 Americans were killed and 71 injured, compared to 289 British dead and 2,000 injured.

On to the White House

After the war, Jackson became a U.S. senator from Tennessee. In 1828, this popular and honored hero was elected the seventh president of the United States. He was the first president to come from a poor family who lived west of the Appalachian Mountains, and he

TOPICAL TIDBIT

"A Corrupt Bargain"

Andrew Jackson first ran for president in 1824. The election was so close that the House of Representatives had to decide the winner. Jackson had the most votes of four candidates. However, the candidate with the second-most votes, John Quincy Adams, made a deal with the third-place candidate, Henry Clay. Clay gave his votes to Adams, so Adams became president. Jackson and his supporters were so angry, they accused the new president of making a "corrupt [rotten] bargain." Four years later, they beat John Quincy Adams and had their revenge.

was hugely popular with the common people. Jackson said that the White House belonged to the people. He welcomed people to visit the White House, and come shake his hand at any hour of the day or night.

Jackson strongly believed that each state had the right to determine its own laws. However, he also thought that each state had to be loyal to the U.S. When South Carolina threatened to ignore a federal law, Jackson said that he would send the army to enforce it. "Our federal Union—it must be preserved," he said. South Carolina backed down, and the Union was saved.

Jackson won a second term as president in 1832. After he left office in 1837, he retired to his plantation in Tennessee. When he died eight years later, on June 8, 1845, he was hailed as a champion of the people who had never been afraid to fight for what he believed in. ◇

LIFE EVENTS

1767
Andrew Jackson is born in the Waxhaws region of South Carolina.

1780
At 13, Jackson joins the American army during the American Revolution and is captured by the British.

1788
Jackson moves to Nashville, Tennessee.

1796
Jackson is elected U.S. representative from Tennessee.

1815
During the War of 1812, Jackson leads U.S. troops to victory at the Battle of New Orleans.

1828
Jackson wins the first of two terms as president of the U.S.

Thomas Jefferson
Creator of a Nation
(born 1743 • died 1826)

Thomas Jefferson combined his intelligence, beliefs, and clear, dramatic writing style to give us the Declaration of Independence—one of the most important documents in history. Later, as the third president of the United States, he made a deal that expanded the nation's borders, changing the face of our nation forever.

> "The price of liberty is eternal vigilance."
> —Thomas Jefferson

A Privileged Childhood

Thomas Jefferson was born in Albemarle County, Virginia, on April 13, 1743. Thomas was a shy child who did not like to speak in public. He was often teased at school and scolded by the teacher. However, education was important to the boy's parents. So when Thomas was 10 years old, he was sent to a boarding school. There, he added Latin, Greek, and French to his studies.

When Thomas was 14, his father died suddenly. As the oldest son, Thomas had to return home and take charge of the family. Despite his new responsibilities, he continued to read and study on his own. When he was 17, he left home again, to attend the College of William and Mary. Two years later, he went to law school. By 1768, he was a member of Virginia's House of Burgesses, part of the colony's governing body.

Rebellion!

During the 1760s, the American colonists began to argue with Great Britain over the burden of many taxes and laws. In the spring of 1774, Jefferson and a few other members of the House of Burgesses suggested that each colony send representatives to a Continental Congress. The Congress would discuss freedom from Great Britain. Jefferson wrote a document called *A Summary View of the Rights of British Americans*. In it, he said that the colonies did not have to remain under British rule. After it was published, Jefferson's name was placed on a list of "dangerous subjects" by the British government.

The Declaration of Independence

In May 1776, Jefferson was asked to compose a Declaration of Independence from Great Britain. It took him 17 days to write. The finished document begins with words that have become immortal. It says that "all men are created equal" and that they have "certain unalienable rights; . . . [including] life, liberty, and the pursuit of happiness." The Declaration of Independence became much more than just an explanation of why the colonists wanted their freedom. It became one of the most important documents ever written.

The American Revolution—war with Britain over the American colonies' right to independence—had begun at Lexington and Concord, Massachusetts, on April 19, 1775. However, it was the signing of Jefferson's Declaration on July 4, 1776, that marked the birth of a new and independent nation.

During this time, Jefferson served on Virginia's state legislature. He worked to reform Virginia's laws of inheritance, allow freedom of religion, and provide a free education to everyone.

In 1779, he was appointed governor of Virginia. The following year, the British army attacked the state and marched to Jefferson's home, Monticello, to take him prisoner. Warned in time, Jefferson managed to escape into the wilderness on horseback.

President Jefferson

In 1782, Jefferson's wife Martha died. To get over his sorrow, he threw himself back into politics. He served in the Continental Congress, then traveled to France to replace Benjamin Franklin as America's ambassador there. He returned to the U.S. in 1789, when President George Washington asked him to be Secretary of State—a high government official who handles relations between the U.S. and other countries. Jefferson later served as vice president under President John Adams. Then, on March 4, 1801, Jefferson took office as the third president of the United States.

During his two terms as president, Jefferson did a

great deal to expand the U.S. In 1803, he purchased the Louisiana Territory from France for $15 million, a historic deal that doubled the size of the country. Soon afterward, he sent a team led by two adventurous men, Meriwether Lewis and William Clark, to explore the continent from the Mississippi River to the Pacific Ocean.

Education for All

In 1808, Jefferson decided that he had been president long enough. He retired to his plantation at Monticello and turned his energies to starting a state university. The University of Virginia welcomed its

TOPICAL TIDBIT

The Louisiana Purchase

France's Louisiana Territory was a huge area of the North American continent. It stretched from New Orleans all the way north to the Canadian border, and from the Mississippi River west to present-day Montana. At first, Jefferson simply wanted to buy the important port city of New Orleans from France's dictator, Napoleon. As it turned out, Napoleon was planning a war to conquer Europe and needed money to finance it. He offered to sell not just New Orleans but *all* of Louisiana Territory for the bargain price of $15 million—less than 3¢ an acre!

first class in 1825. To Jefferson, this was one of the greatest achievements of his life.

By 1826, 83-year-old Jefferson was very ill, but he was determined to see the 50th anniversary of the signing of the Declaration of Independence. On the evening of July 3, Jefferson asked his doctor, "Is it the Fourth?" The doctor replied, "It soon will be." Thomas Jefferson went back to sleep. He died the next day—July 4, 1826, the 50th anniversary of his great achievement. He was buried at Monticello and hailed as one of the greatest architects of America's freedom. He has since become a hero to freedom lovers the world over. ◇

LIFE EVENTS

1743
Thomas Jefferson is born in Albemarle County, Virginia.

1776
Jefferson drafts the Declaration of Independence.

1789
President George Washington appoints Jefferson U.S. Secretary of State.

1801
Jefferson is elected the third president of the U.S.

1803
Jefferson makes the Louisiana Purchase, doubling the size of the U.S.

1826
Jefferson dies on the 50th anniversary of the Declaration of Independence. (So does John Adams— his fellow Declaration signer and former U.S. president.)

John Paul Jones
"I Have Not Yet Begun to Fight!"
(born 1747 • died 1792)

No one was more important in creating the United States Navy than a young sailor named John Paul Jones. His brave deeds made him the greatest naval hero in U.S. history.

A Love of the Sea

The future hero was born John Paul, on July 6, 1747, near the bay of Solway Firth in Scotland. Young John spent many hours watching the ships on the bay, playing on the docks, and sailing small boats.

When John turned 13, he was apprenticed to a British ship owner and went to sea on a ship called the *Friendship*. During his seven-year apprenticeship, he made many trips to America and the West Indies. Although John had to do unpleasant jobs, such as scrubbing the decks and emptying garbage, he loved life aboard ship.

Escape to America

John Paul became captain of his own ship in 1768, when he was 21 years old. In 1772, he was captain and part owner of a bigger ship, the *Betsy*. Soon afterward, an unfortunate incident occurred that changed his life forever.

Late in 1772, the *Betsy* docked on the island of Tobago in the West Indies. Several crew members demanded their pay in advance. Captain Paul refused, and a fight broke out between him and a member of the crew. The crewman ran toward Paul with a club. In the struggle, the captain killed the sailor with his sword. Knowing that his life would be in danger from the man's family in Tobago, Paul left his ship and his belongings behind and fled to America. He also changed his name—to John Paul Jones.

> "Every officer should feel in each fiber of his being an eager desire to [copy the] . . . determination and dauntless scorn of death which marked John Paul Jones above all his fellows."
>
> —President Theodore Roosevelt, dedicating Jones's grave at Annapolis, Maryland, in 1906

Jones Goes to War

Jones settled in Virginia, and soon became friends with Thomas Jefferson of Virginia and Joseph Hewes of North Carolina. Both Jefferson and Hewes were delegates to the Second Continental Congress. On December 7, 1775, Hewes gave Jones a commission as a first lieutenant in the Continental Navy. By accepting this position, Jones cut his ties with Great Britain.

War broke out between the American colonies and Great Britain in 1775. In 1776, Jones was captain of a ship called the *Providence*. He and his crew captured 16 enemy ships, rescued an American ship, and destroyed part of the British fishing fleet in Canada.

The following year, Jones was given command of a new ship, the *Ranger*. The *Ranger* made a daring run to Great Britain, where Jones and his crew captured or sank several ships and seized 200 prisoners. The prisoners were later exchanged for 228 American sailors who had been captured by the British. The British government was furious at Jones's activities. It sent several ships to capture him, but no one was ever able to catch the talented sea captain.

Some of the freed American prisoners joined the

TOPICAL TIDBIT

Jones and the U.S. Navy

After the American Revolution ended, the U.S. decided to disband the Continental Navy. Keeping it seemed too expensive to the young country. Jones argued strongly against doing this. Then, almost immediately, there was trouble. Pirates began attacking U.S. merchant ships off Africa's Barbary Coast and holding the crews for ransom. President George Washington had to admit that John Paul Jones was right. The U.S. established a permanent navy in 1798.

crew of Jones's next ship, the *Bonhomme Richard*. On September 23, 1779, Jones's fleet came across a group of 42 British merchant ships protected by a warship named the *Serapis*. The *Serapis* had more guns and sailors than the *Bonhomme Richard*, but Jones was determined to sink it and capture the ships it protected. A fierce sea battle followed, with cannon blasting, fires burning, and men shouting. Both ships were badly damaged. When the captain of the *Serapis* asked Jones if he were ready to surrender, Jones shouted back a reply that soon became famous: "I have not yet begun to fight!" After three and a half hours, the British captain finally surrendered. Jones had won the battle, but his ship was so badly damaged that it sank the next day.

A Hero Across the Atlantic

After the battle, Jones went to France, which was an ally (friend) of America. He was hailed as a hero there, and his bravery encouraged France to give even more support to the American colonies. Back at home, Jones was considered the greatest fighting captain in the American navy, and was given a Congressional gold medal. Once the Revolution was over, however, things didn't work out so well for the fighting captain. Jones came to feel that he wasn't appreciated in his new country. A brief appointment to the Russian navy was a disaster. Finally, in low spirits and bad health, Jones moved to France.

In 1792, President George Washington and his Secretary of State, Thomas Jefferson, appointed Jones as a commissioner to Algiers, a city in North Africa controlled by pirates. They wanted Jones to free American prisoners being held there for ransom. They also wanted him to establish a treaty between the U.S. and Algiers. Jones would have been honored and pleased by this assignment, but he never got the chance to accept it. He died in Paris on July 18, 1792, before news of the job reached him.

Jones was buried in Paris but, in 1905, his body was taken to the U.S. and reburied at the Naval Academy Chapel in Annapolis, Maryland. It was a fitting resting place for America's first naval hero. ◇

LIFE EVENTS

1747
John Paul is born in Scotland.

1768
Paul becomes captain of his own ship.

1772
Paul kills a mutinous crew member and flees to America. He changes his name to John Paul Jones.

1775
Jones becomes a first lieutenant in the Continental Navy.

1779
During a fierce battle at sea, Jones refuses to surrender, saying, "I have not yet begun to fight!"

1792
Jones dies in Paris. His body lies in an unmarked grave until 1905, when it is moved to the U.S. Naval Academy in Annapolis, Maryland.

Mother Jones
(Mary Harris Jones)
"The Grandmother
of Agitators"
(born 1830 • died 1930)

During the 1800s and 1900s, workers all over the U.S. fought bitter, often bloody, battles to win their rights and improve working conditions. One of the greatest heroes of this battle was Mary Harris Jones— a woman who looked like a sweet little grandmother. In truth, this "grandmother" was a fiery speaker and an inspiration to workers everywhere. They called her Mother Jones.

> "I'm not a humanitarian, I'm a hell-raiser."
> —Mother Jones

A Family Tradition

Mary Harris was born in Cork, Ireland on May 1, 1830. Her family had a tradition of fighting for their rights against the British. Her grandfather had been an Irish freedom fighter, and he was hanged for his activities. In 1835, Mary's father was forced to flee from Ireland and take his family to Canada.

Mary grew up in Toronto, Ontario. After she graduated from high school, she moved to the U.S. to find work. She taught school in Michigan, but did not like "bossing little children," so she quit her job and moved to Chicago to become a dressmaker. In 1861, she married George E. Jones, an ironworker. Jones was a member of a labor union. He taught his wife all about the struggles that workers had to go through every day at their jobs.

Starting Over

By 1867, Mary Jones was living a happy, quiet life with her husband and their four children. Then the family fell ill with yellow fever. Within a week, her husband and all her children had died of the disease.

Jones left Chicago for a time, then returned and resumed her career as a dressmaker. But in 1871, disaster struck again when the Great Chicago Fire roared through the city. Jones lost everything she owned. Once again, she was forced to start a new life.

Everyone's Mother

Jones became involved in the labor movement and joined a group called the Knights of Labor. Soon, her whole life revolved around the workers and their struggle for a decent life. Jones traveled from city to city to meet with workers. She lived with them in tent colonies or rundown tenement houses. When someone asked her where she lived, she answered, "Wherever there is a fight." Because she had no family of her own, the workers became her family. In turn, they began calling her "Mother." In time, she was known all over the country as Mother Jones.

Jones was especially interested in the difficult working conditions of coal miners. She attended her first United Mine Workers (UMW) convention in 1901 and worked for the organization until 1922. Her tireless labor to improve life for the miners earned her a new nickname: "the miners' angel."

Mother Jones had a gift for attracting attention from the press, the public, and the government. In

1902, she led a march of miners' wives into the Pennsylvania coalfields. There, the women used brooms and mops to chase away strikebreakers. In 1903, she led a "children's crusade" of several hundred workers from the textile mills of Pennsylvania to President Theodore Roosevelt's home in New York—a journey, on foot, of 100 miles. Her march brought attention to the evils of child labor and helped end the practice of sending very young children to work at dangerous jobs.

Jones faced many difficulties in her work, but refused to back down. She was arrested after a protest in West Virginia in 1913, when she was 83 years old. Striking mine workers and mine guards had exchanged gunfire, and people were killed. In an

TOPICAL TIDBIT

The Children's Crusade

The "children's crusade," a protest of 1903, was inspired by the plight of America's textile workers. At the time, much of the work done in textile mills was done by children. They worked 60 hours a week. It was dangerous work: Many children were missing fingers that had been torn off by machines. The Secret Service managed to keep most of the children's crusade marchers away from the mansion of President Theodore Roosevelt—but not all. Mother Jones dressed three of the boys in better clothes, slipped onto a train with them, and showed up at the President's door!

effort to discourage her cause, the authorities charged Mother Jones with conspiring to commit murder. She was convicted and sentenced to 20 years in prison! Her trial captured the public's interest and led to a U.S. Senate investigation of conditions in the West Virginia coal mines. Meanwhile, the governor of West Virginia set Mother Jones free.

Mary Harris Jones continued to travel around the country until 1926, when she was 96 years old. She organized strikes, gave speeches, and did whatever she could to help the cause that she believed in so strongly.

She died in Silver Spring, Maryland, on November 30, 1930, at the age of 100. Mother Jones is buried in the Union Miners Cemetery in southern Illinois—among the coal miners she always called her family. ◇

LIFE EVENTS

1830
Mary Harris is born in Cork, Ireland.

1867
Now Mary Jones of Chicago, she loses her husband and children in a yellow fever epidemic.

1871
Jones loses everything in the Great Fire and becomes involved with the Knights of Labor.

1901
Known as Mother Jones, she becomes an organizer for the United Mine Workers.

1913
Jones is arrested during a miner's strike in West Virginia.

1921
Jones, 91, is invited to the Pan-American Federation of Labor in Mexico. She dies at age 100.

Chief Joseph
"I Will Fight No More Forever"
(born 1840? • died 1904)

Few Native American tribes were as peaceful or friendly to white Americans as the Nez Perce. Yet this tribe became part of a desperate fight against the U.S. government to retain its freedom. The hero of this struggle was the tribe's leader, Chief Joseph.

A Peaceful Tribe

Joseph was born around 1840 in the Wallowa Valley of Oregon. His name in the language of the Nez Perce was Hin-mah-too-yah-lat-kekt, which means "Thunder Rolling Down the Mountain." However, the boy's father, chief of the Nez Perce, had been given the name Joseph by a white missionary, so the son became known as Young Joseph.

Joseph's tribe, the Nez Perce, were very peaceful and helped many white explorers and settlers. When Young Joseph was 15, his father even made an agree-

ment that his people would never harm white settlers. In return, the U.S. government promised that
the tribe could stay in the Wallowa Valley forever.

The government broke that promise in 1863, after
gold was discovered on the Nez Perce's land. Soon
the area was filled with white settlers, who put pres-

sure on the government to force the Nez Perce off their land. Young Joseph's father still refused to leave his homeland.

In 1871, when Young Joseph was 31, his father died. The young man became leader of the Nez Perce and so earned his most famous name—Chief Joseph. Five years later, the U.S. government told Chief Joseph that he and his tribe had to leave their land for a reservation in Idaho. Chief Joseph did not want to go to war over the government's order, so he reluctantly agreed. Before the tribe could leave, however, he received some disturbing news. Some U.S. soldiers had stolen hundreds of horses and killed two Nez Perce. Several Nez Perce warriors had fought back, killing 18 whites in a surprise attack. Suddenly, the war that Chief Joseph had tried to avoid seemed to be near.

> "The earth is the mother of all people, and all people should have equal rights upon it."
>
> —Chief Joseph, in Washington, D.C., in 1879

Chief Joseph had to make a big decision. Should he take his family and move to the reservation? Should he join the Nez Perce in battle with the U.S. Army? Chief Joseph decided instead to take the tribe to Canada, which was an English colony then. If his people could make it over the border to Canada, they would be safe from the U.S. government.

On the Run

The Nez Perce began their long flight. Hard at their heels was General Oliver Howard and his soldiers, whose orders were to capture Chief Joseph and his tribe. The Nez Perce were hopelessly outnumbered in their fight against the Army. Chief Joseph had only 200 warriors, few rifles, a limited supply of bows and arrows, and almost 600 women and children to protect. General Howard had thousands of soldiers and plenty of weapons and supplies.

Despite being outnumbered, Chief Joseph put up a brave fight. His warriors attacked army camps at night. He confused the soldiers by changing direction, to throw them off course. He avoided direct conflict as much as possible, but when the two armies did meet in battle, the Nez Perce were so skilled that they were able to drive the government troops away.

TOPICAL TIDBIT

From Enemies to Admirers

Many of the soldiers who pursued the Nez Perce to their surrender at Bear Paw came to greatly respect Chief Joseph. Lieutenant Charles Erskine Scott Wood of the U.S. Army wrote of how shocked he was when the Nez Perce were sent to the "strange and unwholesome land" of the Indian Territory instead of back to their own country. Throughout his life, Wood made appearances before groups urging justice for the Nez Perce.

A Sad Ending

The perilous journey continued across Oregon, Washington, Idaho, and into Montana. They traveled more than 1,000 miles in 115 days. Then, in October 1877, just 30 miles from the Canadian border, it came to an end. The tribe had stopped to rest at Eagle Creek in the Bear Paw Mountains of Montana. They were cold, starving, and tired. Suddenly, soldiers rushed into the camp. Some of the terrified Nez Perce, including Joseph's nine-year-old daughter, ran into the wilderness, where most died from cold or hunger. The rest were trapped in the camp, where many were shot to death.

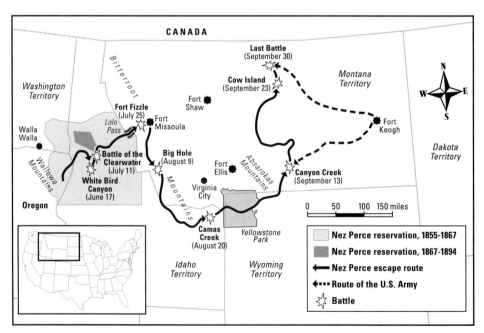

This map shows the route of Chief Joseph's 1877 flight toward freedom.

Chief Joseph could take no more. He climbed onto his horse and rode slowly toward the white men to surrender. His mournful speech ended with words that are still remembered today: "I am tired; my heart is sick and sad. From where the sun now stands, I will fight no more forever."

The Nez Perce were not sent to the reservation in Idaho, as originally promised, Instead, the government sent them to Indian Territory in Oklahoma—a harsher place. Most of the Nez Perce got sick there and died, including all of Chief Joseph's remaining children. Later, a broken-hearted Joseph and some of the tribe were forced to march to a reservation in Washington. Chief Joseph lived there until his death in 1904. To the end, he led his people with dignity and bravery. ◇

LIFE EVENTS

1840
Hin-mah-too-yah-lat-kekt, or Young Joseph, is born in the Wallowa Valley, Oregon Territory.

1871
Young Joseph becomes chief.

1876
The U.S. government orders the Nez Perce to move to a reservation in Idaho.

1877
Chief Joseph leads the Nez Perce toward Canada. They are caught and sent to a reservation in Oklahoma, where many die.

1885
The Nez Perce are moved to Washington Territory.

1904
Chief Joseph dies, still in exile from his native land.

John F. Kennedy
A Profile in Courage
(born 1917 • died 1963)

John F. Kennedy was in poor physical health and almost constant pain. He served as U.S. president for less than three years. Yet he has become one of America's most fascinating and heroic public figures.

Wealthy Beginnings

John Fitzgerald Kennedy was born in Brookline, Massachusetts, on May 29, 1917, the second of nine children. John's father was a successful banker and businessman who later served as U.S. ambassador to England. The family was rich and powerful, and there was a lot of competition to be the best. John was a sickly child, and he later developed Addison's disease. Still,

> "If a free society cannot help the many who are poor, it cannot save the few who are rich."
>
> —John F. Kennedy, from his inaugural address, January 20, 1961

he never let his poor health stop him from taking part in sports, adventures, and family activities.

John's favorite school subject was history. In 1936, he went to Harvard University to study politics. During his senior year, he wrote a paper about England's role in World War II. It became a best-selling book called *Why England Slept*. Later, he wrote a book of essays about brave people called *Profiles in Courage*. It won a Pulitzer Prize, an important honor in literature.

World War II Hero

In December, 1941, the U.S. began fighting in World War II. Even though he had a bad back from a 1939 football injury, John Kennedy joined the Navy and was sent to the South Pacific. Soon he was the commander of a type of small warship called a PT boat.

In August 1943, Kennedy's boat, *PT 109*, was ripped in half by a Japanese ship. Kennedy helped his men swim to a nearby island. Despite his bad back, he pulled an injured sailor through the water to safety, then swam to another island to get help. Kennedy's brave deeds won him honors as a hero.

John F. Kennedy aboard the *PT 109*.

World War II ended in 1945, and Kennedy returned to Massachusetts. A year later, he ran for a seat in the U.S. House of Representatives as a member of the Democratic Party. Massachusetts loved this handsome, brave, young war hero, and he won the election easily. Kennedy served in the U.S. House and then in the Senate for 14 years.

Top Job

In 1960, Kennedy ran for president of the United States. Before the election, Kennedy and his rival, Richard Nixon, took part in the first televised debate between presidential candidates. The nation responded to Kennedy's youth, vigor, and charm,

TOPICAL TIDBIT

"I Am a Berliner"

Soon after he became president, John Kennedy was faced with a crisis in Berlin, Germany. At that time, the Soviet Union controlled the eastern half of the city with a harsh Communist government. Then, in 1961, Nikita Khrushchev, the Soviet premier, had a wall built to keep the people of East Berlin from escaping to democratic West Berlin. Kennedy visited West Berlin, where he made a famous speech to cheering crowds. "Today, in the world of freedom," he said, "the proudest boast is *Ich bin ein Berliner* [I am a Berliner]." In the end, democracy prevailed—the Berlin Wall was finally torn down in 1989.

which came across on TV. That helped him win the election. At 43 years old, he was the youngest person ever elected U.S. president. He also was the nation's first Roman Catholic president.

Kennedy faced many problems during his presidency. One of the most serious was a dispute with the Soviet Union over missiles placed in Cuba, an island country only 90 miles from Florida. The U.S. demanded that the Soviets remove the missiles. Kennedy refused to back down during this tense time and, finally, the missiles were removed.

Kennedy also faced challenges at home. During the 1960s, African Americans were fighting for equal rights. Kennedy was a strong supporter of the civil-rights movement. He sent government troops to the South to help enforce black students' right to attend schools that had been for whites only. Kennedy also tried to change laws and and other systems that discriminated against black people.

During his presidency, Kennedy also started the space program that eventually put Americans on the moon. Another Kennedy accomplishment was the founding of the Peace Corps, an organization that sends American workers all over the world to help poor people improve their living conditions. Kennedy was determined to make America—and the world—a better place. One of his most famous sayings was, "Ask not what your country can do for you, ask what you can do for your country."

A National Tragedy

On November 22, 1963, Kennedy and his wife Jacqueline were riding through the streets of Dallas, Texas, in an open car. Suddenly, shots rang out and the President slumped over in his seat. He had been shot by a sniper named Lee Harvey Oswald. Less than an hour later, Kennedy died at a Dallas hospital. He was 46 years old.

People around the world were stunned at Kennedy's death. The nation mourned, and Americans watched televised news reports about the assassination and funeral for hour after hour. The country was in a state of shock.

John F. Kennedy is buried at Arlington National Cemetery in Virginia. An eternal flame marks his grave, just as his accomplishments burn on in our nation's history. ◇

LIFE EVENTS

1917
John Fitzgerald Kennedy is born in Brookline, Massachusetts.

1940
Kennedy publishes *Why England Slept.*

1943
Kennedy helps save the men of *PT 109* when their boat is hit by a Japanese ship in the South Pacific.

1946
Kennedy wins his first elected office, as Congressman from Massachusetts.

1960
Kennedy is elected the 35th president of the United States.

1963
Kennedy is assassinated in Dallas, Texas.

Bob Kerrey
A Life of Public Service
(born 1943)

Bob Kerrey's life was completely ordinary—until he was severely injured during the Vietnam War. After his recovery, he served his country in a different way, as an elected member of our government.

School and the Navy

Joseph Robert Kerrey was born in Lincoln, Nebraska, on August 27, 1943. He had an ordinary childhood, going to school and playing with friends. After graduating from high school, Bob went to the University of Nebraska at Lincoln. Kerrey graduated from there in 1966 with a degree in pharmacy.

In 1966, the U.S. was fighting a war in Vietnam. Kerrey had been brought up to be patriotic. To him, fighting for his country was the right thing to do. So he joined the Navy and volunteered for the elite SEALs (the **SE**a, **Air**, and **Land**) team, a unit of specially trained commandos. When he finished his training, Lieutenant Kerrey was sent to Vietnam.

A Life-changing Injury

In Vietnam, Kerrey became the leader of his SEALs team. One day, the team was assigned to capture several of the enemy on an island in Nha Trang Bay. Kerrey knew that they would have to surprise the enemy to succeed. So he and his soldiers climbed a 350-foot cliff to a ledge above the enemy camp.

As Kerrey and his men approached the camp, they were spotted and fired upon by the enemy. A grenade exploded at Kerrey's feet. The blast threw him backward against the rocks. Although badly injured and in great pain, Kerrey managed to call for help on his radio. Then he calmly directed his men to keep firing on the enemy camp as they made their escape. Finally, a U.S. helicopter arrived and flew Kerrey to safety. However, his right leg had been so badly injured that it had to be amputated.

Kerrey received the Congressional Medal of Honor, the highest military honor given by the U.S., for his courage and leadership. However, he became angry over his country's participation in the war, and about losing his leg. The patriotism that he had felt toward the U.S. was gone.

> **"There is no force more liberating than the knowledge that you are fighting for others."**
>
> —Bob Kerrey, at the 2000 Democratic National Convention

Then, while recuperating in a military hospital in Philadelphia, Kerrey began to realize how much his government was doing for him. He knew that everyone helping him was there because of government work. "A law was passed in the U.S. Congress, and some president signed that law, authorizing . . . those people to do what they could to save my life and give me a fighting chance to put my life together," Kerrey later said. "This is a great nation to do that."

A New Way to Lead

After being discharged from the hospital in 1972, Kerrey put his leadership skills to work building a chain of successful restaurants and health clubs. By 1982, however, he was looking for a change. He ran for governor of Nebraska, and won. Kerrey wanted to become part of the government because he believed that people needed to work together to improve their lives. "Things don't just get better on their own," he pointed out.

Kerrey was a popular governor, even though he was a Democrat and most Nebraskans were Republican. During his four-year term, he improved the state's finances and started many programs to improve education, job training, and the environment. In 1988, he

TOPICAL TIDBIT

The Medal of Honor

The Congressional Medal of Honor is America's highest military honor. The first such medal, for naval heroes, was created by Congress in December 1861. Congress created a medal to honor army heroes in February 1862. The first person ever to receive the army decoration was Private Jacob Parrott. In April 1862, Parrott was part of "Andrew's Raiders," a group of volunteers from an Ohio brigade that went behind Confederate lines to steal a supply train. Parrott was among a group of six soldiers who managed to survive. All received the Medal of Honor.

decided to move on to higher office. Instead of running for re-election as governor, he won the position of U.S. senator from Nebraska.

Kerrey remained in the Senate until 2000. During that time, he worked to support family farms and health care. He also spoke out against war and nuclear weapons.

Kerrey ran unsuccessfully for president in 1992, and worked on Bill Bradley's presidential campaign in 2000. During an appearance in the 2000 campaign, someone in the crowd called Kerrey a "cripple" and a "quitter." Kerrey later said that he was not offended by being called a cripple, because he had accepted the fact that he had lost a leg. "On the other hand," he added, "I was offended and provoked to anger when I was called a quitter. That accusation put me in the mood to fight!" For Bob Kerrey, quitting has never been an option. ◇

LIFE EVENTS

1943
Joseph Robert Kerrey is born in Lincoln, Nebraska.

1966
Kerry graduates from college and volunteers to be a Navy SEAL during the Vietnam War.

1970
Kerry is awarded the Congressional Medal of Honor for his bravery in battle.

1982
Kerry is elected governor of Nebraska.

1988
Kerry wins the first of two terms as senator from Nebraska. He retires in 2000.

Billie Jean King
Equality on
the Tennis Court
(born 1943)

For most of the 20th century, female athletes were not treated as well as men. Then Billie Jean King came along and changed the world of sports forever.

Not Your Average Tennis Player

Billie Jean Moffitt was born on November 22, 1943, in Long Beach, California. Billie Jean played softball, basketball, and football with the other kids in the neighborhood. When she was 11, she began taking tennis lessons.

Billie Jean did not seem like a tennis player. She was short and pudgy. She could not see the ball unless she was wearing thick eyeglasses. She was once kicked out of a team picture for

> "The main thing is to care. Care very hard, even if it is only a game you are playing."
>
> —Billie Jean King

wearing shorts and a T-shirt instead of a short white tennis dress, like the other girls. Billie Jean also talked to herself while she played. If she won a point, she let out a whoop. If she did something wrong, she yelled at herself. No one in Long Beach had ever seen a tennis player like her before.

Billie Jean may have seemed odd, but she could play tennis. By 1958, when she was 15, she was ranked fifth in the U.S. for girls 15 and under. By age 17, she was ranked fourth among all U.S. women.

Despite Billie Jean's athletic ability, no college offered her a scholarship. In those days, women could not make enough money to support themselves playing tennis professionally. So she became a part-time athlete. During fall and winter, she worked and went to college. In spring and summer, she played tennis.

Equal Treatment for All

By 1965, Billie Jean Moffitt had married Larry King and started to make a name for herself. By 1968, she had won three Wimbledon singles titles, the U.S. Nationals, and the Australian championship. She was the number-one female tennis player in the world. Even though Billie Jean King was very successful, she still had to work another job—as a tennis instructor for $32 a week—to make ends meet.

King was angry that men received more prize money than women did. In 1970, she received $600 for winning the Italian Open. The male winner got $3,500.

To protest the unfairness in prizes, King decided to start her own tennis tournament. She convinced the Virginia Slims cigarette company to put up the prize money. Then she and nine other women skipped a U.S. Lawn Tennis Association (USLTA) event to play in the new Virginia Slims Tournament. This was the first tennis tournament just for women.

The USLTA suspended the women, but that did not stop them. In January 1971, the Virginia Slims Tournament expanded into the Virginia Slims Tour. That year, 29 tournaments were scheduled, with at least $10,000 in prize money for each event.

In 1972, King won the French Open, Wimbledon, and the U.S. Open. That year, *Sports Illustrated* magazine named her its first Sportsperson of the Year.

The "Battle of the Sexes"

Despite the popularity of women's tennis, many people still believed that women could not be equal to men in sports. One such person was a male tennis player named Bobby Riggs. In 1973, he said that no woman could win a match against a man. Then he challenged King to play him. She agreed.

On September 20, 1973, Riggs and King met in the Houston Astrodome for a winner-take-all, $100,000

TOPICAL TIDBIT

Althea Gibson

Before Billie Jean King, Althea Gibson had already made her mark in the world of tennis. A black American in a sport dominated by whites, Gibson set "firsts" everywhere she played. In 1950, she was the first African American to be invited to play at Forest Hills in New York. She competed at Wimbledon in 1951, won the women's doubles in 1956, and the women's singles in 1957 and 1958—all as the first black person to do so.

"Battle of the Sexes." Even though Riggs was 25 years older than King, most people thought that he would win. However, as 30,000 people watched in the Astrodome and 50 million more watched at home on TV, King soundly defeated him 6-4, 6-3, 6-3.

King retired from tennis in 1984. During her career, she won 20 Wimbledon titles, four U.S. Open titles, and many other championships around the world. She was voted into the International Women's Sports Hall of Fame in 1980, and the International Tennis Hall of Fame in 1987. In 1990, *Life* magazine named her one of the "100 Most Important Americans of the 20th Century." Only three other athletes, all men, made that list.

Billie Jean King once said, "Everything I do is about equal opportunity. Let's celebrate our differences." She dedicated her life and career to breaking down barriers to equality. ◇

LIFE EVENTS

1943
Billie Jean Moffitt is born in Long Beach, California.

1961
Moffitt and tennis partner Karen Hantz win the women's doubles tournament at Wimbledon.

1966
Now Billie Jean King, she wins her first women's singles title at Wimbledon.

1973
King defeats Bobby Riggs in the "Battle of the Sexes" match.

1984
King retires from competitive tennis.

1987
King is inducted into the International Tennis Hall of Fame.

Martin Luther King Jr.
A Dream of Equality
(born 1929 • died 1968)

The 1950s and 1960s were a time of great tension and division between blacks and whites in the U.S. Many people dedicated their lives to ending segregation (separation by race) and winning equal rights for all races. One man, Martin Luther King Jr., became a national figure who gave his life in the fight for justice.

A Religious Family

Martin Luther King Jr. was born in Atlanta, Georgia, on January 15, 1929. His father, Martin Luther King Sr., was the pastor of the Ebenezer Baptist Church in Atlanta, and the family spent many hours in church. The boy, known as M.L., loved to listen to his father preach. He could see that his father's words had a powerful effect on everyone who listened to him.

M.L., who skipped several grades in school, was only 15 when he enrolled at Morehouse College in

Martin Luther King Jr. visited poor black families in Mississippi and throughout the South, urging them to register to vote.

Atlanta. He decided to become a minister, like his father. Being a minister, he thought, would allow him to help the black community.

Boycott!

After graduating from Morehouse, King attended Crozer Theological Seminary in Pennsylvania and Boston University in Massachusetts, earning a PhD and the title "Doctor." Then he took a job as pastor of the Dexter Avenue Church in Montgomery, Alabama.

Soon after Dr. Martin Luther King Jr. arrived in

Montgomery, the city became the center of national attention. The law in Montgomery said that black people riding on public buses had to give up their seats to white people. On December 1, 1955, a black woman named Rosa Parks was arrested when she refused to give up her seat. The black community decided to boycott (stop using) the buses until the law was changed. King became one of the leaders of this boycott. He was arrested several times, and his house was bombed. Despite the danger, King refused to get angry. He said that the black community "must meet our white brothers' hate with love." He encouraged everyone to act peacefully, no matter how much violence they faced.

Finally, on November 13, 1956, the U.S. Supreme Court said that the Montgomery bus law was unfair,

TOPICAL TIDBIT

Letter From the Birmingham Jail

King was arrested with many others during protests to integrate public facilities in Birmingham, Alabama, in 1963. During this time, a group of white ministers released a statement criticizing his methods. King needed to go slowly and do things quietly, they said. Furious, he wrote a long letter in reply. "We know through painful experience," he wrote from his cell, "that freedom is never voluntarily given by the oppressor; it must be demanded by the oppressed." King was in solitary confinement, so his soon-to-be famous *Letter From the Birmingham Jail* had to be smuggled out by his lawyer—written in the margins of the city newspaper.

and that blacks had the same rights to ride the buses as whites. The boycott ended, and King and the black community had won an important victory.

"I Have a Dream!"

The victory against the Montgomery bus law inspired King and other civil-rights supporters to fight segregation in other areas. King traveled around the country, giving speech after speech. He

> "Injustice anywhere is a threat to justice everywhere."
> —Martin Luther King Jr., in his *Letter From the Birmingham Jail*

had a powerful speaking voice that moved his listeners to action. King always said that people should act peacefully and with dignity. If they were arrested, they should go to jail quietly. If they were beaten or threatened, they should not fight back. King knew that refusing to use violence took a lot of courage. He called his ideas "the weapon of love." It took time, but a growing number of people around the country—both black and white—supported King's nonviolent efforts. Slowly, the unfair segregation laws began to change.

On August 28, 1963, King spoke before 250,000 people at the March on Washington. He told the crowd, "I have a dream today!" His dream was that, someday, "little black boys and little black girls will join hands with little white boys and little white girls

Martin Luther King Jr. delivers his famous "I Have a Dream" speech.

and walk together as sisters and brothers. . . . I have a dream that my four little children will one day live in a nation where they will be judged not by the color of their skin but by the content of their character."

In October 1964, King was awarded the Nobel Peace Prize. Once a year, this high honor is given to a person who has worked to bring peace to the world.

Tragedy in Memphis

Over the years, King went to jail many times, and many people tried to hurt him. Yet he never lost his faith in nonviolence. On April 3, 1968, King went to Memphis, Tennessee. That night, he told a crowd, "I've been to the mountaintop, and I've seen the Promised Land. I may not get there with you. But . . . we as a people will get to the Promised Land."

The next day, King and some of his friends and co-workers were standing on the balcony outside his motel room. Suddenly, a shot rang out. Moments later, Martin Luther King Jr. was dead. He was only 39 years old.

The whole world mourned the loss of Martin Luther King Jr. In his short life, King helped change many laws and hearts. More important, he showed the world that peace and nonviolence can triumph over anger and hatred. ◇

LIFE EVENTS

1929
Martin Luther King Jr. is born in Atlanta, Georgia.

1955
King leads the black citizens of Montgomery, Alabama, in boycotting city buses.

1957
King helps start the Southern Christian Leadership Conference (SCLC).

1963
King's letter from jail is published and wins fame. He makes his "I Have a Dream" speech at the March on Washington.

1964
The Civil Rights Act of 1964 is passed. King is awarded the Nobel Peace Prize.

1968
King is assassinated in Memphis, Tennessee.

Maggie Kuhn
Never Too Old
(born 1905 • died 1995)

For most of her life, Maggie Kuhn led a quiet, normal existence. However, when she was 65 years old, she began the most important work of her life: winning equal rights for the elderly.

A Political Family

Maggie Kuhn's parents lived in Memphis, Tennessee. They were white, but Maggie's mother hated the segregation laws in Memphis so much that she didn't want her daughter to be born there. So Mrs. Kuhn traveled to Buffalo, New York, to stay with her parents, where Margaret Eliza Kuhn was born on August 3, 1905.

The Kuhns later returned to Memphis. When Maggie was a teenager, the family moved to Cleveland, Ohio. Maggie enrolled at Case Western Reserve University in Cleveland to study English and sociology.

Along with her parents' hatred of segregation, members of the family also worked to win voting

rights for women. Maggie shared her family's interest in making things better for all people. During her years at Case Western Reserve, she helped start a campus chapter of the League of Women Voters, an organization that supports the right and responsibility of all people to vote.

A Working Woman

After graduating from college in 1926, Kuhn began working at the Cleveland YWCA. Her job included setting up programs for young working women. As Kuhn talked with these women, she discovered that they worked long hours in offices and factories, but received little pay. This made her angry, so she dedicated her life to helping people who were treated unfairly.

During the 1930s, Kuhn moved to New York, New York, where she continued to work for the YWCA. Then, in 1945, she accepted a job with the United Presbyterian Church. Kuhn coordinated many church activities, including programs on women's rights, racism, and discrimination against the elderly. She also wrote articles for the church's magazine and was an observer at the United Nations.

> "Old age is not a disease—it is strength and survivorship, triumph over all kinds of . . . disappointments, trials, and illnesses."
>
> —Maggie Kuhn

Kuhn worked for the United Presbyterian Church for 25 years. She loved her job and was very good at it. However, in 1970, when she turned 65, she was forced to retire. Like many organizations at that time, the church had a rule that no one over age 65 could work there.

Fighting Back

Kuhn was furious at having to quit a job she loved. She knew that she was not too old to work, even if society said otherwise. "If you are not prepared, retirement at 65 makes you a nonperson," she said. "It deprives you of the sense of community that has previously defined your life."

Kuhn decided to fight back. In 1971, she and six retired friends formed a group to fight against age discrimination. The group started meeting in a church basement in Philadelphia, Pennsylvania. Kuhn and her friends called themselves the Consultation of Older and Younger Adults for Social Change. The organization grew and started to become more widely known. Because most of the members were elderly, one television reporter referred to them as the Gray Panthers. The name stuck, and soon Kuhn and her Gray Panthers were famous around the country.

The Gray Panthers

From the start, Maggie Kuhn was the organization's leader and its most outspoken member. She wanted everyone to realize that being old did not make a person stupid, helpless, or inferior. Her message was that older people had to take control of their lives and work actively for causes in which they believed. She believed that the elderly are in a unique position to create change. "We who are old have nothing to lose!" she wrote. "We have everything to gain by living dangerously! We can initiate [start] change without jeopardizing jobs or family. We can be the risk-takers."

Although the Gray Panthers were focused on the rights of the elderly, the group also had younger members. Most of all, Kuhn wanted to bridge the gap between young and old, and show people of all ages how they could work together to solve social problems. The group also tackled many such problems as the abuse of people living in nursing homes, negative images of the elderly on television, and the lack of public transportation for the handicapped. Into the 1990s,

TOPICAL TIDBIT

The Gray Panthers

Maggie Kuhn's group, the Consultation of Older and Younger Adults for Social Change, was truly a daring organization when it began in 1971. The name was not very catchy, however. The reporter who dubbed them the "Gray Panthers" solved that problem—everyone remembered it after that! He was comparing Kuhn's group to a radical black-power group of the 1960s called the Black Panthers. The Black Panthers were controversial because they had guns and spoke of violence as a way to achieve their goals. Maggie Kuhn and her elderly comrades were not about to use violence, but their ideas were as radical in their way.

the Gray Panthers fought for a national health-care system and a clean environment.

Kuhn remained active in the Gray Panthers until her death on April 22, 1995, at 89. She had asked that her gravestone be inscribed with these words: "Here lies Maggie Kuhn, under the only stone she left unturned."

Through her hard work and dedication, Maggie Kuhn helped many people realize that old age does not have to mean an end to an active life. Instead, it is a time when a person can achieve his or her deepest dreams and help make the world a better place. ◇

LIFE EVENTS

1905
Margaret Eliza Kuhn is born in Buffalo, New York.

1926
Maggie Kuhn begins work at the YWCA in Cleveland, Ohio, and learns of the poor working conditions of young women.

1945
Kuhn begins work for the United Presbyterian Church in New York.

1970
On reaching age 65, Kuhn is forced to retire.

1971
Kuhn and others start an organization, dubbed the Gray Panthers, to fight age discrimination and other problems.

1995
Maggie Kuhn dies at age 89.

Robert E. Lee
Confederate General
(born 1807 • died 1870)

Robert E. Lee loved his home state of Virginia more than almost anything else. When Virginia went to war against the U.S. government, Lee became its strongest military leader in a struggle that tore the nation apart.

A Military Tradition

Robert Edward Lee was born on January 19, 1807, in Westmoreland County, Virginia. His father, Henry Lee, had fought in the American Revolution and been governor of Virginia from

1791 to 1794. Young Robert idolized his father and wanted to be a military hero, just like him.

When Robert was 11, his father died. Soon afterward, his mother got sick. Because his older brothers had left home, the young man was left with the care of his mother and his two sisters. At the same time, he also went to school. That was a lot of responsibilities for an 11-year-old, but Robert did his best.

When he finished school, the family didn't have enough money to send him to college. However, he was able to win an appointment to the U.S. Military Academy at West Point, New York. Robert was thrilled about the appointment. Not only would he receive a free education, but he would learn how to be a soldier.

He entered West Point in 1825. He spent four years marching and learning military drills and strategy. He graduated second in his class.

Divided Loyalties

Robert E. Lee held several different jobs early in his military career. He was in an engineer corps that built new forts, fought in the 1847 war between the U.S. and Mexico, and commanded a cavalry (horseback) unit in Texas.

By the late 1850s, slavery was tearing the U.S. apart. Many people in the North believed that slavery was morally wrong. Many people in the South believed that slaves were necessary to care for crops and do other jobs. Southerners said that they would secede (break away from) the U.S. and form their own government if slavery were outlawed.

On April 12, 1861, the Civil War began when the U.S. Army's Fort Sumter in South Carolina was captured by Confederate soldiers of the South. When President Abraham Lincoln asked Lee to be a field general in the Union army, Lee faced a difficult choice. His home state of Virginia was part of the Confederacy. Should he take the important job that Lincoln had offered him and fight against the South? Or should he fight for Virginia, even though he, personally, was against slavery and secession?

> "It is well that war is so terrible, or we should get too fond of it."
>
> —Robert E. Lee, at the battle of Fredericksburg, 1862

Finally, Lee refused Lincoln's offer, saying, "I cannot raise my hand against my birthplace, my home, my children." Lee hoped to avoid fighting, but accepted an offer from the governor of Virginia to lead Virginia's army. Later, he became the commanding general of the Confederate forces.

The War Between the States

Lee was the best general in the South, and his Army of Northern Virginia won many battles. His troops successfully defended the Confederate capital in Richmond, Virginia. Lee also used clever strategy to win the battle of Chancellorsville in May 1863, even though the Confederate troops were outnumbered by the Union troops.

Part of the reason Lee was a good general was that he cared about his soldiers. He treated them with kindness and respect, and looked after them as best he could. Unlike most officers, Lee even slept on the ground beside his men and ate the same food they did.

Despite Lee's best efforts, the Confederates could not win the war. The South was running out of supplies, rifles, clothes, and food. Many people had been killed and their homes destroyed. Lee knew that the fighting had to stop. On April 9, 1865, he surrendered to the Union army's General Ulysses S. Grant

TOPICAL TIDBIT

Stonewall Jackson

Robert E. Lee's most trusted general, and one of the great heroes of the Confederacy, was Thomas "Stonewall" Jackson. A fearless commander, he got his nickname at the first Battle of Bull Run by holding as steadily as a stone wall against attackers. Lee used Jackson's smaller division to make lightning strikes against Union forces. The two Southern generals were brilliant together. But in the dusk following their greatest victory, at Chancellorsville, one of Jackson's men mistook him for a Northern soldier, and shot him. Jackson died a week later. Things were never right for the South afterward.

at Appomattox, Virginia. After that, Lee urged Southerners to forget the war and work for peace and unity.

A New Career

After the war, Lee was not sure how he would make a living. In September 1865, he was offered a job as president of Washington College in Lexington, Virginia. Lee worked hard to rebuild the college, which had been closed during the war. He succeeded so well that, after his death, the college was renamed Washington and Lee University in his honor.

Robert E. Lee died in Lexington on October 12, 1870, at age 63. He is remembered as one of the most respected and skilled generals in U.S. history—a man who did his duty and loved his home. ◇

LIFE EVENTS

1807
Robert Edward Lee is born in Westmoreland County, Virginia.

1829
Lee graduates second in his class from West Point.

1858
Lee's unit puts down the slave rebellion of John Brown in Harpers Ferry, Virginia.

1861
The Civil War breaks out. Lee becomes commander in chief of the Army of Northern Virginia.

1865
Union General Ulysses S. Grant accepts Lee's surrender, ending the Civil War.

1870
Robert E. Lee dies in Lexington, Virginia.

John L. Lewis
Mining for Change
(born 1880 • died 1969)

John L. Lewis rose from the coal mines to become the most powerful labor leader in the U.S. His dedication to the labor movement improved working conditions for thousands of men and women.

Life in the Mines

John Llewellyn Lewis was born on February 12, 1880, in Lucas, Iowa, where his father worked in the coal mines. After Mr. Lewis joined a strike against the owners of one of the mines, he was blacklisted. This meant that none of the other mines would hire him. Young John spent much of his childhood moving

> "I have pleaded our case, not in the quavering tones of a feeble [beggar], but in the thundering voice of the captain of a mighty [army], demanding the rights to which free men are entitled."
>
> —John L. Lewis

John L. Lewis *(left)* in 1937, signing an agreement with mine operators.

with his family from one town to another, as his father struggled to find a job.

When John was 12 years old, he left school and began working in the mines himself. Mining was dangerous, backbreaking labor. Miners worked underground in darkness, with little room to move or air to breathe. They knew that, at any moment, the walls of the mine shaft where they were digging could collapse and kill everyone inside. Workers also had to live in company-owned housing, and they were paid in money that wasn't good anywhere but in company stores. Company stores, which sold them all their food and supplies, could charge whatever prices they wanted—usually much more than for the same things sold elsewhere. This system kept miners poor, and made them totally dependent on their employers.

In time, John Lewis left home and worked at several different jobs. Still, he could not forget the struggles of the miners. In 1906, 26-year-old Lewis went back into the mines. This time, however, he wasn't just there to dig coal. He was determined to make a difference.

A New Union

Lewis became active in the United Mine Workers of America (UMWA). The UMWA was a miners' union that worked for higher wages and better conditions for its membership. By 1920, Lewis was president of the UMWA. At that time, the union had more than 400,000 members. Then an economic depression hit, and many miners lost their jobs. By 1932, the UMWA's membership had dropped to 150,000.

In 1933, the nation had a new president, Franklin D. Roosevelt. Roosevelt was determined to put the American people back to work after the Depression. He gave labor unions more rights than they'd had in the past. Lewis jumped on this opportunity to add to his union. Gathering an army of union organizers, he traveled to mining towns around the U.S. Soon, UMWA membership had reached more than 500,000.

Next, Lewis turned his attention to other industries. He went to the country's largest labor union, the American Federation of Labor (AFL), and tried to get the AFL to unionize the steel industry. However, the AFL represented skilled workers, such as carpenters and electricians. Many of its leaders and members were not interested in the unskilled workers employed in such industries as coal and steel.

After a bitter fight at its 1935 national convention, the AFL voted not to admit industrial workers. Furious, Lewis joined a few other unhappy AFL

TOPICAL TIDBIT

"Sixteen Tons"

"Sixteen Tons," sung by Tennessee Ernie Ford, was a hit record all over the country in 1955. It told the story of a fictional coal miner. "You load 16 tons, and what do you get? Another day older and deeper in debt," said the character in the song. ". . . I owe my soul to the company store." The song was written in 1946 by Merle Travis, the son of a miner from Muhlenberg County, Kentucky. It is full of phrases that Travis had heard growing up in Kentucky—including one of his father's favorite sayings: "I can't afford to die. I owe my soul to the company store."

leaders to form a new union, called the Congress for Industrial Organization (CIO).

By the end of 1937, the CIO had almost four million members in the glass, rubber, steel, and automobile industries. Lewis called it "the greatest mass maneuver of organized industry and organized labor in all history. Its results," he said, "will affect the lives of thousands yet unborn."

More Demands

Lewis resigned from the presidency of the CIO in 1940, but continued to lead the UMWA. During the first half of the 1940s, the U.S. was involved in World War II. Other labor unions had agreed not to ask for higher wages until after the war. However, Lewis believed that mine workers still had to support their families, so they should receive better pay. To achieve this, he led several strikes.

So many people were angered by Lewis's threat to stop coal production during the war that he became known as "the most hated man in America." Lewis did not care what people thought of him. His only concern was that his miners get more benefits. By 1949, the coal miners had the best employment contracts of all industrial workers in the U.S.

Conditions began to change during the 1950s. Homes and businesses began to use gas, oil, and electricity, and the use of coal declined rapidly. At the same time, new machines were invented that could dig coal faster, costing many miners their jobs. By the mid-1950s, membership in the UMWA was again down to 150,000.

In 1960, Lewis resigned from the presidency of the UMWA. He was 80 years old and had been leading the union for 40 years. He kept active in UMWA affairs by serving as chairman of the UMWA's Welfare and Retirement Fund.

John L. Lewis died in Washington, D.C., on June 11, 1969, after a lifetime of working to make conditions better for America's workers. ◇

LIFE EVENTS

1880
John Llewellyn Lewis is born in Lucas, Iowa.

1911
Lewis becomes an organizer for the American Federation of Labor (AFL).

1920
Lewis is made president of the United Mine Workers of America (UMWA).

1935
Lewis and several AFL leaders start the Congress for Industrial Organization (CIO).

1942
Lewis pulls the UMWA out of the CIO.

1960
John L. Lewis resigns from the UMWA. He dies nine years later.

Meriwether Lewis and William Clark

Into the Unknown

(Meriwether Lewis: born 1774 • died 1809)
(William Clark: born 1770 • died 1838)

Imagine setting off on a journey into the wilderness. You have no idea what lies in the land ahead. There is no speedy way to send word back home, and no way to ask for help. You and your companions are completely on your own, facing harsh and unknown conditions. Those were the circumstances that Lewis and Clark faced when they set off into the American West in 1804. The bravery and fortitude of those explorers changed the shape of America.

Meriwether Lewis

Meriwether Lewis was born near Charlottesville, Virginia, in 1774. His family members were wealthy plantation owners, and Lewis had a comfortable childhood. In school, he especially enjoyed studying plants and animals and was a sharp observer of nature.

Those interests and the knowledge that he gained then would come in handy during his journey west.

Lewis joined the Army in 1795 and served under Lieutenant William Clark. The two became friends.

In 1801, President Thomas Jefferson selected Lewis as his personal secretary. Later, he offered Lewis the opportunity to explore the West as the leader of a Corps of Discovery.

William Clark

William Clark was also from Virginia, born in Caroline County in 1770. When he was about 10 years old, his family moved to the Kentucky frontier.

William's older brothers had both served in the army, and he, too, decided on a military career. He became a well-respected officer. He also served as a scout on dangerous missions into the Western frontier.

In 1803, President Jefferson bought the Louisiana Territory from the government of France. The "Louisiana Purchase" was a huge parcel of land stretching west from the Mississippi River. Adding this territory to the U.S. immediately doubled the size of the country. The timing was right for exploration. Jefferson decided to send Meriwether Lewis.

William Clark was living on his family's plantation in Kentucky in 1803 when he received a letter from his friend, Meriwether Lewis. Lewis wanted his friend Clark as a partner in exploring the Northwest continent. He wrote to Clark, telling him that "the aims are to meet and begin trading with Indian tribes, to discover new plants and animals, and to make new maps." In addition, Jefferson thought that exploration was necessary to prevent foreign countries, such as England, France, Spain, and Russia, from claiming land in America.

Clark was eager to go. He immediately wrote back to Lewis: "I will cheerfully join you."

The Journey West

Preparations for the trip took almost a year. Supplies were gathered, and about 48 men were hired to make the journey. A boat had to be built to carry the expedition and over a ton of supplies, including books, medicine, scientific equipment, mapmaking tools, and gifts for the Native Americans they would meet on the journey. Finally, on May 21, 1804, the group, known as the Corps of Discovery, left St. Louis, Missouri. Clark's African American slave, a man named York, was part of the team.

Lewis and Clark divided their leadership responsibilities. Lewis was in charge of obtaining samples, drawing pictures, and recording observations about the plants, animals, and people they met on their journey. Lewis took his job so seriously that he got sick when he tasted a sample of soil that contained arsenic, a deadly poison. Clark was the mapmaker, and also negotiated with Native Americans.

By October 1804, the expedition had traveled up the Missouri River and reached Fort Mandan, in present-day North Dakota. They spent a bitterly cold

winter there among friendly Native American tribes,
and attended many Native ceremonies. Lewis and
Clark took careful notes and recorded everything in
their journals.

Lewis and Clark left their winter camp in April
1805. Their group now included a young Shoshone
Indian woman named Sacagawea *(SAK-uh-jah-WEE-uh)*, her French-Canadian husband, and their

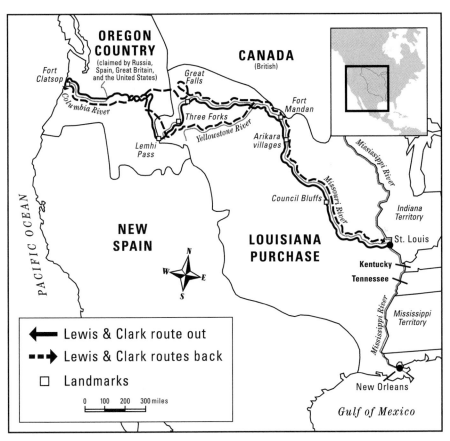

Lewis and Clark took these routes to the Pacific Ocean and back.

infant son. Sacagawea helped Lewis and Clark by talking with Native Americans along the way and negotiating with them for horses and supplies.

Lewis and Clark faced many dangers on their journey. The expedition had to cross waterfalls and rushing rivers. They almost lost their supplies when canoes turned over in river rapids. Several of the men were chased by a grizzly bear. One bad storm included hailstones so large that a team member reported in his journal: "If one had struck a man on the naked head, it would have killed him. The men saved themselves by getting under a canoe."

> I do not think I exaggerate when I estimate the number of buffalo which could be [seen] at one view to amount to 3,000."
>
> —Meriwether Lewis, writing in his journal about his first buffalo sighting

In early September 1805, the expedition reached the Bitterroot Mountains in what is now northern Idaho. There, they traveled on "some of the worst roads that a horse ever passed on the sides of steep and stony mountains, some covered with snow." Several of the expedition's horses fell and were injured. There was no food to be found in the mountains, so several times the expedition members had to kill and eat their own horses to survive.

After crossing the mountains, Lewis and Clark and their team traveled west along the Snake River into what is now Washington state. Then they journeyed along the Columbia River in what is now Oregon. Finally, on November 18, 1805—almost 18 months after leaving St. Louis—Lewis and Clark finally reached the Pacific Ocean. They had traveled all the way across the continent of North America.

> "Great joy in camp. We are in view of the ocean, this great Pacific Ocean, which we have been so long anxious to see."
>
> —William Clark, in his journal, November 1805

Heading Home

Lewis and Clark built a camp, called Fort Clatsop, near present-day Astoria, Oregon. The team spent the winter there. (That winter was a wet and miserable time for the team: It rained for 94 out of 106 days!) Then, on March 23, 1806, they began their long journey home. Along the way, the group split up to do more exploring. Clark led one group along the Yellowstone River, while Lewis took the rest of the team along the Marias River into north-central Montana. The two groups reunited in August, then continued on to St. Louis.

By the time Lewis and Clark reached St. Louis on September 23, 1806, the expedition had been gone for so long that everyone thought that the travelers had died on the journey. But only one member had been lost: Charles Floyd, who died (probably of a burst appendix) three months after their journey began.

The team was greeted by cheering crowds, and they became American heroes. A message describing their safe return was sent to President Jefferson, who reacted with "unspeakable joy."

The Corps of Discovery members were richly rewarded for their work. Every member received double pay, along with 320 acres of land. Lewis and Clark received 1,600 acres. Lewis was named governor of the Louisiana Territory, and Clark became a

TOPICAL TIDBIT

Zebulon Montgomery Pike

Lewis and Clark were not the only explorers sent into the Louisiana Territory by President Thomas Jefferson. In the fall of 1805, Lieutenant Zebulon Montgomery Pike led an expedition up the Mississippi River. He sent back a lot of new information about the upper Mississippi Valley. A year later, he was sent into the valley of Arkansas, where he discovered the mountain that today is called Pike's Peak. Pike returned with advice that was ignored: Much of the West was not fit for farming, he said, and should be left to the Indians.

brigadier general of the Louisiana Territory Militia.

Lewis and Clark's journey was an incredible achievement. They traveled more than 7,600 miles along and across rivers, through forests and prairies, and over mountains, making detailed maps of everything they saw. Lewis's careful observations and drawings introduced scientists to 300 animals and plants that they had never seen before. In addition, Lewis and Clark recorded the customs, ceremonies, and languages of more than 50 Native American tribes, and established peaceful relations with almost all of them. Most important, Lewis and Clark opened the West to the United States and helped encourage the young nation to grow.

After the Journey

For Meriwether Lewis, life did not go smoothly after he returned home. He didn't enjoy his job as governor of the Louisiana Territory, and he had financial troubles and many other disappointments in his personal life. He may also have become an alcoholic. On October 11, 1809, 35-year-old Lewis was killed by two gunshot wounds while traveling through Tennessee. Although some residents believed that Lewis was murdered, historians now believe that he killed himself.

William Clark made a different sort of life for himself. He adopted Sacagawea's young son, Jean

Baptiste—who, as an infant, had traveled with his mother as the team trekked across the continent. Clark put the boy through school. As for another expedition member, Clark's slave, York, Clark granted him his freedom in 1832.

Things turned out much better for Clark than for Lewis after their return from the West. Clark became a famous and powerful man. He served as an agent to Native American tribes and negotiated several treaties between them and the U.S. government. He also served as governor of the Missouri Territory from 1813 to 1821. By the time William Clark died at the age of 68 in 1838, he was recognized as one of the finest authorities on the American West. ◇

LIFE EVENTS

1770
William Clark is born in Caroline County, Virginia.

1774
Meriwether Lewis is born near Charlottesville, Virginia.

1795
Lewis serves under Clark in the Army.

1801
President Jefferson asks Lewis to lead an expedition.

1803
Jefferson buys the Louisiana Territory.

1804-1806
Lewis and Clark and their team explore the West.

1808
Lewis is appointed governor of Louisiana Territory. He dies in 1809.

1813
Clark is appointed governor of Missouri Territory. He dies in 1838.

Abraham Lincoln
Holding the Nation Together
(born 1809 • died 1865)

Abraham Lincoln had a poor childhood, little education, and failed in business. Yet he became president of the United States and led our nation through the most difficult time in its history.

A Log-cabin Childhood

Abraham Lincoln was born in a one-room log cabin in Hodgenville, Kentucky, on February 12, 1809. When he was seven years old, the family moved to Little Pigeon Creak, Indiana.

Two years later, Abe's mother died. Times were hard for the family. Then Mr. Lincoln remarried a woman with three children. Abe's stepmother was a kind woman who was fond of her stepson, and encouraged him to learn. Although young Abe rarely went to school (less than a year, in all), he loved to read. Books and newspapers were rare in the wilderness, but he went out of his way to borrow them. He read every chance he could, even while plowing the fields.

Working for a Living

When Abe was 21, the Lincolns moved to Illinois. Abe helped his family build a new log cabin and clear land for a farm. Finally, he decided it was time to go out on his own.

Abe Lincoln moved to the small town of New Salem, Illinois. There he worked at a series of jobs. Later, he opened a general store, but the business failed, partly because he spent more time reading than working. He also ran for the state legislature, but lost the election.

In 1834, Lincoln ran for the legislature again, and this time he won. While serving on the legislature, he decided to become a lawyer. Lincoln studied hard and passed the law exam in 1836. The following year, he moved to Springfield, Illinois, and opened a law office with a friend. By 1846, he was a successful lawyer and a member of the U.S. House of Representatives. Things did not go well for him in Washington, however. Disappointed, he did not run for reelection. At age 40, it seemed as if his political career was over.

Rising in Politics

During the mid-1800s, slavery was one of the most important political issues in the country. In 1856, the antislavery Republican Party formed. Lincoln, originally a member of the Whig Party, joined the new party. Two years later, he entered the race for the U.S. Senate as the Republican nominee.

Lincoln's Democratic opponent was Stephen Douglas, the senator who was running for reelection. Douglas had introduced a bill in Congress to allow slavery in the Louisiana Purchase area. Lincoln argued strongly against doing this. The two men traveled all over Illinois, debating the issue. The debates became famous for the two men's skillful speeches.

Douglas ended up winning the election, but Lincoln impressed people everywhere with his public-speaking ability. Four years later, in 1860, the two opponents met again. This time they were running for the presidency—and this time, Lincoln won. He became the 16th president of the United States.

"A house divided against itself cannot stand. I believe this government cannot endure permanently half slave and half free. . . . It will become all one thing, or all the other."

—Abraham Lincoln, in 1858

The Civil War

The South bitterly objected to the new president. By the time Lincoln was sworn in on March 4, 1861, seven Southern states had seceded (withdrawn) from the Union. By the end of May, four more states had joined them. Lincoln strongly believed that the U.S. must be brought back together, even if the only way to restore the Union was to fight a civil war.

During the war, Lincoln endured Southern victories, unfriendly newspaper reports, and many other difficulties, but he never hesitated to provide strong leadership. On January 1, 1863, he signed the Emancipation Proclamation, a document that freed slaves in rebellious Confederate states. "If my name ever goes into history, it will be for this act," he said.

Lincoln is also remembered for what has been called the greatest speech ever given. On November 19, 1863, he stood before 150,000 people in Gettysburg, Pennsylvania. Four months earlier, Gettysburg had been the site of the bloodiest battle of the war. Now part of the battlefield was being dedicated as a national cemetery for the war dead.

Lincoln's Gettysburg Address lasted just two minutes and was only ten sentences long. But its closing plea has never been forgotten: "that this nation, under God, shall have a new birth of freedom—and that government of the people, by the people, for the people, shall not perish from the earth."

TOPICAL TIDBIT

The Emancipation Proclamation

President Lincoln did not enter the Civil War demanding that the South free all of its slaves. But on September 22, 1862, after the bloody battle of Antietam, he warned that he would do so if the Confederacy did not rejoin the Union. So Lincoln issued the Emancipation Proclamation on January 1, 1863, freeing slaves in Confederate states. After the war, the Thirteenth Amendment to the Constitution made it final: Slavery was dead throughout the land.

An Assassin's Bullet

On March 4, 1865, Lincoln was sworn in as president for a second term. In his inaugural address, Lincoln encouraged Americans "to do all which may achieve and cherish a just and lasting peace among ourselves."

Although he had won the war, Lincoln was not able to help the U.S. find that peace. On April 14, 1865—just five days after the South surrendered—he was shot by John Wilkes Booth while he and his wife Mary were attending a play at Ford's Theater in Washington, D.C. Lincoln died the next day. He was the first U.S. president to be assassinated.

The entire nation mourned Abraham Lincoln's death. The U.S. had lost its greatest leader—a man who had known that the Union must be preserved at any cost. ◇

LIFE EVENTS

1809
Abraham Lincoln is born in Hodgenville, Kentucky.

1846
Lincoln is elected to the U.S. Congress from the state of Illinois.

1858
Running for the Senate, Lincoln challenges his opponent, Stephen Douglas, to a series of debates.

1861
Abraham Lincoln becomes the 16th president of the United States. The Civil War breaks out.

1865
The South surrenders and the war ends. Five days later, Lincoln is assassinated by John Wilkes Booth.

Charles Lindbergh
Adventure in the Air
(born 1902 • died 1974)

When Charles Lindbergh took off from Roosevelt Field in Long Island, New York, he was not trying to become a hero. Yet his 33-1/2-hour flight made him the most famous and admired man in America.

A Love of Airplanes

Charles Augustus Lindbergh was born on February 4, 1902, in Detroit, Michigan. He saw his first airplane at a flying exhibition in 1912, when he was 10 years old. From then on, he was fascinated with planes. The Wright Brothers had made the first airplane flight just a few years earlier in 1903, and airplanes were a new and exciting way to travel.

After high school, Charles attended the University of Wisconsin, but he wasn't very interested in college. Then he heard about a flying school run by the Nebraska Aircraft Corporation. Against his parents' wishes, Charles signed up for the course and headed for Lincoln, Nebraska, in 1922.

Barnstorming

After spending six weeks at the Nebraska Aircraft Corporation's flying school, Lindbergh went on tour with several barnstormers. During the early days of aviation, pilots known as barnstormers flew around the country, performing daring tricks and taking people for rides. Lindbergh loved doing this, and became known as a daredevil. He performed dangerous feats, such as walking on an airplane's wing while the plane swooped through the air, or sending the plane plunging toward the ground, only to zoom back into the air at the last second.

In 1924, Lindbergh abandoned his barnstorming career to attend the Army Air Service Training School. Two years later, he got a job flying an airmail route from St. Louis to Chicago.

The Transatlantic Challenge

All the while, Lindbergh was dreaming of a much longer flight. In 1921, a wealthy Frenchman offered a $25,000 prize to the first aviator who made a non-stop flight between New York and Paris, France. Lindbergh prepared himself for the challenge. He decided that a light plane carrying very little cargo would be the best choice. He also decided to fly alone. By carrying few materials and no co-pilot, there would be more room for fuel.

At 7:30 a.m. on May 19, 1927, Lindbergh's plane, the *Spirit of St. Louis*, lifted into the sky above New York. The plane carried 450 gallons of fuel, a rubber boat, some water, five sandwiches, a compass—and Charles Lindbergh.

For hour after hour, Lindbergh flew through rain, fog, and ice storms. Weather conditions were not the

> "I saw a fleet of fishing boats. . . . I flew down almost touching the craft and yelled at them, asking if I was on the right road to Ireland. . . . An hour later, I saw land."
>
> —Charles A. Lindbergh, describing the end of his historic flight

biggest problem Lindbergh faced, however. The greatest danger was that he might fall asleep. To stay awake, he opened the plane's windows to let cold air inside. He stamped his feet and sang songs. He also decided not to eat any of his sandwiches, so his empty stomach would keep him awake.

At 10:22 p.m., Paris time, he touched down at Le Bourget Airport. A crowd of 100,000 cheering people surrounded the plane. Suddenly, Lindbergh was a hero around the world. When he returned to America—by ship, with the *Spirit of St. Louis* traveling with him in the cargo hold—he was greeted by adoring crowds and parades held in his honor.

Tragedy and Controversy

Lindbergh had become an international celebrity, but he had trouble living with his fame. He was a private man and a loner who didn't like being the center of attention.

It wasn't long before the hero's fame led to tragedy. In 1932, his two-year-old son was kidnapped and killed. It was the most shocking crime of its time. The news media followed every step of the investigation and trial of the man arrested for the crime. Lindbergh hated the constant public fascination with him and the case. To get away from it all, he moved his family to England.

By 1941, Lindbergh's popularity had turned sour. The U.S. was about to enter World War II, but Lindbergh was an outspoken critic of America's war effort. He joined an organization called America First, and made speeches around the country, urging the U.S. to stay out of the war. For that reason, and because he had accepted several invitations to Nazi Germany,

TOPICAL TIDBIT

The Spirit of St. Louis

Everything about the *Spirit of St. Louis* was designed for maximum lightness, speed, and distance. It was a monoplane, meaning that it had one pair of wings and only one engine. It had been built to hold five people, but Lindbergh had the passenger seats were removed and extra gas tanks installed in their place. There was not even room for a radio! Eventually, Lindbergh gave his plane to the Smithsonian Institution in Washington, D.C., where it hangs to this day.

many people believed that Lindbergh agreed with the Nazis' brutal policies.

During the war, Lindbergh worked for several airlines and served as an adviser for new fighter planes. Later, he became active in efforts to preserve the environment and save endangered animals. He died in Hawaii on August 26, 1974. Despite the controversy that surrounded his activities before World War II, Charles Lindbergh is still honored as one of America's most daring adventurers. ◇

LIFE EVENTS

1902
Charles Augustus Lindbergh is born in Detroit, Michigan.

1927
Lindbergh flies across the Atlantic by himself in the *Spirit of St. Louis.*

1932
Lindbergh's two-year-old son is kidnapped and killed. Bruno Richard Hauptmann is arrested for the crime.

1941
Lindbergh's speeches against the war effort make him unpopular. President Franklin D. Roosevelt asks him to resign from his Air Corps Reserve job.

1953
Lindbergh's book *The Spirit of St. Louis* wins the Pulitzer Prize.

Douglas MacArthur
Never Surrender
(born 1880 • died 1964)

Douglas MacArthur was a man who liked to be in charge. His talent for leadership led him to become one of the most important American military figures of the 20th century.

An Army Life

Douglas MacArthur was born on January 26, 1880, near Little Rock, Arkansas. He spent his early childhood in Fort Selden, New Mexico, where his father commanded an army unit that protected settlers. Douglas later recalled that "my first memory was the sound of bugles. . . . I learned to ride and shoot even before I could read or write—indeed, almost before I could walk or talk." The MacArthur family moved many times over the next few years, following the father's army assignments.

Douglas was not very interested in school. Then, in 1893, he enrolled in the West Texas Military Academy. Douglas enjoyed the discipline of the

General Douglas MacArthur *(right)* with President Harry S. Truman.

school and did well there. He decided that he wanted to make the army his career, just as his father had.

In 1898, Douglas received an appointment to the U.S. Military Academy at West Point. He was one of the best students in the school's history. In 1903, Douglas graduated first in his class.

To the Philippines

MacArthur's first assignment was to work with a group of army engineers in the Philippines. Although he later worked as an aide to President Theodore Roosevelt in Washington, D.C., and had several other U.S. assignments, MacArthur loved the Philippines and was determined to return there someday.

During World War I, MacArthur fought in France. Because of his bravery and great personal style, he won more medals than any other American soldier in World War I.

After the war, MacArthur held several important jobs. He was superintendent of West Point from 1919 to 1922. Later, he served as Army Chief of Staff from 1930 to 1933. However, his wish to return to the Philippine Islands was about to come true.

> "I have returned. By the grace of almighty God, our forces stand again on Philippine soil."
>
> —General Douglas MacArthur, at Leyte, Philippines, on October 20, 1944

At this time, the Philippines was a U.S. territory, but it was scheduled to become an independent nation in 1946. In 1935, the president of the Philippines asked MacArthur to lead the U.S. military group that would prepare the islands for independence. MacArthur was happy to accept.

MacArthur loved living in the Philippines. How-

MacArthur *(in sunglasses)* returns to the Philippines in 1944—after scoring important victories against Japan during World War II.

ever, storm clouds were gathering over the islands. On December 7, 1941, the U.S. was plunged into World War II when Japan attacked a U.S. naval base at Pearl Harbor, Hawaii. That same day, Japanese forces also attacked the Philippines. MacArthur's air force was destroyed, and many of his men were killed. U.S. President Franklin D. Roosevelt ordered MacArthur to escape to Australia. As he left the Philippines, MacArthur promised, "I will return."

World War II—and After

MacArthur dedicated the next three years to winning the war against the Japanese. His forces captured one Pacific island after another in brilliant tactical maneuvers. In October 1944, MacArthur finally kept his promise: He waded onto the shore of Leyte, one of the Philippine islands. Over the next few months, his troops recaptured the rest of the Philippines as well.

On September 2, 1945, MacArthur accepted the Japanese surrender. At long last, World War II was over. For the next five years, MacArthur served as Supreme Commander of the Allied Powers in Japan. Under his leadership, the Allied armies helped Japan rebuild its shattered cities and become one of the world's leading democratic powers.

TOPICAL TIDBIT

Truman and MacArthur

The 1951 clash between President Harry S. Truman and General Douglas MacArthur was a long time in coming. MacArthur had publicly criticized the way the President was conducting the Korean War. MacArthur also was making moves that threatened to pull China into the war. When Truman called the General back to the U.S., after a career of 52 years, Americans were divided over which man they blamed. Even so, MacArthur's farewell speech before Congress will never be forgotten.

Fading Away

In 1950, North Korea invaded South Korea, beginning the Korean War. MacArthur called that war a "last gift to an old warrior." Once again, he commanded an army, leading United Nations forces to help South Korea.

MacArthur achieved several military victories, but publicly criticized U.S. President Harry S. Truman's decisions about how the war should be won. On April 11, 1951, Truman removed MacArthur from his command.

MacArthur returned to a hero's welcome in the U.S. He lived quietly in New York until he died in 1964, at the age of 84. In his 1951 farewell speech to Congress, MacArthur had said that "old soldiers never die, they just fade away." However, his name has not faded from history. He is still remembered as one of America's greatest military leaders. ◇

LIFE EVENTS

1880
Douglas MacArthur is born near Little Rock, Arkansas.

1935
MacArthur serves as Philippines military adviser.

1941
War erupts in the South Pacific. MacArthur is forced to withdraw from the Philippines.

1944
MacArthur returns to Leyte to retake the Philippines.

1945
MacArthur accepts the surrender of Japan's Emperor Hirohito.

1951
MacArthur is forced to retire. He dies in 1964.

Malcolm X
Freedom Can't Wait
(born 1925 • died 1965)

Malcolm X was a controversial figure in American history. He took his anger at racism and the way black Americans were treated and eventually turned it into something positive as he encouraged black people to take control of their lives.

A Rough Childhood

He was born Malcolm Little on May 19, 1925, in Omaha, Nebraska. Malcolm's family lived in poverty. They also faced danger from white hate groups because Malcolm's father followed a leader named Marcus Garvey. Garvey wanted black Americans to establish a separate nation in Africa, believing that blacks could never win equality in the U.S.

When Malcolm was a child, the family moved to East Lansing, Michigan, hoping to escape from racism. Soon after they arrived, however, their house was burned down by the Ku Klux Klan, a white racist group. Then, in 1931, Malcolm's father was

killed under mysterious circumstances, probably by a gang of white men.

Malcolm's mother was unable to care for the family. Malcolm was placed in a foster home. When he was a teenager, his half-sister, Ella, got custody of him. He moved to her home in Boston, Massachusetts. As a young boy, Malcolm had been an excellent student. Soon after moving to Boston, however, he began getting into trouble. He quit school and started breaking into apartments, stealing, and selling stolen goods.

A Life-changing Experience

In January 1946, Malcolm was arrested for theft and sentenced to 10 years in prison. While in prison, he heard about a religion called the Nation of Islam, led by a man named Elijah Muhammad. The Nation of Islam was a form of Islam that had been adapted by and for African Americans. It taught that blacks were descended from a powerful race called Original Man. Malcolm studied this religion and its founder. The Nation's beliefs offered him guidance, discipline, a sense of belonging—and pride as a black man.

Malcolm grabbed this opportunity to make a fresh start in life. Like many members of the Nation of Islam, he changed his last name to X. The *X* represented the African name that his ancestors had lost when they were brought to America as slaves.

Malcolm X was released from prison in 1952. He became assistant minister of the Nation of Islam's mosque in Detroit. Two years later, he went to New York to become chief minister of the mosque there. Malcolm became an inspiring speaker who converted many people to the Nation of Islam—also known as the Black Muslims. He spread a message of self-respect, encouraging black people to stop trying to please whites. Instead, he said, blacks should take pride in themselves and their history, and build strong communities.

> "Yes, I'm an extremist. The black race . . . is in extremely bad condition."
>
> —from *The Autobiography of Malcolm X*

The teachings of the Nation of Islam and its leader, Elijah Muhammad, were very controversial. Among other things, they said that African Americans should defend themselves and claim their rights—and if

Malcolm X with a copy of the newspaper that he founded in 1961.

peaceful methods didn't work, they could use violence. This upset many white people. Other black leaders also disapproved of Malcolm's words—including Martin Luther King Jr., who believed in using only nonviolent methods to end racial inequality.

Shocking Words and Changing Ideas

In 1963, President John F. Kennedy was assassinated. Malcolm X said that the President had gotten what he deserved because of the "climate of hate" that whites stirred up toward blacks. That upset many Americans. Elijah Muhammad was furious at Malcolm X, and suspended him for 90 days. In return, Malcolm was angry at the way the Nation of Islam treated him. A conflict had been brewing for a long time. Elijah Muhammad was jealous of the attention that Malcolm was receiving, and Malcolm disapproved of Muhammad's conduct as a minister. In 1964, Malcolm X left the Nation to form the Organization of Afro-American Unity (OAAU).

Soon after forming the OAAU, Malcolm X went to Africa and to Mecca, the holy site of Islam in Saudi Arabia. There, he proclaimed his faith in traditional Islam rather than the Nation of Islam. He took a new name: El Hajj Malik Shabazz.

Malcolm X's opinions about white people changed during his trip to Mecca. He saw that people of all colors worshipped Allah (the Islamic name for God), and could work together in peace and with respect for one another. When he returned to America, he said

TOPICAL TIDBIT

The Autobiography of Malcolm X

By 1963, Malcolm X knew that time was short. Whenever he had a moment in his hectic schedule, he dictated his life story to a writer named Alex Haley. Malcolm did not live to see *The Autobiography of Malcolm X* become one of the most influential books of its time—or to see Haley to write another important book, *Roots*.

that he no longer believed that all white people were racist. He also made a gesture of peace to Martin Luther King Jr., saying: "What's important is that we both believe in the same things: equality, peace, and justice for our people. Our methods differ but we are both in the same battle."

Danger and Death

Malcolm's break with the Nation of Islam made him new enemies. Despite death threats, however, he kept making public appearances. Speaking out for justice, he said, was his duty.

On February 21, 1965, as Malcolm X prepared to speak at a meeting at the Audubon Ballroom in Harlem, three gunmen linked with the Nation of Islam shot him to death. Death did not silence Malcolm X, however. His message of black power, community, and self-respect lives on, and continues to inspire many people. ◇

LIFE EVENTS

1925
Malcolm Little is born in Omaha, Nebraska.

1952
Little converts to the Nation of Islam and changes his name to Malcolm X.

1954
Malcolm X becomes head of a Nation of Islam temple in Harlem.

1961
Malcolm X founds *Muhammad Speaks*, the Nation of Islam's newspaper.

1964
Malcolm X makes a pilgrimage to Mecca and breaks with the Nation of Islam.

1965
Malcolm X is assassinated.

Francis Marion
The Swamp Fox
(born 1732 • died 1795)

For most of his life, Francis Marion was an average farmer. Then the American Revolution turned him into a skilled fighter—and an American hero.

An Ordinary Life

Not much is known about Francis Marion's early years. Historians believe that he was born in 1732, in Berkeley County, South Carolina. For most of his life, Marion farmed the rich South Carolina land.

In 1760, many men in South Carolina formed a militia (volunteer army) to fight the Cherokee Indians. Marion joined the militia, and served until 1761. Then he went back to farming.

South Carolina at War

In 1775, the American colonies were moving toward war against Great Britain. Marion took part in South Carolina's first revolutionary convention.

The convention organized two regiments of men to fight against the British. Marion was put in charge of one of those regiments.

On June 28, 1776, Marion and his men chased the British fleet out of Charleston's harbor. Getting rid of the British ships turned out to be a tremendous help to the colony during the war.

For the next three years, Marion organized and trained his men. Then, in September 1779, he took part in a campaign to drive the British out of Savannah, Georgia. The colonists were defeated. Marion publicly announced that if his forces had been allowed to strike more quickly, they might have been able to capture the city.

"The Swamp Fox"

Things got even worse for the American side in 1780, when the British captured Charleston. Marion was one of the few officers to escape. He quickly gathered about 200 of the best men he could find. The group called itself Marion's Brigade, and set out to attack the British.

Because the British army was so much larger, Marion knew that he and his men couldn't face it head-on. The only way to fight it was to strike quickly and withdraw before they could react. For the next two years, he and his men used the dense Carolina swamps as their base. Rushing out from their hiding place, Marion's Brigade launched many surprise

> "Well now, Colonel Doyle, look sharp. For you shall presently feel the edge of our swords!"
>
> —Francis Marion's warning to the British commander

attacks on the British army. Then they disappeared back into the swamps.

Conditions in the swamp were harsh. Like his men, Marion slept on the ground, without any blankets or tents to protect him. But the small army's methods were effective. Colonel Banastre Tarleton, the most feared British leader in South Carolina, was forever frustrated that Marion kept slipping through his fingers. "As for the damned old fox," the colonel said, "the devil himself could not catch him!" From then on, Marion was known as "the Swamp Fox."

Later, Marion helped other military leaders capture British posts along the Santee River. He also commanded a regiment that helped drive the British out of South Carolina for good.

TOPICAL TIDBIT

Guerrilla Warfare

Francis Marion's band of "irregulars" practiced a kind of fighting called guerrilla *(guh-RIL-uh)* warfare. Small armies throughout history have used this tactic to strike at, and often defeat, larger armies. The American colonists had to rely on methods such as this to beat the British troops, who were more numerous and had much better weapons. The story of Marion and other guerrilla-style fighters of that war was later used as the basis for *The Patriot*, a movie starring Mel Gibson.

After the War

When the American Revolution ended in 1783, Marion was thanked by Congress for his "wise, gallant, and decided conduct." It also gave him a pension (retirement money) for his military service. Marion went on to serve two terms as a state senator, in 1782-1786, and 1791-1794. During his terms, he was known as a dignified, polite, and kind-hearted man who spoke out against harsh punishments for South Carolina residents who had helped the British during the war.

Francis Marion died in Berkeley County, Virginia, on February 27, 1795. His determination and courage during one of the most dramatic periods in U.S. history make him a true American hero. ◇

LIFE EVENTS

1732
Francis Marion is born in Berkeley County, South Carolina.

1775
Marion is a delegate to the South Carolina Provincial Congress.

1776
American independence is declared. Marion, a captain in the 2nd South Carolina Regiment, drives the British out of Charleston harbor.

1780
Marion's Brigade attacks the British from hiding places in the Carolina swamps.

1783
The American Revolution ends. Marion later serves as a state senator and commander at Fort Johnson. He dies in 1795.

John Marshall
A Legal Leader
(born 1755 • died 1835)

John Marshall was the fourth chief justice of the U.S. Supreme Court. His legal rulings were so brilliant that they are still used to settle disputes today.

A Talented Man

John Marshall was born on September 24, 1755, in a log cabin in the wilderness of western Virginia. His parents were related to, or friends with, some of Virginia's most important families. His mother was a distant cousin of Thomas Jefferson, and his father had been friends with George Washington since the days when the two had gone to school together.

John never attended school. Instead, he studied at home with his father. Later, his father hired a tutor to live with the family and teach his 15 children. By the time John was 12, he had memorized most of the few books his family owned. By the age of 19, he was studying law at home.

Marshall was 20 years old when America went to

war against Great Britain. He joined Virginia's militia and fought in several major battles. More important, he stopped considering himself a Virginian. Instead, he considered "America as my country" and believed that a strong central government was necessary to keep the states united.

In 1782, 27-year-old Marshall was elected to Virginia's state legislature. He became well-known as a successful lawyer, judge, and a strong supporter of the

353

U.S. Constitution. In spite of his success, however, Marshall dressed casually and sloppily. This led many people to underestimate his intelligence and power.

In 1798, George Washington personally asked Marshall to help John Adams, who was about to become the second president of the United States. Marshall agreed. First, he took part in an important mission to France. Later, he served as Adams's secretary of state.

> "The people made the Constitution and the people can unmake it. It is the creature of their own will, and lives only by their will."
>
> —John Marshall

Appointment to the High Court

In 1801, President Adams was about to give up his office to the newly elected third president, Thomas Jefferson. One of Adams's last acts as president was to nominate a new chief justice of the Supreme Court. Adams trusted Marshall, so the two men met to determine who would make a good chief justice. After discussing several other candidates, Adams turned to Marshall. "I believe I must nominate you," he said.

Marshall served as chief justice for 34 years. His most important goal was to make the U.S. Constitution the highest law of the land. This was not as easy to do as it sounds, however, because people often disagreed about what the Constitution meant. In those cases, Marshall decided, it was up to the Supreme Court to interpret the Constitution and determine the law. He also declared that the Supreme Court could set aside any law that it considered to be unconstitutional.

Because the U.S. was a young country, it was important to create a strong legal system and establish fair and just laws. By using the Constitution as the basis for all American laws, Marshall gave the U.S. a legal foundation that is still in place today.

Not everyone agreed with Marshall's decisions. Many people thought that he had too much power, and that he was giving the Supreme Court too much authority over other branches of government. However, Marshall remained influential and strong

TOPICAL TIDBIT

A Key Decision

One of the most important decisions ever made by the Supreme Court was *Marbury* v. *Madison* in 1803. (The *v.* in a court case's name stands for "versus," which means "against.") The case raised a crucial question: Who decides whether a law passed by Congress is constitutional—that is, whether it fits with our Constitution? John Marshall argued strongly that the Constitution itself gave this role to the Supreme Court. The decision established the power of the Supreme Court in the U.S. government.

throughout his long career. Today, most historians agree that his legal leadership gave the U.S. government stability and strength.

John Marshall died on July 6, 1835, just two months before his 80th birthday. Several years earlier, John Adams had called Marshall his gift to the American people. Nominating John Marshall, said Adams, was "the proudest act of my life." Adams's gift gave the young country a model of legal genius—a man whose rulings still affect our lives today. ◇

LIFE EVENTS

1755
John Marshall is born near Germantown, Virginia.

1788
The Constitution establishes the Supreme Court to interpret the laws of the land.

1801
President John Adams appoints Marshall the fourth chief justice of the U.S. Supreme Court.

1803
Chief Justice Marshall issues the important decision of *Marbury* v. *Madison*. It establishes the Supreme Court's power to interpret the Constitution.

1835
Marshall dies after 34 years as chief justice.

Thurgood Marshall
Mr. Civil Rights
(born 1908 • died 1993)

As a lawyer, Thurgood Marshall fought tirelessly for civil rights. As the first black justice of the U.S. Supreme Court, he challenged inequality and helped bring fair treatment to people of all races.

Not Afraid to Fight

Thurgood Marshall was born on July 2, 1908, in Baltimore, Maryland. He was named for his grandfather, Thoroughgood. Young Thurgood's parents knew that education was important. They wanted his older brother to be a doctor, and decided that Thurgood would be a dentist.

Thurgood's father loved to debate. He taught his son how to fight with words—and made sure that Thurgood could back up every argument with facts. He also taught the boy not to back down from trouble. If anyone ever insulted him because of the color of his skin, Thurgood had orders to fight back.

Thurgood often got into trouble at school for not paying attention in class. As punishment, he had to stay after school and learn part of the U.S. Constitution. He soon memorized most of that important document, which is the basis for the country's laws.

Separate and Unequal

By the time Marshall was attending Lincoln University, an all-black college in Pennsylvania, he knew that he didn't want to be a dentist. He had decided to become a lawyer. After college, he wanted to go to law school at the University of Maryland. However, only white students could go there. Instead, Marshall attended Howard University, a well-known black school in Washington, D.C. He graduated at the top of his class. Then he went home to Baltimore and opened a law office there.

Two years later, Marshall represented a young black man named Donald Murray. Murray wanted to go to law school at the University of Maryland—the same school that had turned Marshall away. At the trial, Marshall argued that the U.S. Constitution said that

Murray had a right to attend whichever school he wanted. The judges agreed, and Marshall won his case. He was so happy, he danced outside the courtroom.

In 1940, Marshall became head of the legal and education division of the National Association for the Advancement of Colored People (NAACP). The NAACP is an organization that works toward fair treatment for all Americans. Marshall's tireless work with the NAACP gave him a new nickname: "Mr. Civil Rights."

Many of Marshall's legal battles were aimed at ending school segregation— the practice of requiring children of different races to attend separate schools. At the time, the law said that states could segregate as long as facilities for blacks were "equal" to those for whites. "Separate but equal" was the accepted idea. Time after time, however, Marshall was able to prove in court that public schools for blacks and white were *not* equal. Black schools were given less money; they had fewer, older books and supplies; and were unequal in other ways as well.

> "Our whole constitutional heritage rebels at the thought of giving government the power to control men's minds."
>
> —Thurgood Marshall

In 1952, Thurgood Marshall went before the U.S. Supreme Court to argue the most important case of his career. The name of the case was *Brown* v. *the Board of Education of Topeka, Kansas*.

A black girl named Linda Brown wanted to go to a white school in her neighborhood in Topeka, Kansas. It was closer to her home, and it was a better school. Marshall argued that she had every right to attend the white school, because segregation was against the Constitution. On May 17, 1954, the U.S. Supreme Court justices agreed. The Court ruled that school segregation was both harmful and illegal.

The Court's decision dealt with schools, but it had a far-reaching effect. The ruling that "Separate is not equal" in schools gave new power to the civil-rights movement. It was used to knock down other unequal treatment by race—in public transportation, stores and restaurants, jobs, housing, and many other areas.

TOPICAL TIDBIT

Charles Hamilton Houston

The Supreme Court decision that created the "separate but equal" rule was *Plessy* v. *Ferguson* (1896). Charles Hamilton Houston (1895-1950), an African American who was the grandson of slaves, dedicated his life to fighting this decision. Even before Thurgood Marshall, Houston was one of the most important lawyers of the 20th century. His efforts helped lay the path for victories he would not live to see. "We were just carrying his bags, that's all," Thurgood Marshall said after he won the *Brown* case.

The Highest Court in the Land

During the 1960s, Marshall served on the U.S. Court of Appeals and as Solicitor (lawyer) General of the United States. He used these positions to make sure that civil-rights laws were obeyed.

In 1967, President Lyndon Johnson appointed Marshall to the Supreme Court. Johnson said, "I believe it is the right thing to do, the right time to do it, the right man, and the right place." Thurgood Marshall was the first African American to serve on the Court. He held that post for 24 years. During that time, he worked to win equal treatment for all Americans.

Poor health forced Marshall to retire in 1991. He died two years later, on January 24, 1993. Thousands of people paid their respects as his body lay in state in Washington, D.C. They were honoring a man who had changed the lives of millions of American schoolchildren—for the better. ◈

LIFE EVENTS

1908
Thurgood Marshall is born in Baltimore, Maryland

1936
Marshall becomes special counsel for the NAACP.

1940
Marshall wins the first of 29 cases before the U.S. Supreme Court.

1954
Marshall wins the historic case of *Brown* v. *Board of Education* before the Supreme Court.

1967
President Lyndon Johnson nominates Marshall to the Supreme Court. He serves until 1991 and dies in 1993.

John McCain
Bravery Under Pressure
(born 1936)

John McCain has faced pressure in many forms—as a naval pilot, a prisoner of war, and a politician. No matter what situation life has placed him in, he has always stood firmly for what he believes in.

Growing Up in the Navy

John Sidney McCain III was born on August 29, 1936, in the Panama Canal Zone. His father and grandfather were both commanders in the U.S. Navy, so it probably was no surprise when John also decided on a naval career.

Young John did not take school very seriously, however. He much preferred having good times with his friends. Even when he was admitted to the U.S. Naval Academy in Annapolis, Maryland, and faced more serious studies, John did not settle down. When John McCain graduated from the Naval Academy in 1958, he was fifth from the bottom of his class.

Trouble in Vietnam

McCain trained to be a naval aviator (flier). He was a good pilot, and soon earned a reputation for keeping calm under pressure. Once, while McCain was sitting in his fighter jet on the deck of the aircraft carrier *Forrestal*, another jet accidentally fired a missile that hit his plane. He escaped—then rushed back to help injured airmen.

During the 1960s, the U.S. was fighting a war in Vietnam, a country in Asia. John McCain, by now a veteran pilot, volunteered for duty. Vietnam would prove to be the most challenging and difficult experience of his life.

> "I had a lot of time [in the prisoner-of-war camp] to think and I came to the conclusion that one of the most important things in life is to make some contribution to your country."
>
> —John McCain

In 1967, McCain's plane was shot down over Hanoi, North Vietnam's capital city. He was seriously injured when the plane crashed into a lake. Then a crowd of people dragged him out of the water and attacked him. By the time policemen pulled McCain away from the crowd, he had broken bones and other injuries.

At first, he was taken to a prison hospital, but his injuries were not treated. He was in such bad shape that many people thought that he would die. Then his captors found out that his father was an American naval hero. After that, his injuries were treated, and he eventually left the hospital for the main prison.

The prison was a notorious place, where conditions were harsh and prisoners were tortured and beaten. The prisoners' sarcastic name for the place was

Hanoi Hilton. (Hilton is the name of a chain of fine hotels—nothing like what the prisoners faced.) In prison, McCain was frequently beaten and tortured. His guards wanted him to say that he was a spy and that the U.S. was an evil country. McCain refused to do so for a long time, but the torture finally became too much for him. To his great shame, he signed a paper that said that he was a spy, even though it was not true.

Because McCain's family was important in the U.S. military, the North Vietnamese offered to release him. However, McCain thought that it was unfair for him to go home ahead of other prisoners who had been at the Hanoi Hilton for a longer time. So he refused the offer of release. McCain and many other

TOPICAL TIDBIT

The U.S.S. *Forrestal*

In 1967, Lieutenant Commander John McCain was assigned to the aircraft carrier U.S.S. *Forrestal*, off the coast of Vietnam. On July 29, as he was preparing to take off on a bombing mission, a missile was accidentally fired from a nearby plane, striking one of his fuel tanks. McCain just barely escaped from his burning plane. Then, as he tried to help a fellow pilot whose flight suit had burst into flames, another explosion knocked him back 10 feet. In all, 134 men died that day. It was the worst noncombat-related accident in U.S. naval history.

prisoners of war were finally released in 1973, when the U.S. agreed to stop the war. McCain had been imprisoned for five and a half years.

Taking Up Politics

McCain received many awards for his bravery in Vietnam, including the Silver Star, Legion of Merit, Purple Heart, and Distinguished Flying Cross. He retired from the U.S. Navy in 1981, after a 22-year career. Then he decided to serve his country in a different way—as an elected official. McCain first represented Arizona as a Republican in the House of Representatives from 1983 to 1986. In 1986, he was elected to the U.S. Senate.

As a senator, McCain has served on the Senate's Armed Services Committee and the Indian Affairs Committee, working to help veterans and Native Americans. He also has worked hard for campaign finance reform. McCain believes that there are too many special-interest groups (powerful, wealthy people and industries) influencing government. This means that ordinary people are not given a fair chance to be heard.

In 1999, McCain decided to run for president. In his presidential campaign, as in his career as a senator, his main message was a call for campaign finance reform. McCain pointed out that the way politicians raise and spend money gives an unfair advantage to big busi-

nesses and other wealthy con-
tributors. He also called for
new laws that would limit large
contributions, and would help
candidates finance their campaigns without compromising
their values.

Although many Americans
responded to McCain's message
of reform, he did not win
enough votes to successfully
challenge George W. Bush for
the Republican nomination.
After McCain dropped out of
the race, however, he continued
to spread his message, and
gained increasing support in
the U.S. Congress for his campaign reform program. ◇

LIFE EVENTS

1936
John Sidney McCain
III is born in the
Panama Canal Zone.

1958
McCain graduates
from the Naval
Academy.

1967
McCain is shot
down over North
Vietnam. He spends
the next five and a
half years as a
prisoner of war.

1982
McCain is elected to
the U.S. House of
Representatives.

1986
McCain is elected to
the U.S. Senate.

1999
McCain runs for
president.

1999
Senator McCain
continues to call for
campaign finance
reform in Congress.

John Muir
Man of the Wilderness
(born 1838 • died 1914)

John Muir is known as "the father of our national parks." Because of his dedication and hard work, we can enjoy the beauty of our country's wild places.

A Farm Boy

John Muir was born in Dunbar, Scotland, on April 21, 1838. Even as a little boy, John loved nature. He spent hours walking along the seashore and racing through the woods. He also enjoyed reading about the wilderness in America. Someday, he dreamed, he would go see that wilderness for himself.

That dream came true sooner than he thought. When John was 11, his family moved to Wisconsin. John loved the woods there, but spent most of his time working on his family's farm. Along with his brothers and sisters, he cleared land, planted seeds, and harvested crops. Mr. Muir was very strict and made his children work 16 hours a day. If he caught John reading, he punished him and told him to get back to work.

John Muir *(right)* with President Roosevelt in Yosemite Valley, California.

Leaving Home

By the time he was 22 years old, John Muir knew that he didn't want to be a farmer. Even though he had barely gone to school, he enrolled in the University of Wisconsin, in Madison. He enjoyed college, but didn't take enough courses to graduate.

In 1863, he left school and went to Canada to explore the woods and study the plants that grew there. When his money ran out, he returned to the U.S. to work.

A Life-changing Accident

In 1866, Muir was working in Indianapolis, Indiana. While he was fixing a machine, he injured his eye and went blind. Muir was terrified at the thought of losing his sight. The damage was not permanent, however; after a month, his sight returned.

The accident made Muir question how he had been spending his life and what he wanted to do with the rest of it. He decided that he had spent enough time working in cities. Now that he had his eyesight back, he was determined to spend his life doing what he really cared about: studying nature. He decided to travel to South America and study all the plants he saw along the way.

To begin with, Muir walked 1,000 miles to the Gulf of Mexico in Florida. Along the way, he kept a journal about what he saw. (The notebook was later published in book form.) In 1868, he sailed to Cuba and spent a month there. Again, he wrote down everything he observed, and marveled at how perfectly everything in nature worked together.

> "Going to the mountains is going home. . . . Mountain parks and reservations are useful not only as fountains of timber and irrigating rivers, but as fountains of life."
> —John Muir

The Sierra Club

In March 1868, Muir went to California and spent the next few years exploring the wild places of the west. When he got his first look at the Yosemite Valley in east-central California, he was so over-whelmed by its beauty that he shouted for joy. Yosemite Valley remained Muir's favorite place.

During his travels, Muir saw that the natural world was being destroyed. Timber companies were cutting down forests. Ranches were being built in the valleys, and sheep and cattle were destroying the plants that grew there. Muir began speaking out about the need to save the wilderness. "People need beauty as well as bread," he wrote. In 1892, he and some friends formed an organization called the Sierra Club. The Sierra Club's mission was to pre-

TOPICAL TIDBIT

The Sierra Club

The Sierra Club is named for the Sierra Nevada Mountains of California, which John Muir loved. (His book *My First Summer in the Sierra* is a journal of camping and exploring those mountains in 1869.) The Sierra Club was originally formed in 1892 to sponsor outings in the mountains. Soon, however, Muir and his friends turned to political action to preserve the Sierra Nevada. This led to other conservationist efforts. Today, the Sierra Club continues to fight to save our nation's natural beauty.

serve nature all around the world.

After a while, government leaders began to listen to his words. California passed laws to protect the mighty redwood forests. The Sequoia and Yosemite national parks were established. Muir's work led President Grover Cleveland to protect more than 21 million acres of wilderness.

In 1903, Muir took President Theodore Roosevelt hiking in the Yosemite Valley. After that inspiring trip, Roosevelt doubled the number of national parks, preserving 145 million acres of wilderness.

John Muir spent his last years at his home in Martinez, California. He died on December 24, 1914, at the age of 76. His house in Martinez is now a national historic site. However, a more fitting tribute to this conservationist is a redwood forest a few miles outside of San Francisco, California. The name of that forest is Muir Woods. ◇

LIFE EVENTS

1838
John Muir is born in Dunbar, Scotland.

1868
Muir first visits the Yosemite Valley in California.

1892
Muir is co-founder and first president of the Sierra Club.

1890
The Sequoia and Yosemite national parks are established.

1908
The U.S. government establishes the Muir Woods National Monument in Marin County, California. Muir dies in 1914.

Audie Murphy
Bravery in Battle
(born 1924 • died 1971)

When Audie Murphy was a boy in Texas, it didn't look as if he would become a hero. Then this poor farm boy went off to fight in World War II, and became an American legend.

Audie Murphy's sister, Billie Tindol, with the stamp honoring her brother.

Dirt-poor Beginnings

Audie Leon Murphy was born in Hunt County, Texas, on June 20, 1924. His parents were poor sharecroppers. A sharecropper is a farmer who lives and works on another person's land.

Audie's family was so poor that they couldn't send him to school. Instead, he had to work. He picked cotton to earn money. Audie also learned how to use a rifle at a very young age. He used this skill to hunt for food to add to the family's table.

Off to War

In 1942, America had just started fighting in World War II. Audie Murphy wasn't quite 18 years old yet, but he enlisted in the Army. After training in the U.S., he was sent to fight in Europe. Over the next three years, Murphy fought in nine major campaigns in North Africa, Italy, France, and Germany. He was wounded three times and decorated for bravery several times.

January 26, 1945, became the most important day in Audie Murphy's life. On that day, he was commanding Company B in the woods of Germany. Suddenly, they were attacked by six German tanks and several hundred soldiers. Murphy ordered his men to seek safety in the woods. Then he climbed on top of a burning tank destroyer and began firing its machine gun on the advancing German army. For the next hour, Murphy single-handedly held off 250 German soldiers. Even after he was shot in the leg, he continued to fight.

Finally, Murphy ran out of ammunition. Then he retreated into the woods, where his company was waiting for him. He led his men in a counterattack that finally drove the Germans away.

Soon after Murphy's brave stand, he was awarded the Congressional Medal of Honor. He received 25 other medals as well, making him the most decorated hero of World War II. France and Belgium also gave medals to Murphy. After the war, however, he gave all of the medals away to his family because, he said, "I never felt that the medals entirely belonged to me. My whole unit earned them."

> "Freedom is what America means to the world. And to me."
> —Audie Murphy

Audie in Hollywood

Murphy was released from the army in 1945. He was featured on the cover of *Life* magazine and invited to Hollywood. He struggled for several years to find work as an actor. Finally, in 1950, he signed a contract with the Universal-International movie studio. Over the next 15 years, Murphy starred in 26 films for Universal, most of which were Westerns.

Murphy also wrote a best-selling book about his war experiences, called *To Hell and Back*. The book was made into a movie in 1955, starring Murphy as himself. The film version of *To Hell and Back* was Universal's biggest moneymaker for the next 20 years.

Murphy left Universal in 1965 and spent the next five years making movies for other studios. He made a total of 44 feature films.

Hard Times

Even though he was a war hero and a Hollywood star, life was not perfect for Audie Murphy. His wartime experiences caused him to suffer from post-traumatic stress syndrome (serious after-effects from

TOPICAL TIDBIT

To Hollywood and Back

Audie Murphy returned to the U.S. a hero. But what does a hero do when he hangs up his uniform? As it turned out, Murphy's face helped him answer that question. In 1945, the actor James Cagney saw Murphy's photo on the cover of *Life* magazine and invited him to Hollywood. Like any other actor, Murphy struggled for a time. He even slept in a gymnasium for a while. Luckily for Murphy, his contract with Universal Pictures changed everything. *To Hell and Back*, the 1955 movie based on his book, was Universal's biggest film until *Jaws* in 1975.

a bad experience). He was often depressed and had trouble sleeping. Murphy wanted to help other war veterans suffering in the same way, so he often spoke out about his personal problems. He also urged the U.S. government to study the emotional impact of war on veterans.

Murphy's life came to an early end. On May 28, 1971, while on a business trip, the small plane in which he was flying crashed into the side of a mountain near Roanoke, Virginia. He was 46 years old.

Audie Murphy was buried with full military honors in Arlington National Cemetery. Every year, thousands of people still visit his grave. ◇

LIFE EVENTS

1924
Audie Leon Murphy is born in Hunt County, Texas.

1941
The U.S. enters World War II. Murphy joins the Army the following year.

1945
Murphy wins the Congressional Medal of Honor for bravery in action in France.

1949
Murphy's autobiography, *To Hell and Back*, and his first film, *Bad Boy*, are released.

1971
Murphy dies in a plane crash and is buried in Arlington National Cemetery.

Thomas Paine
Inspiring a New Nation
(born 1737 • died 1809)

Thomas Paine was born in England and did not come to America until he was 37 years old. Yet his patriotic writings made him one of the most beloved and important leaders of American independence.

Life in Great Britain

Thomas Paine was born on January 29, 1737, in Thetford, England. His father was a member of the Quaker religion, and Thomas was raised to believe in peace and equal treatment for all. He enjoyed reading books about America, and dreamed of traveling there someday.

Tom's youth was not promising. He was able to attend school only until he was 13 years old. Then he went to work in his father's shop, making women's corsets. However, he was restless and wanted adventure, so he ran away from home when he was 16. For the next four years, young Tom Paine worked as a sailor aboard several warships. When he returned to

England, he worked at several different jobs. One was as a tax collector.

In 1772, other tax collectors asked Paine to write a pamphlet to convince the government to give them a raise. Paine's writing was strong and forceful. He discovered that he had a talent for political writing. But the pamphlet did not have the effect that Paine and the others had hoped for. First, the tax collectors did not receive their raise. Second, Paine was fired from his job. On top of that, he was having problems in his marriage, and was separating from his wife. Things did not look good for Thomas Paine.

A New Life

Then Paine met Benjamin Franklin, who was in London at the time. Franklin became a good friend and major influence in Paine's life. He urged Paine to seek his fortune in America. So, at age 37, he set sail for the colonies to make a new start in life, with letters of introduction from Benjamin Franklin.

Franklin's letters opened many doors for Paine. He soon found work tutoring the sons of Philadelphia's most important citizens. He also became involved in the growing movement for America's independence from Britain.

> "We fight not to enslave, but to set a country free, and to make room upon the earth for honest men to live in."
>
> —Thomas Paine, in *The American Crisis*, number 4, 1777

On January 10, 1776, Paine published a 50-page pamphlet called *Common Sense*. That essay became one of the most important pieces of political writing ever composed. In it, Paine took the complicated issues of the struggle between America and Great

Britain and made them easy for ordinary citizens to understand. "We have it in our power to begin the world over again," he wrote. Paine's words convinced many Americans to support independence, and made him a hero. His pamphlet sold 500,000 copies in the first three months—an amazing number at a time when many people could not read.

Paine continued writing after America declared its independence in July 1776. While the American army struggled through the early months of the war, Paine published a series of 16 pamphlets called *The American Crisis*. Beginning with the now-famous words, "These are the times that try men's souls," Paine went on to explain how and why the fight for

TOPICAL TIDBIT

Tom Paine's *Common Sense*

When *Common Sense* appeared in January 1776, the colonists were divided over the issue of independence from England. Many Americans did not want to be independent. Others wanted independence, but did not want to go to war over it. Thomas Paine's stirring words made a huge difference in the debate. Many people read *Common Sense*, then gave it to others, who also passed it on. It was being read aloud in public places, and General Washington ordered it read to his troops at Valley Forge. In the end, it served as a model for the most important document of all, the Declaration of Independence.

independence was important. His words helped inspire the American people to continue—and eventually win—the war against Great Britain.

Paine supported the Revolution in other ways as well. American troops were poorly paid and often had to go without even basic supplies. Besides contributing his own money to help them, Paine and an associate made a trip to France to plead for aid. They returned with money and clothes for the soldiers, and ammunition for their weapons.

Back to Europe

Although Paine loved America, his adopted home, he went back to Europe in 1787. He had designed an iron bridge and wanted to show it to the Royal Society in London and the Royal Academy of Sciences in Paris. While in Europe, Paine became inspired by the French Revolution. He wrote a stirring pamphlet called *The Rights of Man*, encouraging the British people to overthrow their monarchy (rule by kings and queens). The British government charged Paine with treason, a crime of disloyalty. He escaped to France in 1792, before he could be arrested.

In France, Paine was given a hero's welcome and made an honorary French citizen. However, he soon became a victim of the political troubles there. In 1793, he was imprisoned and sentenced to death. Fortunately for Tom Paine, France's political climate changed yet again, and he was released from prison 10 months later.

Home Again

Paine remained in France until 1802, when President Thomas Jefferson invited him to return to the U.S. He spent his last seven years in New York. To the last, he continued to write against injustice and ignorance.

When Thomas Paine died on June 8, 1809, he had been almost forgotten by the American public. Today, however, we recognize his importance in the fight for American independence. As John Adams said when he heard of Paine's death, "I know not whether any man in the world has had more influence on its inhabitants or affairs for the last 30 years than Tom Paine." ◇

LIFE EVENTS

1737
Thomas Paine is born in Thetford, England.

1776
Paine publishes *Common Sense*, an argument for American independence.

1776-1783
Paine publishes *The American Crisis*, 16 pamphlets supporting the American Revolution.

1791
Paine's *The Rights of Man* is published.

1793
While in prison in France, Paine begins writing *Age of Reason*, another important work.

1802
Paine returns to the U.S., where he dies in 1809.

Rosa Parks
A Quiet Hero
(born 1913)

For most of the 20th century, black people in the South were forced to live separate lives from white people. People of different races were not allowed to sit in the same sections in movie theaters, swim in the same pools, eat at the same restaurants, or even sit together on public buses. In the mid-1950s, that began to change, thanks to a woman named Rosa Parks.

Growing Up Apart

Rosa Louise McCauley was born in Tuskegee, Alabama, on February 4, 1913. Her father left the family when Rosa was young. Because her mother had to work full-time to support her family, Rosa and her younger brother were raised by their grandparents.

Like other black children in the South, Rosa went to a blacks-only segregated school. There were few books and supplies, and the teachers were poorly paid. Such schools often had no heat, or even desks to sit at.

When Rosa was 11, she and her mother moved to

Rosa Parks with E. D. Nixon, one of the leaders of the bus boycott.

Montgomery, Alabama, so Rosa could continue her education. However, she had to leave high school to take care of her grandmother and mother when they became ill. Rosa didn't finish school until years later, after she had married a barber named Raymond Parks. Besides holding down regular jobs, Raymond and Rosa worked for the NAACP, an organization that campaigns for equal rights for African Americans.

A Seat on the Bus

After Rosa Parks left school, she got a job working at a shirt factory. Later, she worked as a seamstress in a department store. She was on her way home from that job on Friday, December 1, 1955, when her life changed forever.

Like many blacks in the city, Parks rode a public bus to and from work. That evening, the bus was full. When a white man got on, the bus driver did something that was considered acceptable at the time: He ordered Parks to give up her seat. Tired of being pushed around, Parks refused. When the driver threatened to call the police, she calmly replied, "You may do that." A police officer boarded the bus and arrested her.

> "All I was doing was trying to get home from work."
>
> —Rosa Parks

By the time Raymond Parks and a friend came to get Rosa Parks out of jail, word of her arrest had spread through Montgomery's black community. Some community leaders asked all the city's blacks to boycott (refuse to use) the buses on Monday. The boycott was a huge success. Black leaders, including a young minister named Martin Luther King Jr., decided to continue the boycott. Days stretched into weeks, then months. Every day, empty buses rolled through the city while its black citizens walked or shared rides to get around.

The boycott made many of Montgomery's white citizens very angry. Rosa Parks and other black leaders were threatened. Some blacks were attacked. Others, including Parks and her husband, were fired from their jobs. The bus company, the police, and the city government did everything they could think of to force an end to the boycott. But the black community held firm—and stayed off the buses.

Rosa Parks' legal case went all the way to the U.S. Supreme Court. Finally, on November 13, 1956, the Supreme Court declared that segregation on buses was against the law. A month later, Montgomery received a written order from the Supreme Court to integrate the buses. The next day, blacks and whites sat together on the buses.

TOPICAL TIDBIT

Behind One Hero, Many Others

The story of the Montgomery bus boycott is one of many heroes. When Rosa Parks was arrested, her mother called E. D. Nixon, president of the local NAACP. Nixon had long wanted to challenge the segregation laws, but had been looking for the right person to defend in court. Rosa Parks, a model citizen, was perfect. Late that night, Jo Anne Robinson and a group of NAACP women came up with the idea for the boycott. The boycott needed a leader so, the next day, a group of local ministers chose a newcomer: a young minister named Martin Luther King Jr.

A New Home

Many whites in Montgomery were angry that the boycott had succeeded in changing the law. After the boycott ended, Rosa Parks and her family moved to Detroit, Michigan. Parks stayed active in the civil-rights movement. She traveled around the country, making speeches and appearing at rallies and meetings. From 1965 to 1988, she also worked as an assistant to Congressman John Conyers of Michigan.

In 1987, Parks founded the Rosa and Raymond Parks Institute for Self-Development. Its goal is to provide education for young people. Parks knew that developing a sense of self-worth and confidence is important for all children.

Rosa Parks has been called "the mother of the civil-rights movement." She has received many awards for her work, and continues to inspire Americans today. ◇

LIFE EVENTS

1913
Rosa Louise McCauley is born in Tuskegee, Alabama.

1943
Now Rosa Parks, she becomes the secretary of the Montgomery, Alabama, chapter of the NAACP.

1955
Parks is arrested for refusing to give up her seat to a white person, sparking the Montgomery bus boycott.

1956
The U.S. Supreme Court rules that Alabama's bus-segregation laws are unconstitutional.

1999
Rosa Parks is awarded the Congressional Gold Medal of Honor, the highest civilian honor in the U.S.

George S. Patton
"Old Blood and Guts"
(born 1885 • died 1945)

During World War II, few American generals had as powerful a reputation as George S. Patton. His skill in handling armies made him one of the greatest combat leaders of modern times.

Young Soldier

George Smith Patton Jr. was born on November 11, 1885, in San Gabriel, California. His great-grandfather and grandfather had served in the U.S. Army, and his father was a graduate of the Virginia Military Institute (VMI). From his earliest days, all George wanted was to be a soldier.

He was a poor student, especially in math and spelling. Most of his education came at home. His parents finally enrolled him in a private school when he was 12 years old.

George was determined to attend the U.S. Military Academy at West Point, but his family was sure that he wouldn't be able to pass the written exam to get

in. Instead, George enrolled at VMI, his father's old school. After studying there for a year, he was able to enter West Point without taking the written exam.

Although George had to repeat his first year at West Point, he impressed his professors with his determination and dedication to military life. His motto was, "Do all you can, not only all you have to do."

After graduating in 1909, George Patton was given command of a cavalry unit. He soon had a reputation as a demanding, tough leader who expected perfection from his men.

Into Battle

Patton's first taste of battle came in 1916. He served as an aide to General John J. Pershing during a border skirmish with Mexico. Patton also was on Pershing's staff during World War I. After the war, Patton commanded several tank and cavalry units, then served as chief of cavalry from 1928 to 1932.

In 1940, it seemed likely that the U.S. would get caught up in World War II, which started in Europe in 1939. Patton was ordered to Fort Benning, Georgia, to command the 2nd Armored Division. Under his leadership, the division became the most feared unit in the U.S. Army.

In July 1942, Patton was put in charge of the

> "Wars may be fought with weapons, but they are won by men. It is the spirit of the men who follow and of the man who leads that gains the victory."
>
> —George S. Patton

Allied invasion of North Africa. The following year, he was ordered to take charge of an inexperienced American unit that had just been defeated at Kasserine Pass in Tunisia. Patton wasted no time whipping the unit into shape. Along with hard work and discipline, he treated his men with respect and made sure that they had the best food, equipment, and uniforms. On March 16, 1943, Patton successfully led his men against German and Italian troops.

Patton was now a hero in the U.S. and its allied countries. He became even more famous when he took part in the Allied invasion of the island of Sicily in July 1943. His Seventh Army captured western Sicily in 12 days. Three weeks later, the entire island was in the hands of the Allies.

Controversy and Success

Patton's no-nonsense attitude was an advantage in battle. Off the field, however, it sometimes got him into trouble. Shortly after the invasion of Sicily, Patton paid a visit to a hospital. When he saw one soldier who appeared to be healthy, he asked the man what was wrong with him. The soldier began to cry and said that his nerves were shot from the fighting. Patton angrily slapped the man across the face with one of his gloves and demanded that he be sent back into battle.

News of that incident caused an uproar among

other army officers and the American public. Patton made a public apology, but many people still called for him to be dismissed. However, Dwight Eisenhower, supreme commander of the Allied forces, could not do without his best general. He placed Patton in background roles for several months, then put him in command of the Third Army. Patton's Third rolled across northern France after D-Day, crushing the German armies. His fierce, relentless progress secured his reputation as one of the U.S. Army's greatest generals.

When the war in Europe ended in May 1945, the Third Army was ordered to occupy part of Germany. Patton soon caused another controversy when he publicly suggested that the Allied forces go to war against the Soviet Union. (During World War II, the

TOPICAL TIDBIT

"When in Doubt, Attack!"

General Patton waged war boldly, with everything he had. "When in doubt, attack," he used to say. Patton was an expert in tank warfare, and loved moving tanks in mass formations. He hated to have to stop and wait for orders or supplies. His Third Army traveled with thousands of trucks that carried tons of supplies, including huge quantities of gasoline, so that the tanks wouldn't run out. They swept across northern France in the summer of 1944 with a speed that was stunning.

Soviet Union had fought with Britain, France, the U.S., and other Allies. After the war, however, Soviet leaders began cracking down on freedom in areas that they controlled.) Patton's unpopular opinion led to his removal as commander of the Third Army. Instead, he was put in charge of a unit that was recording the history of the war.

A few months later, on December 9, 1945, George S. Patton's car was struck by an army truck on a narrow German road. He was severely injured and died on December 21. The general was mourned by his men, who called him "a man you would go to hell and back for." ◇

LIFE EVENTS

1885
George Smith Patton Jr. is born in San Gabriel, California.

1917
Patton is an aide to General Pershing in World War I.

1943
Patton leads the Sicilian campaign during World War II.

1944
Patton's soldiers sweep across France and fight in the Battle of the Bulge in Belgium.

1945
Patton dies of injuries suffered in a car accident.

Robert Peary and Matthew Henson
Arctic Explorers
(Robert Peary: born 1856 • died 1920)
(Matthew Henson: born 1866 • died 1955)

During the early part of the 20th century, explorers from all over the world were determined to be the first to reach the North Pole. The men who finally accomplished this incredible feat were two close friends from America, Robert Peary and Matthew Henson.

Robert Peary

Robert Edwin Peary was born on May 6, 1856, in Cresson, Pennsylvania. His father died when Robert was just two years old, and the boy and his mother moved to Maine, where her family lived. Robert and his mother were very close, and she encouraged him to read and dream about adventure.

After graduating from Bowdoin College in 1877 with an engineering degree, Peary got a job with the Coast and Geodetic Survey. He moved to Washing-

Robert Peary

ton, D.C., to work as an engineer. In 1881, he joined
the Navy and made several trips to Nicaragua, where
he worked on a project to build a canal.

Peary loved to browse in bookstores. One day, he

found an old book about the Greenland Ice Cap, an 8,000-foot-thick sheet of ice in the Arctic that covers most of Greenland. The Ice Cap had never been explored. Peary was seized with the idea of crossing it.

He borrowed $500 from his mother and booked passage on a whaling ship that was traveling to Greenland. He made it to the island on June 6, 1886. For the next six weeks, Peary and a Danish sailor named Christian Maigaard explored a portion of the Ice Cap. On July 19, they were forced to give up their journey when

> "I shall find a way or make one."
> —Robert Peary

their food began to run out. However, Peary was pleased at his adventure. He was more determined than ever to explore the forbidding Arctic.

Matthew Henson

Matthew Alexander Henson was born on August 8, 1866, in Charles County, Maryland. An African American, he was the son of free-born sharecroppers. When Matthew was four years old, his family moved to Washington, D.C. Soon afterward, his parents died. Matthew and his siblings were raised by an uncle.

Matthew left home when he was 12 years old and went to work as a cabin boy on a ship. Over the next

Matthew Henson

five years, he traveled to China, Japan, and North Africa. During these trips, he studied geography, mathematics, history, and foreign languages with the help of the ship's captain. It was an extraordinary education for a young black man. When the captain died, however, Henson had to find other work.

For several years, Henson worked various jobs, but he longed to go back to sea. He was working as a clerk for a furrier when he meet Robert Peary. The two shared a love of adventure and travel, and became friends. When Peary asked the 22-year-old Henson to serve as his valet on his next expedition to Nicaragua, in 1888, Henson quickly agreed. On the trip, Henson acted as a mechanic, navigator, carpenter, and interpreter. His value to the expedition was much greater than expected.

> "The lure of the Arctic is tugging at my heart. To me the trail is calling."
> —Matthew Henson

To the Pole!

When Peary and Henson returned from Nicaragua, Peary turned his attention back to the Arctic. He asked Henson to accompany him on future expeditions, and Henson agreed. In 1891, they began a series of journeys to Greenland, with the goal of making their way all the way to the top of the world—the North Pole.

In 1893, Peary's wife accompanied them to Greenland. While there, she gave birth to their daughter, Marie—the first white child born in the Arctic Circle.

During another trip, Peary lost nine of his toes to frostbite. Yet he was not ready to quit. "A few toes aren't much to give to achieve the Pole," he said.

In 1904, Peary was given $100,000 to lead another expedition to the North Pole. He had a powerful ship built that could cut through ice. He also hired Eskimo drivers and sled-dog teams. On March 2, 1906, the expedition set off. On April 21, harsh conditions and lack of supplies forced Peary and Henson to turn back—only 174 miles from the North Pole.

Robert Peary was 50 years old. Time was running out for him. He decided to make one more attempt to reach the North Pole.

In July 1908, the explorers and their crew boarded their new ship, the *Roosevelt*, and set sail. After making a base camp in the Arctic, Peary left most of his men behind for a final push to the Pole. He chose Henson to go with him, saying, "Henson must go all the way. I can't make it without him."

By April 1909, Peary and Henson, along with four Eskimo helpers, were traveling across the frozen Arctic Ocean. For five days, they fought howling winds, thin ice, and temperatures that fell as low as 59 degrees below zero. Walking was especially difficult for Peary, because he had lost so many toes. Finally, on April 6, 1909, they reached their goal. "The Pole at last!" Robert Peary exclaimed. Matthew Henson was right beside him at that historic moment.

Heroes!

Peary and Henson were true heroes. When they returned to the U.S., however, they found that receiving a hero's welcome was not so simple. To their surprise, Dr. Frederick A. Cook, who had been with them on an earlier trip to Greenland, was claiming that he had made it to the North Pole in 1908.

Peary and Henson took this route to the North Pole in 1908-1909.

Although this claim was later proven false, Cook had already received many honors. The public was too confused to give Peary and Henson the notice they deserved right away.

Another problem was one of pride and racial prejudice. Henson found that Peary was not eager to share credit for their remarkable achievement. Also, because Henson was black, the media and the public ignored his accomplishments while heaping praise on the expedition's white leader.

Robert Peary was promoted to rear admiral in the Navy and received honors from scientific societies around the world. He died on February 20, 1920, and was buried in the national cemetery at Arlington, Virginia.

For Matthew Henson, recognition came slowly. In

TOPICAL TIDBIT

Cook's Claim

Dr. Frederick Cook's claim that he had beaten Peary and Henson to the North Pole shocked the explorers. They learned that it was not true. Henson talked with the two Eskimos who were supposed to have gone with Cook. They laughed and denied that it had happened. Back in the U.S., Peary protested Cook's claim and the National Geographic Society investigated. Cook's story was found to be a hoax. Cook disappeared for a while, but was later sent to jail for 14 years for selling fake stock in oil wells.

1912, he wrote a book about his adventures, entitled *A Negro Explorer at the North Pole*. The next year, President William Howard Taft ordered that Henson be given a position as a clerk at the U.S. Customs House in New York. Only late in life did Henson began receiving honors, including medals from the U.S. Congress, the Defense Department, and the Chicago Geographic Society. In 1954, President Dwight D. Eisenhower received Henson and his wife at the White House.

Henson lived the rest of his life quietly in New York City. He died on March 9, 1955, and was buried in the Bronx. In 1987, however, his body was moved to lie beside Peary's at Arlington. It is a fitting resting place for a man whose monument reads, "Matthew Alexander Henson, co-discoverer of the North Pole." ◇

LIFE EVENTS

1856
Robert Edwin Peary is born in Cresson, Pennsylvania.

1866
Matthew Alexander Henson is born in Charles County, Maryland.

1886
Peary makes his first trip to Greenland.

1888
Peary hires Henson for an expedition to Nicaragua, their first journey together.

1891
Henson accompanies Peary on an expedition to Greenland.

1909
Peary and Henson reach the North Pole.

1920
Robert Peary dies.

1955
Matthew Henson dies.

William Penn
Free to Worship
(born 1644 • died 1718)

William Penn could have lived an easy, privileged life in England. Instead, the founder of Pennsylvania and Delaware dedicated his life to creating a place where people could practice their religion without fear of imprisonment or death.

Born Into Trouble

William Penn was born in London, England, on October 14, 1644. At that time, England was being torn apart by a civil war between the king, who led the Church of England, and a religious group called Puritans, who opposed the king's religious ideas. William's father was a rear admiral in the navy, fighting under the Puritans' leader, Oliver Cromwell.

Cromwell and the Puritans won control of England in 1649. Six years later, Cromwell granted William's father an estate in Ireland. The family moved to Ireland in 1656. One day, young William learned about the Quaker religion from a family friend.

William Penn, meeting with Native Americans.

Quakers believe that people should live simple, quiet lives. They are against war and inequality. William soon became a firm believer in these ideals.

In 1660, William Penn enrolled at Christ Church College at Oxford University. Oxford's students were required to attend Church of England services. When Penn refused to do so, he was expelled in 1662.

Jailed for His Beliefs

By 1668, Penn had become a Quaker and was preaching around London. After he wrote a pamphlet attacking the Church of England's beliefs, he was arrested and thrown into prison at the Tower of London. During his imprisonment, he wrote *No Cross, No Crown*. That essay called for an end to religious persecution.

> "Any government is free to the people under it where the laws rule and the people are a party to the laws."
>
> —William Penn

Penn's father won his release eight months later. However, Penn continued to preach against the Church of England. Once again, he was arrested, but a jury refused to find him guilty. Five months after that, Penn was in prison again. This time, he had refused to sign an oath saying that he would not take up arms against the king.

Penn spent a few years organizing Quaker meetings in Germany and Holland. By the time he returned to England in 1672, laws against religious freedom were even stricter. Penn realized that he could no longer live in England if he wished to practice his religion.

Penn applied for a land grant in America. On March 4, 1681, he received a charter naming him Absolute Proprietor of "Penn's Woods," the area that is now the state of Pennsylvania. (The name *Penn-*

sylvania means "Penn's woods.") A year later, the land area that makes up present-day Delaware was added to Penn's grant.

A New Home

Penn set sail for America and arrived in New Castle, Delaware, late in 1682. He reached the site of present-day Philadelphia a few weeks later. For the next three years, Penn offered free land to settlers of every religion. The promise of being able to worship freely made Pennsylvania one of the most popular and successful colonies in America.

Penn was not able to spend much time in his new home. He soon had to go back to England to settle

TOPICAL TIDBIT

"Bushell's Case"

On August 14, 1670, London authorities padlocked the Quakers' meeting house to keep them out. When William Penn arrived, he simply preached to the several hundred people gathered in the street outside. The police arrested Penn for the false charge of inciting a riot. A jury, led by Edward Bushell, refused to convict him—so the judge ordered the jury imprisoned! In the end, however, the lord chief justice ruled that the jury was justified in reaching its own verdict, independent of the judge's will. "Bushell's Case" became a landmark in English legal history.

an argument over the colony's boundaries. While he was there, he got in trouble with the British government again, and was charged with treason (disloyalty to his country). The charges were dropped in 1693, but Penn did not return to America until 1699.

By the time Penn arrived back in Philadelphia, it had 5,000 residents and was the second-largest city in the American colonies. However, Penn had to return to England once again, in 1701. He had heard a rumor that colonies with individual owners, such as Pennsylvania, would be taken over by the British government. That didn't happen, but Penn soon found that he had other problems.

Penn owed a large sum of money to his former business manager, Philip Ford. Ford had recently died, and his family wanted the money back. They threatened to take

LIFE EVENTS

1644
William Penn is born in London, England.

1666
Penn leaves the Church of England to join the Quakers.

1669
Penn writes *No Cross, No Crown* while in prison for his religious views.

1670
A jury sets Penn free in what becomes known as "Bushell's Case."

1681
Penn receives a land grant for an area called Pennsylvania in the American colonies. He goes there in 1682.

1701
Penn returns to England for the final time. He dies in 1718.

Pennsylvania as payment. Penn asked the British government to buy his colony, but the government refused. Penn was arrested and taken to debtors' prison. Fortunately for him, he was able to borrow money from his Quaker friends to pay the debt.

After nine months in prison, Penn was released. Penn never made it back to Pennsylvania. He and his family moved into a small house in Ruscombe, England, where Penn died on July 30, 1718. His family kept the official charter of Pennsylvania until the American Revolution, when all the colonies became free states.

William Penn spent only about four years in the colony that bears his name. However, his vision of a land where people could worship freely and peacefully helped shape America into the land it is today. ◇

Oliver Hazard Perry
"The Enemy Is Ours!"
(born 1785 • died 1819)

Oliver Hazard Perry was so eager to command a naval fleet in battle against the British, he built his own ships. This resourceful officer became one of the greatest heroes of the War of 1812.

A Young Sailor

Oliver Hazard Perry was born in Kingston, Rhode Island, on August 23, 1785. His father had fought against the British during the American Revolution and later became a captain in the Navy. Oliver made his first trip to sea at age 15, traveling with his father.

By the time Oliver Perry was 17, he was an experienced Navy man. He was promoted to lieutenant and sailed to the Mediterranean to fight in the war between the U.S. and the Barbary pirates of northern Africa. The war was almost over by the time he got there, though, so he missed the chance to go into battle.

Perry returned to Rhode Island and was put in charge of building gunboats. These small ships were

used to keep English trading ships from reaching U.S. ports. Knowing how to build the boats would come in handy for Perry in the future.

The Battle of Lake Erie

Perry finally got a chance to go into battle when the U.S. began fighting against Great Britain in the

War of 1812. On February 13, 1813, Perry was ordered to take control of Lake Erie from the British. There was just one problem: When Perry reported to his post, there were no ships for him to command.

Perry got right to work. Despite the fact that it was winter and the ground was covered with snow and ice, he and his men began building ships. They used every bit of material that they could find, including barn doors. Perry and his crew built five ships, and were able to get four more sent to them from Lake Ontario.

By July 4, Perry's ships were ready to sail. They traveled to the site of present-day Sandusky, Ohio, and waited for the British to arrive. On September 10, 1813, the Battle of Lake Erie began.

> "The chief merit of the American commander [Perry] and his followers was indomitable courage, and determination not to be beaten."
> —Theodore Roosevelt

Perry's ships were outnumbered, but his guns were more powerful than the guns on the British ships. The two navies fired mercilessly at each other all morning. Perry's flagship, the *Lawrence*, was badly damaged, and most of its crew was killed or wounded. However, Perry refused to give up. He simply moved onto another of his ships, the *Niagara*, and kept on fighting.

As the hours passed, the British ships suffered

tremendous damage. At three in the afternoon, the British captain finally surrendered. Perry sent word of the victory to General William Henry Harrison, commander of the American forces in the Great Lakes. "We have met the enemy and they are ours!" Perry wrote.

A National Hero

Perry was only 27 years old when he won the Battle of Lake Erie. Until then, few people outside of the Navy had ever heard of him. His victory at Lake Erie made him a national hero. The U.S. Congress awarded him $80,000 in prize money and decorated him with a specially made gold medal.

The British also admired Perry because he treated

TOPICAL TIDBIT

The Battle of the Thames

The Battle of the Thames on October 5, 1813, was the deciding fight of the War of 1812. After the British were defeated at Lake Erie, they retreated to Ontario, Canada. U.S. General William Henry Harrison followed with an army of 3,500 troops. Seven hundred British troops were assisted by 1,000 Indian warriors led by the great Tecumseh. The armies clashed on Canada's Thames River. Tecumseh and his men fought furiously, but after he was killed, the battle was all but over. The British fled or surrendered.

his prisoners very well. He even spent $1,000 of his own money to make sure that they received excellent care. Perry also looked out for the wounded British captain and other casualties.

After the Battle of Lake Erie, Perry served directly under General Harrison. Perry even fought on horseback in the Battle of the Thames, which ended any threat of invasion from British troops in Canada. Whether on land or sea, Perry was a powerful fighter.

After the war ended, he served in the Mediterranean and the West Indies. Oliver Hazard Perry died of yellow fever on his 34th birthday, August 23, 1819, after a mission to Venezuela. He was buried in Port-of-Spain, Trinidad, but six years later his body was reburied in Newport, Rhode Island. The man who had changed the course of U.S. history at the Battle of Lake Erie had finally come home. ◇

LIFE EVENTS

1785
Oliver Hazard Perry is born in Kingston, Rhode Island.

1812-1814
The U.S. and Great Britain oppose each other in the War of 1812.

1813
Perry leads his men to victory in the Battle of Lake Erie.

1816
Perry commands the U.S.S. *Java* in the Mediterranean Sea.

1819
Perry dies of yellow fever aboard ship.

John J. Pershing
General of the Armies
(born 1860 • died 1948)

Few army leaders have received as many honors as John "Black Jack" Pershing. His leadership during World War I made a difference on the battlefield and gave him a reputation as a courageous and fair commander.

A Simple Childhood

John Joseph Pershing was born on September 13, 1860, near Laclede, Missouri. His father laid track for the railroad, and also had a small farm. The family had little money and lived in a simple shanty.

John worked hard on his father's farm, and soon had a reputation as a dependable, sensible young man. He had no interest in being a soldier, but he did want a good education. So when he heard that an exam was being given for admission to the U.S. Military Academy at West Point, he decided to take the test. John was admitted to the Academy, and graduated in 1886. Although John Pershing wasn't

the best student there, he was elected president of the class for his excellent leadership qualities.

Early Army Days

After leaving West Point, Pershing was assigned to a fort in New Mexico. He later served in other western forts and fought several battles against hostile Native Americans.

In 1891, at age 31, Pershing became a professor of Military Science at the University of Nebraska. While teaching, he also studied law and graduated from the law school in 1893. He later taught at West Point and worked for the War Department.

Pershing got his nickname, "Black Jack," early in his military career, while serving with an African American unit called the Buffalo Soldiers. Unlike many white officers of that time, Pershing respected and admired black soldiers. Later, as a commander in World War I, he made sure that black soldiers were assigned to combat, rather than being limited to less important duties.

Pershing was decorated for bravery during the Spanish-American War of 1898. During the early 1900s, he served on many overseas assignments, including the Philippines and Japan. By 1916, he was a brigadier general,

> "His ramrod bearing, steely gaze, and confidence-inspiring jaw created almost a caricature of nature's soldier."
>
> —General Douglas MacArthur

and back in the U.S. fighting in a border war with Mexico. Pershing's wealth of experience soon came in handy: During World War I, he tackled the most challenging and important role of his career.

The American Expeditionary Forces

When the U.S. declared war on Germany in 1917 and entered World War I, Pershing was sent to Europe. His job was to command the American Expeditionary Force (AEF) and help French and British troops fight against Germany. This was a difficult job, because the U.S. had no standing army. It needed time to train men before sending them into battle. Also, France and Great Britain expected U.S. soldiers to fight with their armies. However, Pershing insisted that U.S. troops fight in their own units, under their own officers and their own flag.

Pershing was able to assemble an army of 500,000 men by 1918. Their most important battle was fought at Saint-Mihiel in France in September 1918. When the Americans won, they became the first U.S

TOPICAL TIDBIT

"Our Black Heroes"

The charge up San Juan Hill outside Santiago, Cuba, on July 1, 1898, is the most famous battle of the Spanish-American War. It made Theodore Roosevelt and his Rough Riders famous. But the Rough Riders did not do it alone. The African American soldiers of the 9th and 10th Cavalry were right beside them. Five of the cavalry men won the Congressional Medal of Honor. John J. Pershing, who commanded the 10th Cavalry, said proudly, "We officers could have taken our black heroes in our arms."

army to win a victory in World War I without any help from European soldiers.

Pershing became famous for his strict, yet fair, leadership, and was much admired by his men and the American people. In 1919, after the end of the war, Congress created the rank of General of the Armies for Pershing. This title made him the highest-ranking military officer in U.S. history.

After the War

Pershing remained an important figure after World War I. He served as Army Chief of Staff from 1921 until his retirement in 1924. During this time, Pershing designed the modern U.S. Army.

In 1931, Pershing published a book about his wartime experiences. *My Experience in the World War* won a Pulitzer Prize and became a best-seller.

Pershing's health failed in

LIFE EVENTS

1860
John Joseph Pershing is born near Laclede, Missouri.

1898
Pershing commands a unit of black troops during the Spanish-American War.

1916
Pershing leads U.S. troops against Pancho Villa, a Mexican rebel.

1917
The U.S. enters World War I. Pershing builds a U.S. army that turns the tide for the Allies.

1919
Congress creates the title of General of the Armies for Pershing.

1931
Pershing's auto-biography wins a Pulitzer Prize. He dies in 1948.

the late 1930s, and he was forced to retire from public life. However, U.S. military leaders often asked for his advice, especially in preparing the military for another war.

John J. Pershing died on July 15, 1948, in Washington, D.C. He was 87 years old. Before his death, he had been offered a special memorial in the national cemetery at Arlington, but he refused it. Instead, Pershing was buried with ordinary soldiers at Arlington, with the same, simple government-issued headstone as his men. ◇

Molly Pitcher
(Mary Ludwig Hays McCauly)
Hero of the American Revolution
(born 1754 • died 1832)

When Mary Ludwig was growing up in England's American colonies during the 1760s, she had no idea that they would soon become a new country called the United States of America. She could not have guessed that it would take a war for the colonies to win independence—or that, as "Molly Pitcher," she would become one of that war's most beloved heroes.

Growing Up

The Ludwigs were German immigrants who had moved to Great Britain's American colonies. Their daughter, Mary, was born on the family's dairy farm in Trenton, New Jersey, on October 13, 1754. Mary— or Molly, as she was called—spent her childhood carrying buckets of milk, herding cows out to pasture and back, and helping her family in other ways.

   As Molly was growing up, many colonists were
unhappy about British rule—especially about taxes.
The 1764 Sugar Act raised taxes on products that
colonists shipped to and from Great Britain. The 1765
Stamp Act required colonists to pay taxes on newspapers, legal documents, and other business papers.

As the colonists grew angrier, they began to talk about going to war to win independence from Great Britain.

In 1769, when Molly was 15 years old, she moved to Carlisle, Pennsylvania. There she worked as a servant to a doctor. Later, she met a barber named William Hays, and the two of them married.

Molly Goes to War

In April 1775, war broke out between Britain and the American colonies. The first battles were fought in Massachusetts, but the American Revolution soon spread to the other colonies. Molly's husband joined the colonial army in December 1775. Like many soldiers' wives of that time, Molly followed the army as it marched. The women cooked, cleaned, and took care of sick or injured men.

On June 28, 1778, the American and British armies met at Monmouth, New Jersey. There, on a day that one report called "one of the hottest days ever," the two armies fought the Battle of Monmouth.

"While in the act of reaching for a cartridge, a cannon shot from the enemy passed directly between her legs without doing any other damage than carrying away all the lower part of her petticoat."

—Joseph Plumb Martin, a soldier from Connecticut

The soldiers suffered greatly in the terrible heat. Along with those who fell from wounds suffered in the battle, many men passed out from the heat. One of these men was Molly's husband. He was in charge of firing a cannon, but fainted in the hot sun.

When Molly saw how the American soldiers were suffering, she went to work. The strength she had gained as a girl lugging buckets of milk around the dairy farm served her well that day. She carried buckets of water onto the battlefield and ladled out drinks to the thirsty soldiers. Grateful troops called her "Molly Pitcher" as she refilled her buckets at a nearby stream and went back to the battlefield time and time again. According to some stories, she even took over for her fallen husband, helping to load and fire his cannon.

TOPICAL TIDBIT

Margaret Corbin

Margaret Cochran Corbin was the first woman to receive a pension from the U.S. government as a disabled soldier. She relieved her slain husband at the cannon at the battle at Fort Washington on November 16, 1776. The British fire was murderous and Corbin suffered serious injury. Eventually, the British captured the fort, but the wounded were freed. Corbin never completely recovered from her wounds. She died in 1783. Today, she is buried near the site of the battle in Fort Tryon Park in New York City.

Molly Pitcher's name was not forgotten after the battle. The story of her efforts was retold many times. It may even have become mixed up with stories of Margaret Corbin, another woman who followed her husband to war. When Corbin's husband was killed during the 1776 attack on Fort Washington, New York, she kept firing his cannon until she was wounded.

A Place in History

Whether or not she ever fired a shot, Molly Pitcher became known as a hero of the Battle of Monmouth. Some years after the war, William Hays died and Molly married George McCauley. It was to Mary McCauley that, in 1822, Pennsylvania awarded a pension of $40 a year for wartime bravery. After she died on January 22, 1832, a cannon and a sculpture were placed at her grave in Carlisle, Pennsylvania, to honor her. A monument to Molly Pitcher also stands at the battle site in Monmouth, New Jersey. ◇

LIFE EVENTS

1754
Mary Ludwig, called Molly, is born in Trenton, New Jersey.

1775
William Hays, Molly's husband, volunteers for the colonial army.

1778
At the Battle of Monmouth, Molly earns the nickname Molly Pitcher.

1822
The state of Pennsylvania awards her a pension of $40 a year.

1832
Molly Pitcher dies in Carlisle, Pennsylvania.

Pocahontas
Native American Legend
(born 1595? • died 1617)

Sometimes one simple act of compassion can make a person a hero. That is what happened to Pocahontas, a young Native American girl who saved a man's life—and became a legend.

A Carefree Childhood—Then Change

Pocahontas was born around 1595 in Virginia. Her father was a powerful Native American chief named Powhatan. Pocahontas's real name was Matoaka, but her father called her Pocahontas, which means "playful one."

Pocahontas spent most of her childhood playing. She enjoyed running through the woods and swimming in the cool rivers and streams of her home. In those days, Native Americans had the land to themselves. A few years later, however, that changed.

When Pocahontas was 10 or 12 years old, the first Englishmen came to America. Along with the other Native Americans, Pocahontas watched the newcom-

In this artist's idea of Pocahontas's heroic moment, she kneels before her father, Powhatan, as a warrior with an axe stands over John Smith.

ers build homes and a fort in a settlement that the English called Jamestown. Pocahontas probably wondered if these strange-looking people were friends or enemies. Some of the Native Americans traded with the new settlers, but others were afraid of them.

The Rescue

One day, some of Powhatan's tribe captured Captain John Smith, one of Jamestown's leaders. Powhatan decided to kill Smith. As several warriors got ready to beat Smith to death with heavy clubs, Pocahontas ran forward. As Smith later told it, she threw her arms around Smith's head to protect him. Then she begged her father not to hurt the Englishman. Because there was an old custom that said that a woman could save a prisoner's life, Powhatan agreed.

"Pocahontas was the instrument to preserve this colony from death, famine, and utter confusion."
—Captain John Smith, 1616

Smith stayed with Powhatan's people for a while, and he and Pocahontas became good friends. After he returned to Jamestown, Pocahontas visited Smith. She took corn and other food to the settlers. If not for her help, the Jamestown settlers probably would have starved to death because they had run out of food.

Among the English

In 1609, Smith was injured when a box of gunpowder exploded. He returned to England to get well. After he left, Pocahontas didn't visit Jamestown as often as she had before. Some historians believe that Powhatan would not allow her to go to Jamestown because the Native Americans and the Englishmen had begun to fight with each other.

In 1612, an Englishman named Samuel Argall captured Pocahontas. Argall thought that he could force Powhatan to stop fighting the English if they held his daughter captive. Powhatan loved his daughter, but he refused Argall's terms. So Pocahontas stayed in Jamestown. She began to wear English clothes and follow English habits. In time, she became a Christian and changed her name to Rebecca.

In 1614, Pocahontas married an English settler named John Rolfe. A year later, she gave birth to a boy, who was named Thomas. By then, many people

TOPICAL TIDBIT

Pocahontas's Men

What became of the men in Pocahontas's life? Her father, Powhatan, died in 1618, a year before his daughter. John Smith made one more successful trip to America, and mapped the coast of New England. On another trip, he was captured by pirates but escaped and eventually returned to England. After Pocahontas died, her husband, John Rolfe, returned to Virginia and remarried. He died during an Indian attack in 1622. Thomas Rolfe, son of Pocahontas and John Rolfe, was raised by an uncle in England. He returned to Virginia to claim his family property in 1640.

in England had heard about Pocahontas and wanted to meet her. So she and John Rolfe decided to take their new son to London, to visit Rolfe's family there.

Off to England

Pocahontas was a sensation in England. People came from miles around to meet the "Indian Princess," as she was called. She even met Queen Anne, wife of England's King James I. However, the high point of Pocahontas's trip was when she saw her old friend, Captain John Smith, again. The two, who had not seen each other for eight years, spent hours talking.

In 1617, the Rolfes decided to go back home to Virginia. However, their ship had barely left London when Pocahontas became very sick. The ship landed in Gravesend, England, where Pocahontas died.

LIFE EVENTS

About 1595
Pocahontas is born to the Powhatan tribe near present-day Jamestown, Virginia.

1607
Pocahontas rescues Captain John Smith, a Jamestown settler, from Powhatan warriors.

1613
Captain Samuel Argall takes Pocahontas hostage.

1614
Pocahontas marries John Rolfe, an English settler.

1616
Pocahontas, her husband, and their baby son visit England.

1617
While in England, Pocahontas becomes ill and dies.

A Noble Line

Historians are not sure how much, if any, of the story of Pocahontas saving John Smith's life is true. They do agree, however, that her help was important to the Jamestown colony.

Years later, Pocahontas's son, Thomas, returned to Virginia and became an important settler in the new colony. Through him, many people claim to be descended from Pocahontas, the Indian Princess. ◇

Ernie Pyle
War Correspondent
(born 1900 • died 1945)

For many Americans, World War II was hard to understand. Then Ernie Pyle traveled to Europe's war-torn cities and began writing about the people he met and the things he saw. His simple, down-to-earth writing style gave Americans a clearer idea of what they were fighting for.

A Restless Young Man

Ernest Taylor Pyle was born on August 3, 1900, in the family home in Dana, Indiana. His parents were farmers, but Ernie never liked living and working on the farm. Instead, he dreamed of faraway places where life was more exciting.

In 1919, he enrolled at Indiana University. He soon discovered that he had a natural talent for writing. By his sophomore year, Ernie Pyle was writing for the college newspaper. He realized that journalists didn't just report the news; they could also enlighten and inspire people through their writing.

In 1923, Pyle quit school for a job as a reporter for a newspaper in La Porte, Indiana. Just a few months later, he moved on to a better job with the *Washington Daily News* in Washington, D.C. Pyle worked a number of jobs at the *News*, including reporting, editing copy, and writing a daily aviation column.

In 1935, Pyle became a roving reporter for the *News*. This job was perfect for his restless spirit. It allowed him to make his own schedule, travel to different places, talk with unusual and interesting people, and express his feelings in print. Within a year, Pyle had traveled more than 29,000 miles and visited every state. His columns were published in 24 different newspapers around the country.

The World at War

By 1940, Europe was being torn apart by World War II. In November, Pyle moved to London to write about life during wartime. At the time, London and

TOPICAL TIDBIT

Bill Mauldin

Bill Mauldin was another newspaperman beloved by the men who fought World War II—but Mauldin's work was cartooning. Beginning in 1943 in Sicily, he drew cartoons for the U.S. Army newspaper, *Stars and Stripes*, that showed how the soldiers at the front line really lived. "Fresh American troops flushed with victory . . ." said one caption—while the picture showed men who were tired and covered with mud. Many of Mauldin's cartoons featured two battle-weary characters named Willie and Joe, who grew popular with both the soldiers and the folks back home.

other parts of England were being heavily bombed by Germany. Pyle was deeply affected by the bombings. He wrote moving columns describing his experience. By the time he returned to Washington in March 1941, he had become one of the most popular newspaper columnists in America.

In November 1942, Pyle and a number of other journalists joined U.S. troops in Algeria. Unlike the other reporters, Pyle didn't stay in the officers' quarters and report on military strategy. He stayed with the soldiers on the front lines and wrote about their everyday lives—how they washed their dishes with sand, what kind of food they ate, what it was like to see a friend killed in battle. His columns were full of details about these ordinary young men he called "the guys that wars can't be won without." In turn, the soldiers treated Pyle like a beloved buddy. His columns made the soldiers feel that their sacrifices were appreciated by the folks back home.

> "There was nothing macho about the war at all. We were a bunch of scared kids who had a job to do."
> —Ernie Pyle

By 1943, Pyle was the most popular war correspondent in America. His columns appeared in hundreds of newspapers and were read by millions of people. The columns were also published as a book, called *Here Is Your War*. (Three other books of Pyle's writings were published as well: *Ernie Pyle in England*, *Brave Men*, and *Last Chapter*.)

Pyle didn't care about being famous, though. When he returned to America for a brief vacation in 1943, he couldn't wait to go back to Europe and rejoin the soldiers there.

A New Front

In 1944, Pyle received news that he had won a Pulitzer Prize for distinguished correspondence. Later that year, he wrote his last column from Europe. Then he headed to the other side of the world to write about the soldiers who were fighting against Japan on islands in the Pacific Ocean.

While in the Pacific, Pyle wrote about the 77th Infantry Division's invasion of Okinawa on April 1, 1945. A few days later, he traveled to a

LIFE EVENTS

1900
Ernest Taylor Pyle is born in Dana, Indiana.

1923
Pyle quits school to work full-time as a reporter.

1940
Pyle's reporting from the bombardment of England begins to make him the most popular columnist in America.

1942
Pyle joins U.S. troops in Algeria.

1944
Pyle wins the Pulitzer Prize for his war columns.

1945
The Story of G.I. Joe, a movie based on Pyle's writing, is released. Pyle is killed by Japanese sniper fire on the island of Ie Shima.

Japanese island called Ie Shima to write about an invasion taking place there. On April 18, while he was driving down a road on the island, he was killed by machine-gun fire. He was 44 years old.

News of Ernie Pyle's death stunned America. President Harry S. Truman honored him as a man who "told the story of the American fighting man as American fighting men wanted it told."

Pyle was buried on Ie Shima, along with U.S. soldiers also killed on the island. Later, his body was moved to the National Memorial Cemetery of the Pacific, in Hawaii. A memorial marker stands at the place on Ie Shima where he was killed. "At this spot," says the plaque, "the 77th Infantry Division lost a buddy. Ernie Pyle. 18 April 1945." ◇

A. Philip Randolph
Labor Leader
(born 1889 • died 1979)

For many years, African Americans were not represented by labor unions. A. Philip Randolph changed that, and helped win fair and equal treatment for black workers all over America.

Racial Tensions

Asa Philip Randolph was born on April 15, 1889, in Crescent City, Florida. When he was two years old, his family moved to Jacksonville, Florida. Jacksonville was one of the most integrated cities in the South. Black and whites lived in the same communities, rode the same streetcars, and shopped in the same stores. Blacks also were able to serve as city council members, judges, and in other positions of authority. However, things changed during the early 1900s, as segregation laws erased many freedoms and discrimination flourished.

The Randolph family was very poor. Despite their poverty, Asa's father, a minister, made sure that his

children were proud and self-confident. He encouraged them to stand up to discrimination and to be
leaders in helping others.

Education was also important in the Randolph
family. Asa and his older brother did well in school,

but there wasn't enough money for them to go to college. Instead, Asa worked at a variety of jobs while he tried to decide what he wanted to do with his life.

Organizing Black Workers

In 1911, 22-year-old A. Philip Randolph moved to Harlem, a black community in New York City. He worked at a number of jobs while attending City College at night. In 1917, Randolph and a friend, Chandler Owen, started a magazine called *The Messenger*. It called for more opportunities for blacks in industry. In those days, that was a radical position to take. The government said that *The Messenger* was "the most dangerous of all the Negro publications," because it called for racial equality at home and spoke out against blacks fighting in World War I.

Randolph wanted to see blacks gain political power. He realized that this could happen only if black workers belonged to labor unions. However, most labor unions refused to admit black members.

In 1925, Randolph was asked to advise a group of railroad porters about how to start their own union. Railroad porters were men who carried luggage and performed other services for passengers. They all worked for the Pullman Company, which operated the sleeping cars used on long-distance trains. The porters felt that they were underpaid and badly treated. They were so excited by Randolph's speech that they asked him to lead their new union. He agreed, and more than 200 members signed up at the first meeting.

By the end of 1926, the Brotherhood of Sleeping Car Porters had more than 5,700 members all over the country. They represented more than half of all the porters who worked for the Pullman Company.

The Pullman Company was very angry about the new union. Union leaders were threatened and beaten, and porters who were seen with union organizers were fired. The Pullman Company also sent letters to the black community criticizing Randolph and saying that he was trying to deny jobs to black workers.

> "Let the nation and the world know the meaning of our numbers. We are the advance guard of a massive moral revolution for jobs and freedom."
>
> —A. Philip Randolph, at the March on Washington, 1963

Randolph himself had so little money that he had only one suit to wear, and he and his wife relied on their friends to bring them food.

Despite these hardships, the Brotherhood grew stronger. In 1937, the union won its first major contract with the Pullman Company. Randolph was recognized as one of the most important leaders in the black community and in the U.S. labor movement.

More Victories

Randolph's victories with the Brotherhood were only the beginning of his fight for equality. During the 1940s, Randolph called for the government to pass legislation that prohibited discrimination. His efforts led to the passage of presidential orders banning discrimination in defense industries and federal bureaus (1941) and ending segregation in the military (1948).

Later, Randolph served as vice president of America's largest union, the AFL-CIO, from 1957 to 1977. He also served as the first president of the Negro American Labor Council from 1960 to 1966.

Randolph's most dramatic accomplishment, how-

TOPICAL TIDBIT

The March That Finally Came to Pass

A. Philip Randolph had dreamed for years of a march on Washington. He originally called one for July 1, 1941, to demand racial equality in the nation's defense plants. "We loyal Negro American citizens demand the right to work and fight for our country," he said. President Franklin D. Roosevelt was worried that the U.S. might soon have to join World War II, already being fought in Europe. He asked Randolph to call off the march. When he refused, Roosevelt issued an executive order banning discrimination in defense plants. With that victory won, Randolph tackled other problems—and put off his march for another 22 years.

---

ever, was directing the March on Washington for Jobs and Freedom. On August 28, 1963, nearly 250,000 people gathered on the Mall in the nation's capital to demonstrate for equal rights for blacks. Millions of Americans, watching on TV, saw the power and purpose of the civil-rights movement for the first time. No one would forget the "I Have a Dream" speech that Martin Luther King Jr. made that day. It remains one of the most important speeches in American history.

Randolph's health began to fail during the 1960s. He resigned as president of the Brotherhood in 1968, after 43 years in office. A. Philip Randolph died in New York City on May 16, 1979, at the age of 90. His life had set an example of how dignity and courage could triumph over ignorance and injustice. ◇

LIFE EVENTS

1889
Asa Philip Randolph is born in Crescent City, Florida.

1925
Randolph is founding president of the Brotherhood of Sleeping Car Porters.

1938
Randolph leaves the American Federation of Labor, protesting discrimination.

1941
Randolph's actions lead to the federal ban of job discrimination in defense industries.

1963
Randolph directs the March on Washington for Jobs and Freedom.

1968
Randolph retires from the Brotherhood. He dies in 1979 at age 90.

Paul Revere
The Midnight Rider
(born 1735 • died 1818)

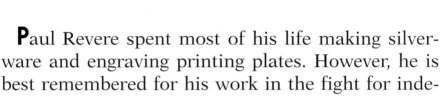

Paul Revere spent most of his life making silverware and engraving printing plates. However, he is best remembered for his work in the fight for independence for the American colonies—especially for his heroic, late-night ride on the eve of the American Revolution.

Paul Revere, Silversmith

Paul Revere was born on January 1, 1735, in Boston, Massachusetts. His father was a silversmith, and Paul learned the family business from him. He earned a reputation as a fine craftsman, and the bowls, pitchers, cups, and tea sets he made were prized by the most important families in Boston.

Revere was also interested in politics. He drew political cartoons and engraved printing plates with political scenes. His most famous engraving showed the 1770 Boston Massacre, when British soldiers fired on a group of angry colonists.

Talk of Revolution

During the early 1770s, many American colonists were angry at Great Britain. They resented having to pay high taxes and follow the laws of a country 3,000 miles away. Revere was among the first to join the movement for independence. He began carrying messages between revolutionaries in the Boston area.

In 1773, the English government passed another harsh tax law, the Tea Act. It would force colonists to buy all their tea from one source: the British-owned East India Company. On the night of December 16, three ships full of East India tea sat in Boston Harbor. A group of about 60 Boston citizens, including Paul Revere, disguised themselves as Mohawk Indians, boarded the ships, and threw about $90,000 worth of tea into the water. Colonists referred to the incident with dark humor as the Boston Tea Party.

England was furious. The British Parliament passed new laws to punish the rebels. Among other things, these laws—known as the Intolerable Acts—shut down the port of Boston until the cost of the tea was paid back. For many Americans, this was the last straw. In September 1774, a group of colonists formed the First Continental Congress in Philadelphia, Pennsylvania. They declared that they would no longer obey British laws.

The Midnight Ride of Paul Revere

In Massachusetts, colonists were ready to fight. Groups of men trained as soldiers. They called themselves "the Minutemen," because they could be ready to fight in a minute. However, it seemed as if these small groups of soldiers would stand little chance against the large British army.

On the night of April 18, 1775, 700 British soldiers began marching from Boston to Concord, Massachusetts. Revere and two other patriots, William Dawes and Samuel Prescott, had to alert the people of Concord that the soldiers were approaching. They waited as American spies watched the roads for the British army. Would the soldiers be coming by land, or would they cross the Charles River by boat?

Finally, one of the American spies climbed to the tower of the Old North Church in Boston. He hung two lit lanterns in the tower so Revere could see them. This was a signal telling Revere that the British army was traveling by ship.

Revere climbed onto his horse. He rode all night, trying to reach Concord before the troops did. As he

TOPICAL TIDBIT

"The Midnight Ride"

Many generations of Americans best know the story of Paul Revere from a famous poem—and have memorized its opening lines: "Listen, my children, and you shall hear of the midnight ride of Paul Revere." Written by Henry Wadsworth Longfellow, "Paul Revere's Ride" was published in the *Atlantic Monthly* magazine in 1863. The poem has some errors. Longfellow's story has Revere making it all the way to Concord without being stopped by soldiers. The poet never mentions Revere's fellow riders—not even Samuel Prescott, who *did* make it to Concord.

passed through the towns and villages along the way, he shouted warnings, telling people that British regular troops were headed their way. Farmers and shop workers quickly got dressed and prepared to fight. Revere stopped in the town of Lexington to warn two of the American Revolution's most important leaders, Sam Adams and John Hancock, that

> ### "The Regulars are coming out!"
> —Paul Revere's warning, April 18-19, 1775

soldiers were coming to arrest them. Adams and Hancock got away just ahead of the soldiers.

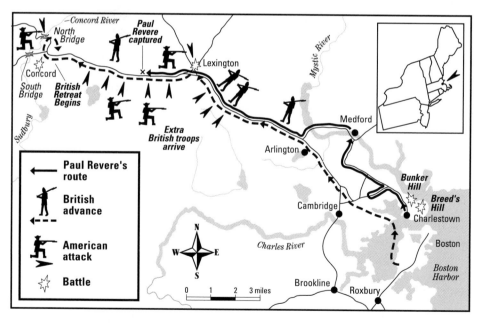

Paul Revere's midnight ride took him this way on April 18-19, 1775.

Revere didn't make it all the way to Concord. A group of British soldiers captured him and held him prisoner for a short time. However, Prescott did make it to Concord in time to warn the citizens. When the British arrived in Lexington, a group of Minutemen was waiting for them. The American Revolution had begun.

Wartime and After

During the Revolution, Paul Revere commanded forts in Boston Harbor and Maine. In 1780, he went back to his life as a silversmith. He engraved printing plates and printed money for the Massachusetts Congress. He also designed the Massachusetts state seal, still used today. He died in Boston on May 10, 1818. His famous ride lives on in poetry and folklore, making him a true American hero. ◇

LIFE EVENTS

1735
Paul Revere is born in Boston, Massachusetts.

1773
Revere takes part in the Boston Tea Party.

1775
Revere makes his famous midnight ride to warn citizens that the English army is on its way.

1776
Revere is put in command of Castle William in Boston Harbor.

1818
Revere dies in Boston.

1863
Henry Wadsworth Longfellow makes Revere forever famous in his poem "Paul Revere's Ride."

Eddie Rickenbacker
Flying Ace
(born 1890 • died 1973)

Eddie Rickenbacker became famous as one of the most daring fighter pilots of World War I. His bravery and style made him one of the war's most popular heroes.

Fast Cars

Edward Vernon Rickenbacker was born in Columbus, Ohio, on October 8, 1890. His parents had emigrated from Switzerland. When Eddie was 13, his father was killed in a construction accident. To help his family, Eddie left school and lied about his age to get a job in a glass factory.

Eddie loved machines and wanted to work with them. He started working in a garage, and later for a car manufacturer. By the time he was 17, Eddie was a well-paid auto mechanic and salesman, even though he had only a sixth-grade education.

In those days, car manufacturers often promoted their cars by racing them. Eddie enjoyed racing, and

was soon a star in the field. In 1911, 21-year-old Eddie Rickenbacker got his first chance to race in the famous Indianapolis 500. By 1916, he was ranked third nationally among U.S. racers, and had set a world record for speed driving.

Taking to the Skies

World War I had broken out in Europe in 1914, but the U.S. did not join the fighting until April 1917. One month later, Rickenbacker was getting ready to compete in the Indianapolis 500 another time, when he received a phone call that would change his life. General John J. Pershing, who was leading the American Expeditionary Forces (AEF) in World War I, wanted Rickenbacker to be his driver in France. Rickenbacker, who was very patriotic, jumped at this unique chance to serve his country.

> **"I'll fight like a wildcat."**
> —Eddie Rickenbacker's motto

While in France, Rickenbacker also worked for Colonel William "Billy" Mitchell, the chief air officer for the AEF. Mitchell encouraged Rickenbacker to apply for pilot training. In March 1918, Rickenbacker received his first assignment as a combat pilot.

Airplanes were only 15 years old in 1918, and World War I was the first time they were used in combat. Aerial combat—planes doing battle in the air—was known as a dogfight. Rickenbacker's first dogfight was on April 19, 1918, when he shot down a German plane. Three weeks later, he was nearly shot down by the enemy, but managed to fly his damaged plane back to the American line before crash-landing on his own airfield.

In September, Rickenbacker was promoted to captain and put in command of a squadron of fighter planes. At first, the other pilots didn't like him because he was from a poor, working-class background. However, Rickenbacker soon won their respect. The other pilots especially appreciated the fact that their captain never asked them to take any risks that he wouldn't take himself.

By the end of the war, Rickenbacker was a flying ace, with 26 victories against German airplanes and balloons—more than any other pilot. He was called America's "ace of aces."

Rickenbacker returned home to a hero's welcome. He was awarded the Congressional Medal of Honor,

TOPICAL TIDBIT

Colonel Billy Mitchell

During World War I and for many years afterward, the U.S. did not have an Air Force that was separate from the Army and Navy. Colonel Billy Mitchell fought the War Department officials for years to create one. He made a lot of people angry along the way. In 1925, Mitchell publicly criticized the War Department for losing a Navy airship, and the Army put him on trial. But Billy Mitchell was a hero to many Americans. His dream of an Air Force finally came to pass, and he was awarded a special Congressional Medal of Honor in 1946.

the highest honor in the U.S. military. Parades and other events were held in his honor. The "ace of aces" also published a book about his wartime experiences.

After the War

After leaving the armed forces, Rickenbacker continued his work in the fields of automobiles and aviation. He worked for General Motors, and later became general manager of the company's Eastern Air Lines. When General Motors sold the airline in 1938, Rickenbacker was able to raise enough money to buy it. Under his control, Eastern grew from a small, unprofitable airline into one of the nation's most successful carriers.

Crash Landing

During World War II, the U.S. government called Rickenbacker back into service. He took a job inspecting air bases all over the world. One of those journeys turned into a dangerous adventure. On October 21, 1942, Rickenbacker and seven other men were aboard a B-17 bomber from Hawaii to New Guinea. The plane crashed into the Pacific Ocean. He and the other men were stranded on rafts in the middle of the ocean.

Everyone in America thought that Eddie Rickenbacker was dead. However, after drifting for 24 days and living on rainwater, a sea gull, and some fish, the survivors—including Rickenbacker—were spotted by an American plane and rescued. Only one of the men died. In 1943, Rickenbacker published a book about that ordeal, *Seven Came Through*.

After World War II, Rickenbacker returned to Eastern Air Lines, where he served as director and chairman of the board until 1963. He died in Zurich, Switzerland, on July 27, 1973, at age 82.

During his life, Eddie Rickenbacker was not only a brave flying ace and war hero, but his work with Eastern Air Lines helped shape the future of commercial aviation. ◇

LIFE EVENTS

1890
Edward Vernon Rickenbacker is born in Columbus, Ohio.

1918
Rickenbacker fights the first of many dogfights over Europe during World War I.

1919
Fighting the Flying Circus, Rickenbacker's book about the war, is published.

1930
Rickenbacker is awarded the Congressional Medal of Honor.

1942
Rickenbacker's plane is forced down over the Pacific. He and six others survive 24 days at sea.

1973
Rickenbacker dies in Zurich, Switzerland.

Sally Ride
First American
Woman in Space
(born 1951)

Until June 18, 1983, every U.S. astronaut who went into space was a man. Sally Ride was the first American woman to leave Earth and soar into space.

An Active Childhood

Sally Kristen Ride was born on May 26, 1951, in Los Angeles, California. Her parents were both teachers. Sally and her younger sister were always encouraged to do their best, even if that meant acting differently than society expected girls to behave.

Sally loved sports, and often talked her way into playing football or baseball with neighborhood boys. Her favorite sport was tennis. By the time she was in high school, she was nationally ranked. Tennis star Billie Jean King saw Sally play, and suggested that she quit school and turn professional. However, Sally had many other interests that she wanted to explore.

One of those interests was science. Sally took as many science classes as she could in high school. Later, she attended California's Stanford University, partly because it had an excellent tennis team, and partly because it had one of the best science programs in the country. After graduating in 1973 with a degree in physics, she did graduate work in astronomy at the University of California at Los Angeles (UCLA).

Reaching the Stars

One day in 1978, while reading the UCLA newspaper, Sally Ride saw an article that said the National Aeronautics and Space Administration (NASA) was looking for scientists who wanted to be astronauts. Ride rushed to apply. So did more than 8,000 other people. Out of that group, NASA chose 208 finalists—including Ride. They went to the Johnson Space Center near Houston, Texas, for interviews and medical exams. A month later, Ride was chosen to join the space program.

> "The thing that I'll remember most about the [space] flight is that it was fun. In fact, I'm sure it was the most fun I'll ever have in my life."
> —Sally Ride

Ride went through tough physical and mental training to become an astronaut. In 1979, she qualified as a mission specialist—someone who conducts experiments and does other tasks on space-shuttle flights.

As one of NASA's first female astronauts, Ride faced some unusual problems. For example, in the early days of the program, astronauts were not issued pajamas for space flights. They just wore their underwear. That would not work with crews made up of both males and females, so NASA had to design in-flight pajamas.

On June 18, 1983, Sally Ride was launched into space aboard the shuttle *Challenger*. As the flight engineer, her job was to make sure that all the shuttle's mechanical systems were working properly. She also worked with another astronaut to launch two communications satellites.

Ride was very affected by flying into space. "You spend a year training just which dials to look at and when the time comes, all you want to do is look out the window," she later said. "It's so beautiful."

Ride's mission was a huge success, and she became a national celebrity. However, she did not consider herself an extraordinary person. Asked about her position as America's first female astronaut, she always pointed out that she was a scientist, not a female scientist.

TOPICAL TIDBIT

The *Challenger*

Sally Ride was not the only female astronaut on the October 1984 *Challenger* flight. On that mission, her childhood friend, Kathryn Sullivan, became the first American woman to walk in space. The last *Challenger* flight made history of another kind. Christa McAuliffe, a schoolteacher, had been chosen to be the first private citizen sent into space. On January 28, 1986, millions of people watched on TV as McAuliffe and her fellow astronauts prepared for takeoff. Moments later came a shocking sight: The *Challenger* blew apart, killing McAuliffe and her six fellow passengers.

In October 1984, Ride made a second *Challenger* flight. Once again, she launched a satellite.

Back to Earth

After her historic flights, Ride continued to work for NASA. She was appointed to the presidential committee that investigated the *Challenger* disaster, after the shuttle exploded during takeoff in 1986. In 1987, she created NASA's Office of Exploration.

Ride left NASA in 1987 and taught science at Stanford University. Two years later, she became a physics professor at the University of California at San Diego, and director of the California Space Institute. Throughout her life, she has been a role model for young people, showing them that they can achieve their most fantastic dreams. ◇

LIFE EVENTS

1951
Sally Kristen Ride is born in Los Angeles, California.

1961
NASA puts the first American, Alan Shepard, into space.

1963
Valentina Tereshkova, a Russian cosmonaut, orbits Earth, becoming the first woman in space.

1978
Ride is accepted by NASA as one of six female astronaut candidates.

1983
Ride's space-shuttle flight makes her the first American woman in space.

1987
Ride creates the Office of Exploration at NASA.

Matthew B. Ridgway
Army Chief
(born 1895 • died 1993)

Many men have been leaders in wartime. One of the most distinguished was Matthew B. Ridgway, who led the U.S. Army in key battles during World War II.

An Army Brat

Matthew Bunker Ridgway was born in Fort Monroe, Virginia, on March 3, 1895. His father was a colonel in the Army and was stationed at the fort. Matthew later wrote that his "earliest memories are of guns and marching men." He grew up on several Army bases around the country and was proud of the fact that he was an "Army brat."

> "There is still one absolute weapon. . . . That weapon is man himself."
> —Matthew B. Ridgway

Matthew dreamed of attending the U.S. Military Academy at West Point, but he failed the geometry test on the entrance exam.

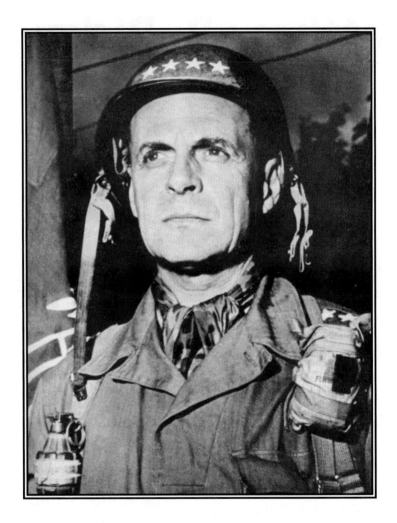

It took one more try for him to pass the test. During his days at West Point, Matthew Ridgway enjoyed athletics and was manager of the football team. He graduated in 1917 and was sent to command an infantry (foot soldiers) company in Texas. Later, he returned to West Point as a Spanish teacher and manager of the athletics program.

Overseas Duty

In 1925, Ridgway was sent to lead an infantry company in Tsientsin, China. In 1927, he was asked to be part of a U.S. mission to Nicaragua, a small country in Central America. The mission was to supervise an election in that war-torn country. Ridgway was chosen for the assignment because he could speak Spanish.

By 1937, Ridgway had been promoted to major and had served on several assignments in Central and South America. He was considered a good leader, and someone who would rise quickly through the Army ranks. From 1939 to 1942, he served in the U.S. War Department's war plans division. This was an important assignment, because many future commanders were chosen from the division's staff.

TOPICAL TIDBIT

"The Busiest Man in the Place"

Matthew B. Ridgway was admired by his superiors, his peers, and his soldiers. His West Point yearbook described him as "the busiest man in the place." Parachuting into danger with his men, he saw more action than any other World War II commander. Easily recognized by the grenades that he kept strapped to his shoulders, he had the ability to inspire soldiers. In December 1951, the 8th Army in Korea was in the middle of the longest retreat in U.S. military history. Ridgway was given command. He turned the situation around, and eventually drove the Chinese out of South Korea.

During World War II, Ridgway took to the air. In 1942, he was a brigadier general commanding one of the Army's first airborne divisions. He won his paratrooper wings, and planned the Army's first major night airborne operation: the 1943 invasion of Sicily.

Ridgway parachuted into battle with his troops during the Allied invasion of Normandy, France, on D-Day, June 6, 1944. Two months later, he was given command of the new 18th Airborne Corps, and led it in battles in the Netherlands, Belgium, and Germany.

Supreme Commander

After World War II ended in 1945, Ridgway served as a military adviser for the U.S. delegation to the United Nations (UN). When the Korean War began in 1950, he was named commander of the 8th Army in Korea. There, he became a common figure on the front lines, inspiring his men to fight as hard as they could.

In 1951, President Harry S. Truman appointed Ridgway to be U.S. commander in chief of the Far East, taking the place of another great general, Douglas MacArthur. Just one year later, Ridgway was promoted to supreme commander of the Allied forces in Europe.

In 1953, he became Army Chief of Staff. Although the position was a great honor, Ridgway called it "the toughest, most frustrating job of my whole career." He was angered by the government's decision to reduce the role of army troops in favor of nuclear weapons. Upset at policies that he believed were weakening the nation's defense, Ridgway retired from the Army in June 1955.

Honors for an Old Warrior

Despite his disagreement with government policies, Ridgway was considered a great warrior and commander. In 1986, he was awarded the Presidential Medal of Freedom for his role in World War II. The citation read: "Heroes come when they are needed. Great men step forward when courage seems in short supply. World War II was such a time, and there was Ridgway."

Matthew B. Ridgway was honored again in 1991, when he received the Congressional Gold Medal. The "great battle leader" died in Fox Chapel, Pennsylvania, on July 26, 1993, at the age of 98. ◇

LIFE EVENTS

1895
Matthew Bunker Ridgway is born in Fort Monroe, Virginia.

1917
Ridgway graduates from West Point.

1943
Brigadier General Ridgway leads an airborne assault of Sicily during World War II.

1944
Ridgway's men parachute into France during the D-Day invasion.

1951
Ridgway succeeds General Douglas MacArthur as commander of the Allied forces in the Far East.

1956
Soldier, Ridgway's memoir, is published. He dies in 1993.

Jackie Robinson
Breaking Baseball's Color Barrier
(born 1919 • died 1972)

When Jackie Robinson was growing up, only white players were allowed to play on major-league baseball teams. When Robinson joined the Brooklyn Dodgers as the first African American player in the major leagues, he changed baseball—and history—forever.

Born Into Poverty

Jack Roosevelt Robinson, the grandson of a slave, was born on January 31, 1919, in Cairo, Georgia. Like other black Americans in the South, the Robinsons faced a great deal of discrimination. At that time, black children and white children had to go to separate schools. Blacks were not allowed to eat in restaurants that served whites. They had to sit in the rear of trains and buses. In almost every part of life, black people were treated as if they were not as good as white people.

Jackie Robinson of the Dodgers, trying to slide in under a tag.

When Jackie was six months old, his family moved to Pasadena, California. There was not as much segregation as in Georgia, but the Robinsons still lived in poverty. Their first apartment had no hot water or electricity, and there was barely enough food to feed everyone. In time, though, Jackie's mother got a job as a cleaning woman and was able to save enough to buy her own home.

A Gifted Athlete

Despite their hard life, the Robinsons were a close and loving family. Jackie did well in school, but the area where he really stood out was sports. He played soccer, baseball, football, basketball, and tennis, and was the star of his high school and college teams. Often, his opponents would try to upset him by using racial slurs—insulting him because he was black. Jackie just ignored them and played as hard as he could. This ability came in handy later in Jackie's life, when he faced the greater challenge of playing major-league baseball.

> "I never cared about acceptance as much as I cared about respect."
> —Jackie Robinson

Breaking the Color Barrier

In 1945, when Robinson was 26 years old, he joined the Kansas City Monarchs. The Monarchs were a baseball team in the Negro Leagues, which were formed because African Americans were barred from playing in the major leagues.

While Robinson was playing for the Monarchs, he came to the attention of Branch Rickey, president of the major-league Brooklyn Dodgers. Rickey wanted to bring black players into the major leagues. After his scouts saw Robinson play, Rickey sent for Robinson.

Rickey asked Robinson if he was willing to break baseball's color barrier. It would not be easy, he warned. Robinson would be insulted and attacked by players and fans who wanted to keep blacks out of major-league baseball. Hardest of all, he could not fight back. Fighting back, Rickey said, could allow bigots to dismiss blacks as untalented or as unworthy of playing in the major leagues. It might set back the integration of baseball for many years. Rickey expected Robinson to just play hard and ignore any abuse that he faced. Robinson agreed to the challenge.

A Dangerous Game

Jackie Robinson played his first game for the Brooklyn Dodgers on April 15, 1947. Being the first black player in a white league was every bit as dan-

TOPICAL TIDBIT

The Negro Leagues

In the years before Jackie Robinson, African American baseball thrived in the Negro Leagues. Some of its greatest talents—such as Satchel Paige, Willie Mays, and Hank Aaron—went on to be major-league Hall of Famers. Other legendary players—including Cool Papa Bell, Buck Leonard, and Josh Gibson, known as "the Babe Ruth of the Negro Leagues"—never got a chance to compete in the big leagues.

gerous as Rickey had told him it would be. Fans threw things at Robinson when he was on the field. Players on other teams spat at him and tried to spike him with their shoes. Pitchers threw fastballs at his head. Some of his own teammates refused to play with him at first. He even received death threats.

> "I had to fight hard against loneliness, abuse, and the knowledge that any mistake I made would be magnified because I was the only black man out there."
>
> —Jackie Robinson

But Robinson refused to show any fear or anger at the way he was treated. Instead, he played baseball with all the intensity he could. During the 1947 season, he led the National League with 29 stolen bases. Players and fans alike admired both his courage and his athletic ability. Baseball fans swarmed to the Dodgers' home stadium, Ebbets Field in Brooklyn, and to other National League parks to see the most exciting player in the game. At the end of the season, sportswriters named him Rookie of the Year.

Robinson played second base and first base in Brooklyn for 10 years. He led the Dodgers to six National League championships and helped them win the World Series in 1955. In 1949, he was voted the Most Valuable Player (MVP) of the National League. Robinson retired from baseball in 1956 with a career batting average of .311. He was voted into the National Baseball Hall of Fame in 1962.

More important than his baseball achievements, Jackie Robinson opened the door for other black athletes. After his success as a Dodger, major-league baseball teams rushed to sign Negro League stars. By 1959, all the major-league teams had at least one black player. There was no going back to the practice of segregation in sports. Today, black athletes are common in almost every sport. Robinson's accomplishments were felt outside of sports, too. He helped the world see that the color of a person's skin has no bearing on his or her abilities. His dignity and skill made a powerful, irreversible impact on baseball—and beyond. ◇

LIFE EVENTS

1919
Jack Roosevelt Robinson is born.

1947
Robinson joins the Brooklyn Dodgers. He is named Rookie of the Year.

1949
Robinson is the National League's Most Valuable Player.

1957
Robinson retires after 10 seasons with the Dodgers.

1962
Robinson is named to the National Baseball Hall of Fame. He dies in 1972.

1997
Robinson's number, 42, is retired throughout the major leagues on the 50th anniversary of his breaking the color barrier.

Eleanor Roosevelt
First Lady of the World
(born 1884 • died 1962)

Eleanor Roosevelt was the wife of U.S. President Franklin D. Roosevelt. However, she was more than just a First Lady. During her life, she became known all over the world for her dedication to improving conditions for poor and disadvantaged people.

Privilege and Pain

Anna Eleanor Roosevelt was born in New York, New York, on October 11, 1884. Her family was very rich and famous. Eleanor's uncle was Theodore Roosevelt, who became the 26th president of the United States when Eleanor was a teenager.

Eleanor was a shy child, always afraid that other people would not like her. She feared many things, including mice and the dark. She also was afraid of failure, but that did not keep her from being generous and caring. Helping the less fortunate was a family tradition. From a young age, Eleanor was taught that it was wrong not to share her nice things with others.

In December 1892, when Eleanor was eight years old, her mother died. A few months later, Eleanor's four-year-old brother also died. Then, in 1894, her father died, too. Ten-year-old Eleanor and her baby brother, Hall, went to live with their grandmother.

Five years later, Eleanor was sent to a boarding school in England. She loved the school, and made many friends there.

Eleanor returned to New York in 1902, when she was 18. Like other rich girls, she began going to parties and dances. However, Eleanor wanted more out of life. She wanted to help people. So she spent her days teaching young people in a slum neighborhood. This job showed her the terrible conditions in which poor people lived, a lesson she never forgot. She spent the rest of her life trying to make things better for them.

> "No one can make you feel inferior without your consent."
> —Eleanor Roosevelt

First Lady to All

In 1905, Eleanor married Franklin Delano Roosevelt, her sixth cousin. He, too, had been raised in wealth and privilege. Eleanor's work with the poor was a great influence on the young man as he moved from law school to corporate work to politics.

During World War I, Franklin served as Assistant Secretary of the Navy in Washington, D.C. Meanwhile, Eleanor directed a Red Cross center that served food to thousands of soldiers. She discovered that she was good at organizing.

In 1929, Franklin was elected governor of New York. Eleanor had helped him win the election by organizing voting drives and speaking at women's meetings. The shy, frightened girl who had been afraid to make a mistake had grown into a confident, capable woman.

In 1932, Franklin Roosevelt was elected the 32nd president of the United States, and the couple moved into the White House. No one had ever seen a First Lady like Eleanor Roosevelt. Other First Ladies had done little to attract attention. Eleanor, however, saw her new position as a chance to help others. "I begin to think there are ways in which I can be useful," she

TOPICAL TIDBIT

Marian Anderson

Eleanor Roosevelt attacked injustice all of her life. In 1939, Marian Anderson, a distinguished African American singer, tried to schedule a concert at Constitution Hall in Washington, D.C. The hall was owned by the Daughters of the American Revolution (DAR), an elite group of women whose ancestors belonged to America's first families. When the DAR refused to let Marian Anderson sing because she was black, Eleanor Roosevelt was furious, and resigned from the group. She helped arrange a new location and another, bigger concert was scheduled. On Easter Sunday, 1939, Marian Anderson sang for an audience of 75,000 people—at the Lincoln Memorial.

wrote to a friend shortly after her husband's election.

Franklin was unable to walk because of a disease called polio. So Eleanor helped him by traveling all over the country to find out how people were living. Eleanor was interested in *all* people—poor people, African Americans, migrant workers, women, and young people. Then she went back to the White House and told her husband what she had seen, heard, and learned. She asked Franklin to help these people live better lives. The once-shy woman said, "I long ago reached the point where there is no living person whom I fear, and few challenges I am not willing to face."

Not everyone appreciated Eleanor Roosevelt's outspoken attitude. She was called "the most dangerous woman in America" by political enemies. Newspaper cartoons made fun of her plain appearance. Elea-

LIFE EVENTS

1884
Anna Eleanor Roosevelt is born in New York, New York.

1905
Eleanor marries Franklin D. Roosevelt, her distant cousin.

1932
Franklin Roosevelt wins his first term as president.

1945
President Truman appoints Eleanor Roosevelt as a delegate to the United Nations (UN).

1948
Eleanor Roosevelt is a major contributor to the UN's Universal Declaration of Human Rights.

1958
On My Own, Eleanor Roosevelt's autobiography, is published. She dies in 1962.

nor ignored the unpleasant things that were said about her, and carried on with her mission of helping people who were less fortunate.

A New Life

After Franklin died in 1945, Eleanor said that she was going to relax and play with her grandchildren. Instead, she became an even more active public figure. President Harry S. Truman appointed her to represent the U.S. at the United Nations. Soon, she was traveling to other countries, working for equal rights and better living conditions for people everywhere. Now she was called "the First Lady of the world." She also wrote a daily newspaper column, called "My Day," as well as several books.

Eleanor Roosevelt died on November 7, 1962, at the age of 78. Today, she is considered one of the most influential women of all time—a First Lady who helped change the world. ◇

Franklin D. Roosevelt
Four-term President
(born 1882 • died 1945)

Franklin D. Roosevelt was born wealthy, and could have spent his life having fun. Instead, he served the nation as its 32nd president for 12 years, leading the nation through two of the worst crises it ever faced—the Great Depression and World War II. In doing so, he changed the way the U.S. government works.

A Spoiled Childhood

Franklin Delano Roosevelt was born on January 30, 1882, in Hyde Park, New York. He was the only child of a very wealthy and important family. His mother adored her son and called him her "darling boy."

Franklin lived by a very strict schedule. He spent most of his day studying with a private tutor, and always ate his meals at the same time. He was allowed to play for just two hours a day, and then only games that had been approved by his mother.

Franklin D. Roosevelt enjoys a moment with one of his daughters and the family dog. The public rarely saw photos of him in a wheelchair.

When Franklin was 14, he was sent away to boarding school. It was his first time away from home, and he had trouble adjusting to his new life. He was a good student, but he had little talent for sports and was often teased by the other students.

Tragedy Strikes

In 1900, Franklin Roosevelt entered Harvard University. After graduating from Harvard, he attended Columbia University Law School in New York, New York. He also married his sixth cousin, Eleanor Roosevelt. After law school, he began working as a lawyer in New York.

However, Roosevelt was bored with his job. Another distant cousin, Theodore Roosevelt—who was now president of the United States—had encouraged him to enter politics. In 1910, Franklin Roosevelt won election to the New York state senate. In 1913, President Woodrow Wilson appointed him assistant secretary of the Navy. Roosevelt played an important role in modernizing the Navy and preparing it for World War I.

Then, on August 10, 1921, Roosevelt's life changed forever. While vacationing with his family at their summer home, he felt chilled. By August 12, his legs were completely paralyzed. He had come down with polio, a crippling disease that usually struck children. Doctors told him that he would never walk again. It seemed as if his political career was over.

Franklin Roosevelt was determined not to spend his life in a wheelchair. For the next three years, he worked hard to strengthen his legs with special exercises. By 1924, he could walk a short distance on crutches. That year, he was asked to give a speech at the Democratic National Convention. Wearing heavy steel braces on his legs and leaning on crutches, Roosevelt walked to the podium. The audience gave him a standing ovation. Roosevelt now had the image of a fighter who would not let anything stop him. His political career was back on track.

In 1928, Roosevelt was elected governor of New York. Four years later, he set his sights on the highest office in the land: the presidency.

New Deals

By 1932, the nation was deep in a terrible economic slowdown known as the Great Depression. Millions of Americans had lost their jobs, and many more lost their savings when banks closed. People were deeply afraid that things would never get better.

> "I see one-third of a nation ill-housed, ill-clad, ill-nourished."
>
> —Franklin D. Roosevelt, in his second inaugural address, 1937

Roosevelt campaigned for president on the promise that he would create "a New Deal for the American people." America was ready for his vision, and he won the election by a landslide. "The only thing we have to fear is fear itself," Roosevelt said in his inaugural address. His optimism and new ideas energized the country.

Roosevelt got to work at once, forming many new government agencies that created jobs for unemployed workers and improved quality of life in many other ways. Later, he helped set up the Social Security program, which pays benefits to retired workers and their families. Slowly, economic conditions began to improve.

President Roosevelt was an immensely important figure in his time. He was a part of the country's daily life, and his "fireside chats" on the radio were listened to by millions of Americans. When people spoke of him, all they needed was his initials: FDR.

Many Americans admired Roosevelt and believed that he had saved the nation. However, others thought that his actions had given the government too much power. They hated Roosevelt so much that they couldn't speak his name at all. Instead, they called him "that man in the White House."

TOPICAL TIDBIT

The Great Beyond

People from all over the U.S. would remember where they were when they heard that Franklin D. Roosevelt had died. There was an outpouring of national grief. FDR's body made a long journey, by railroad, from Georgia to Washington. Everywhere the train went, people stood in tribute at railroad crossings—sometimes hundreds of them in one place. Even America's war enemies sent messages honoring him. "Franklin D. Roosevelt has crossed to the Great Beyond [Heaven]," said the German statement.

The Four-term President

Roosevelt was re-elected in 1936. Then, in 1940, he was elected to a third term. He was the first—and only—U.S. president to serve more than two terms. (After his time in office, the Constitution was amended to limit the president to two terms in office.)

In 1941, the U.S. entered World War II. Roosevelt steered the nation through most of that terrible war, working with other leaders of the Allied forces. He traveled to visit troops in North Africa, making him the first president since Abraham Lincoln to visit U.S. troops in a combat zone.

On January 20, 1945, Franklin D. Roosevelt was sworn in for his fourth term as president. However, it was obvious that his health was failing. On April 12, 1945, he died suddenly while on vacation in Georgia. Millions of people around the nation mourned the loss of their leader—a man who is considered one of the country's greatest presidents. ◇

LIFE EVENTS

1882
Franklin Delano Roosevelt is born in Hyde Park, New York.

1921
Roosevelt is stricken with polio.

1928
Roosevelt is elected governor of New York.

1932
Roosevelt becomes the 32nd president of the U.S.

1941
The Japanese attack Pearl Harbor on December 8. The U.S. enters World War II the next day.

1945
FDR dies in Warm Springs, Georgia.

Theodore Roosevelt
Rough Rider President
(born 1858 • died 1919)

Theodore Roosevelt started life as a frail child, but grew up to be an adventurer, a war hero, and one of the nation's most energetic presidents.

Starting Out Sickly

Theodore Roosevelt was born in New York City on October 27, 1858. He was the oldest son of a wealthy and important family. Teddy had a privileged childhood, and spent a lot of time traveling around the U.S. and Europe.

Teddy loved to read and was fascinated by the natural world. He started a collection of living and dead animals that he called "Roosevelt's Natural History Museum." Its prize specimen was the skull of a dead seal that he had found at a New York fish market.

Young Teddy suffered from asthma, a condition that makes it difficult to breathe. His family did everything they could think of to improve his health. Finally, Teddy's father told him, "You have the mind,

but you have not the body. You must make your body." Teddy began an intense program of running, swimming, and weight-lifting. As his body got stronger, Teddy's health improved.

Public Life

Like many rich children in the 19th century, Teddy Roosevelt studied at home, with private tutors. Later, he graduated from Harvard University. During his days at Harvard, Roosevelt wrote a book called *The Naval War of 1812*. It became required reading at the U.S. Naval Academy.

After graduating from Harvard, Roosevelt attended Columbia University Law School. He also developed a thirst for politics. In 1882, when he was 23 years old, he became the youngest member of the New York State Assembly. Soon he was known for speaking out against injustice and calling for government reform.

> "I am as strong as a bull moose and you can use me to the limit."
> —Theodore Roosevelt

In 1884, two days after the birth of their daughter Alice, Roosevelt's wife died. His mother died on the same day. Overwhelmed by grief, he headed west to the Dakota Territory, where he had a ranch. He spent the next two years there, riding horses and rounding up cattle. Roosevelt enjoyed the beauty of the western landscape and the challenge of staying alive in a rough world.

Roosevelt returned to New York City in 1886. He remarried, wrote several books, and served as head of the U.S. Civil Service Commission from 1889 to

1895. In 1896, he became New York City's police commissioner. Later, he became assistant secretary of the Navy under President William McKinley.

Rough Riding

In 1898, war broke out between the U.S. and Spain. Roosevelt jumped at the chance to fight. He resigned from his Navy position and became colonel of a regiment of mounted soldiers. The troop soon became known as the "Rough Riders."

On July 1, 1898, Roosevelt led his Rough Riders up San Juan Hill in Cuba. Braving gunfire from the Spanish above them, they overwhelmed the enemy and took the hill. The Rough Riders were not the

TOPICAL TIDBIT

Sharing the Land

When Theodore Roosevelt became president in 1901, few Americans had ever even thought about conserving the environment. Roosevelt had the vision to protect natural wilderness areas from overuse by logging, mining, and other industries. To him, it was important to keep the land for the common people. Roosevelt was responsible for protecting such important areas as Muir Woods and the Grand Canyon. In total, he protected almost five times as much land as all 25 previous presidents put together.

only soldiers there that day, but it was their dashing leader who most Americans remembered. Roosevelt later called the victory "the great day of my life." It made him a famous war hero throughout the U.S.

Assassin's Bullets

Roosevelt served briefly as governor of New York, but left the post after only two years to become vice president under President McKinley. Just six months after their March inauguration, McKinley was shot by an assassin. He died a few days later, on September 14, 1901. That day, Theodore Roosevelt became the 26th president of the United States—the youngest man ever sworn in to that office. He was 42 years old.

Roosevelt served two terms as president. During his time in office, he tried to make sure that all Americans had a "square deal." Roosevelt helped labor unions become stronger and forced companies to pay their workers more money. He passed the nation's first pure food and drug law, and fought to break up large corporations, called trusts, that ruined small businesses and charged high prices for their goods. Roosevelt also preserved 145 million acres of wilderness as national parks, created 16 national monuments, and established 51 wildlife refuges.

TR, as he was known, was also a strong presence in foreign affairs. He won the Nobel Peace Prize in 1906 for helping bring an end to a war between

Russia and Japan. His efforts also were responsible for the Panama Canal, on which construction started in 1903.

Later Life

In 1908, Roosevelt finished his second term as president and headed off to Africa on a hunting trip. In 1912, he ran for president again. He had served as a Republican president, but this time he ran as the candidate of the Progressive, or Bull Moose, Party. He won more votes than William Howard Taft, the Republican candidate. However, Woodrow Wilson, the Democratic candidate, won more votes than Taft and Roosevelt put together.

Theodore Roosevelt spent the next few years writing the story of his life and traveling. He died on January 6, 1919, at the age of 60. He is still remembered as a person who lived life to the fullest. ◇

LIFE EVENTS

1858
Theodore Roosevelt is born in New York, New York.

1898
Roosevelt organizes the "Rough Riders" to fight in the Spanish-American War.

1901
President McKinley is assassinated. Vice President Roosevelt is sworn in as president.

1902
After TR refuses to shoot a bear cub, a toy maker introduces the teddy bear.

1905
The Forest Service is created to preserve wilderness areas.

1906
Roosevelt wins the Nobel Peace Prize.

1912
Roosevelt runs for president on the Bull Moose ticket.

Sacagawea
Guide to the West
(born about 1787 • died 1812 or 1884)

In 1804, Meriwether Lewis and William Clark set out to explore what is now northwestern U.S. Early in their two-year journey, they met Sacagawea *(SAK-uh-jah-WEE-uh)*. The young Native American woman became their interpreter and friend—and an essential part of their expedition.

A Young Wife and Mother

Little is known about Sacagawea's childhood. A member of the Shoshone tribe, she probably was born in Idaho around 1787. When she was about 12 years old, she and several other Shoshone women and children were captured by the Hidatsa, another Native American tribe. Sacagawea was sold as a slave to the Mandan tribe, who lived along the Missouri River. The Mandans, in turn, sold Sacagawea to a Canadian fur trapper named Toussaint Charbonneau *(too-SAHN shar-buh-NOH)*.

Charbonneau had several Native American wives.

Sacagawea became one of them, and gave birth to their son, Jean Baptiste (known as Pompey), in 1805. Sacagawea, Charbonneau, and Pompey were living at Fort Mandan, a military camp in what is now North Dakota. That is where they met the men who would change the young woman's life.

The Journey West

In 1804, President Thomas Jefferson had sent Meriwether Lewis and William Clark to explore the northwestern U.S. They were to draw maps, befriend Native American tribes, and draw pictures and collect specimens of plants and animals they found along the way.

When Lewis and Clark reached what is now North Dakota, they knew that they would need to purchase horses from the Shoshone Indians in order to cross the Rocky Mountains. The explorers didn't speak the Shoshone language, so they needed an interpreter to help them. When they heard about Charbonneau and his Shoshone wife, Sacagawea, they hired the two to travel with them on the rest of their journey.

> "We find [that Sacagawea helps us with] the Indians, as to our friendly intentions. A woman with a party of men is a token of peace."
>
> —William Clark, in his journal

Although neither explorer liked the rough, hot-tempered Charbonneau, they found Sacagawea a pleasant and valuable addition to the party.

On April 7, 1805, Lewis and Clark and their new guides left Fort Mandan. With her two-month-old son strapped to her back, Sacagawea helped the explorers any way she could, including finding plants that were safe to eat.

One day in May, a sudden storm almost tipped over Charbonneau's boat. Lewis and Clark watched helplessly from shore as many of their supplies began to float away. Only Sacagawea stayed calm. She sat in the boat and grabbed objects as they floated past. Her quick thinking saved many valuable objects, including the group's medicines and journals of their trip.

In August 1805, Lewis and Clark met a large band of Shoshone near the border of Montana and Idaho. The Shoshone were about to attack. Suddenly, Sacagawea ran forward, yelling and dancing with delight. She had recognized the band's chief as her brother, Cameahwait. They had not seen one another since she was kidnapped. Cameahwait and the other

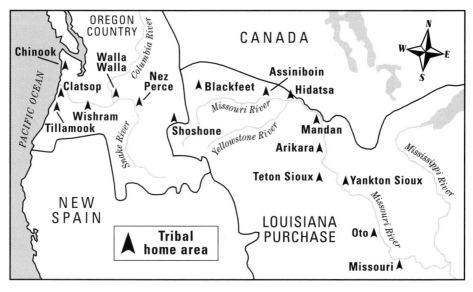

This map shows the home areas of some of the Native American peoples the Lewis and Clark team met on its 1804-1806 journey.

Shoshone were thrilled to see Sacagawea again. They served as protectors to the explorers and later sold horses to them so they could complete their journey to the Pacific Ocean.

What Happened to Her?

On November 18, 1805, Lewis and Clark and their team reached the Pacific Ocean. They spent the winter in Oregon. On March 23, 1806, they began the long journey home. Once again, Sacagawea, Charbonneau, and Pompey traveled with them, and Sacagawea proved to be a great help guiding them back through the mountain passes. In his journal, William Clark called Sacagawea "the Indian woman, who has been

TOPICAL TIDBIT

Meeting the Natives

Lewis and Clark's Corps of Discovery met nearly 50 different tribes of Native Americans on their journey west. Some had never seen a white man. The explorers developed a ritual that they repeated for each group. They explained that the tribe had a new "great father," President Thomas Jefferson, back in the east. Then they gave the Indians gifts and performed a kind of parade, marching in their uniforms and shooting their guns. Sacagawea was important in helping to establish communication between the explorers and the Native Americans they met.

of great service to me as a pilot through this country."

When the explorers reached North Dakota, Sacagawea, her husband, and son remained there while Lewis, Clark, and the rest of their team traveled on to Missouri. No one is sure what happened to Sacagawea after that. Some historians think that she died in 1812. However, years later, a very old woman living on a Shoshone reservation in Wyoming claimed to be Sacagawea. Because she knew many details about Lewis and Clark and their journey, many historians believe her story. That woman died in 1884 and was buried on the reservation. A stone monument marks her grave, honoring her as "a guide with the Lewis and Clark expedition."

However Sacagawea ended up, she has become much more than that a mere guide. Her story of heroism lives on in American history. ◇

LIFE EVENTS

About 1787
Sacagawea is born in what today is Idaho.

About 1800
Sacagawea is kidnapped, sold to Mandan Indians, then to a French fur trapper.

1804
Meriwether Lewis and William Clark start their expedition from St. Louis, Missouri.

1805
Sacagawea meets Lewis and Clark in what is now North Dakota. She, her husband, and baby son accompany the expedition. The team returns in 1806.

2000
The U.S. Mint issues new one-dollar coins, honoring Sacagawea with her picture on the face.

Jonas Salk
Conqueror of Polio
(born 1914 • died 1995)

Today, almost all American children are vaccinated against a disease called polio. Until 50 years ago, however, polio was one of the most feared diseases in the world. It paralyzed or killed tens of thousands of children every year. Today, however, polio is rare—thanks to Dr. Jonas Salk, who developed a vaccine to prevent it.

A Love of Science

Jonas Salk was born on October 28, 1914, in New York City. His parents had emigrated from Russia and didn't have much money, but they had high expectations for their children.

Jonas did well in school and started high school when he was 12 years old. He graduated at 15 and entered City College of New York. Although Jonas was studying law, he had to take a few science classes. He enjoyed those classes so much that he decided not to be a lawyer, after all. He wanted to be a doctor instead.

When Jonas Salk entered the New York University School of Medicine in 1934, the U.S. was in the middle of a terrible economic period known as the Great Depression. Salk's parents had to borrow money to pay for his first year of medical school. After that,

Salk won scholarships and worked part-time to pay for his education.

Most of his classmates planned to become private physicians, but Salk decided to become a researcher. Research was a low-paying profession, but he was excited about the idea of discovering new ways to cure diseases.

Destroying Polio

Salk graduated from medical school in 1939 and soon went to work for Dr. Thomas Francis, a noted scientist. Francis was trying to find a way to prevent influenza (the flu). A form of influenza had killed millions of people around the world in 1918. In his laboratory, Salk helped develop a flu vaccine that was given to American soldiers on their way to fight in World War II.

> "I feel that the greatest reward for doing is the opportunity to do more."
>
> —Dr. Jonas Salk

Along with their influenza work, Salk and Francis studied how to prevent polio. In 1947, Salk took a job at the University of Pittsburgh School of Medicine. There, he continued to investigate the mystery of polio. In a tiny room in the basement of a hospital, he conducted some of the most important research and experiments in modern medicine.

Salk learned everything he could about the different types of polio. For his research, he received money from the National Foundation for Infantile Paralysis (NFIP). That organization, which later became the March of Dimes, had been founded by President Franklin Roosevelt, a victim of polio.

Salk worked to develop what is called a killed-virus vaccine. This means that a sample of live virus is killed with a chemical called formaldehyde. Then it is injected into the body to build up the body's defenses against the disease. Salk's research was a breakthrough. At the time, giving a vaccination with a live virus was thought to be too dangerous, because it might cause the very disease it was meant to prevent.

By 1952, Salk had his polio vaccine. He was so sure of its safety that he tested it on himself and his

TOPICAL TIDBIT

Dr. Albert Sabin

During the years that Jonas Salk was investigating the mysteries of the polio virus, Albert Sabin, a Polish-American microbiologist, was doing the same thing. Salk had the first breakthrough. Then Sabin had one. It was Albert Sabin who figured out how to use a *live* virus in a vaccine—how to weaken it enough so it would not be harmful. Sabin's live-virus vaccine turned out to be better than Salk's killed-virus vaccine. Sabin's was stronger. It had to be given only one time. Best of all for millions of children, it could be taken by mouth, in a sugar cube—meaning no needles!

three children. In 1954, the virus was tested on the public. More than 650,000 children in 44 states received three shots each of Salk's vaccine. Careful records were kept, then sent to Salk's old friend, Dr. Thomas Francis, for study. On April 12, 1955, Francis announced that Salk's vaccine worked. Finally, there was a safe way to prevent polio!

From Polio to AIDS

The development of a safe polio vaccine made Dr. Jonas Salk a national hero, but he just wanted to keep working, developing new vaccines. In 1963, the Salk Institute for Biological Studies opened in La Jolla, California. There, Salk and his staff studied how the human body defends itself against cancer and other diseases.

In 1987, Salk and his scientists began working on two different vaccines for AIDS.

LIFE EVENTS

1914
Jonas Salk is born in New York, New York.

1947
Salk begins his research into polio at the University of Pittsburgh.

1952
Salk conducts important field tests for his killed-virus polio vaccine.

1955
The completed polio vaccine is released for use.

1977
Salk receives the Presidential Medal of Freedom.

1995
Jonas Salk dies. By this time, polio has been wiped out in the Western Hemisphere and greatly reduced worldwide.

One vaccine would protect the body against being infected with HIV, the virus that causes AIDS. The other vaccine would be given to patients who already had HIV, to keep it from developing into AIDS. Salk continued to work into his eighties, hoping to find a way to prevent one of the world's deadliest diseases. He died in La Jolla in 1995.

Salk received many honors for his life's work, including the Congressional Gold Medal and the Presidential Medal of Freedom. However, his greatest honor was the knowledge that, thanks to his dedication, millions of children have been able to grow up healthy and strong. ◇

Alan B. Shepard Jr.
First American in Space
(born 1923 • died 1998)

Today, a journey into space seems almost ordinary. However, in the 1950s and 1960s, sending someone into outer space was a fantastic achievement that many people thought impossible. The first American to leave our planet behind was Alan Shepard.

In the Navy

Alan Bartlett Shepard Jr. was born on November 18, 1923, in East Derry, New Hampshire. Alan attended a one-room schoolhouse and was a popular, athletic, and smart student. He was especially good at math. Alan also had an early interest in planes. He spent many hours during his childhood working at a local airport.

After finishing high school at the Pinkerton Academy in Derry, Alan Shepard went on to study at the U.S. Naval Academy in Annapolis, Maryland. From the start, he wanted to become a naval aviator. First, however, he was required to spend two years

aboard a ship. He served in the Pacific on the destroyer U.S.S. *Cogswell* during World War II.

Shepard began flight training soon after the war ended in 1945. He earned his wings in 1947, then spent several years as a fighter pilot in Europe. He completed more flying courses—at the Naval Test Pilot School in 1951 and the Naval War College in 1957. Then he found himself stuck in a desk job, at the offices of the Atlantic Fleet Commander. However, that soon changed.

Into Space

In 1957, President Dwight D. Eisenhower announced that America's first astronauts would be chosen from Navy test pilots. Shepard eagerly waited for his invitation to join the program, but it never arrived. When Shepard asked why, he was told that he *had* been sent an invitation. It must have been lost in the mail.

After months of tough physical and emotional tests, seven men were named as astronauts in a new program called Project Mercury. Shepard was one of those chosen. The Mercury Seven quickly became national celebrities. "I'm here because it's a chance to serve the country," Shepard told *Life* magazine. "I'm here, too, because it's a great personal challenge."

> "One doesn't think of oneself as being a hero or historical figure. One does it because the challenge is there. . . . I must admit, maybe I am a piece of history, after all."
> —Alan B. Shepard Jr.

After two years of training, Shepard won a dream assignment: He would be the first U.S. astronaut in space. On May 5, 1961, his *Freedom 7* spacecraft was launched into space from Cape Canaveral, Florida. Shepard traveled 116 miles above Earth. Fifteen minutes and 22 seconds later, *Freedom 7* splashed down in the Atlantic Ocean. America's first voyage into space had gone perfectly, and it made Alan Shepard a national hero. His journey was especially inspiring since, less than a month before, the Soviet Union had launched the world's first person into space—a cosmonaut named Yuri Gagarin. Shepard's achievement made Americans proud of their country and its accomplishments.

TOPICAL TIDBIT

"Miles and Miles and Miles"

As the first American in space, everything that Alan Shepard saw and felt was strange and new. He was the first to see Earth from above. (Gagarin's craft had no window.) "What a beautiful view," Shepard said. He could not float in weightless space because he was strapped into his chair—but he watched a loose washer drift lazily in front of his eyes. Later, on the *Apollo 14* mission, Shepard hit golf balls on the moon! He had to do it with one arm because his suit was too bulky. Because of the moon's low gravity, the balls went for "miles and miles and miles," he said.

Disappointment and Triumph

Shepard could hardly wait to go back into space. However, he developed Meniere's syndrome, an inner-ear disorder. It causes dizziness and hearing loss, which meant that Shepard could no longer fly. Even so, Shepard was determined to stay active in the astronaut program. In 1963, he took a desk job as chief of the Astronaut Office. Later, he underwent surgery to correct his inner-ear problems. By May 1969, Shepard was ready to fly again—just in time for the *Apollo* moon landings.

Shepard's wish to return to space finally came true on January 31, 1971. That day, he took off as spacecraft commander of *Apollo 14*. During the 10-day journey—the third mission to land on the moon—Shepard and another astronaut performed scientific experiments and collected

LIFE EVENTS

1923
Alan Bartlett Shepard Jr. is born in East Derry, New Hampshire.

1945
Shepard begins Navy flight training.

1959
NASA chooses Shepard as one of the seven original astronauts for the Mercury program.

1961
Shepard makes a 15-minute suborbital flight aboard *Freedom 7*, becoming the first American in space.

1971
Commanding *Apollo 14*, Shepard walks on the moon.

1974
Shepard retires from the space program.

1998
Shepard dies of leukemia.

almost 100 pounds of samples from the moon. They stayed on the moon's surface for 33 hours—longer than any other *Apollo* mission.

After Shepard returned from his lunar trip, he went back to work as chief of the Astronaut Office until he retired from NASA in 1974. During his career, Shepard spent more than 8,000 hours flying in airplanes, and almost 217 hours in space.

Shepard spent the next 14 years working in business in Houston, Texas. He also served as president of the Mercury Seven Foundation, which provides college scholarships for science students. He died of leukemia in Monterey, California, on July 21, 1998, at age 64. Alan B. Shepard Jr. was a pioneer in a new kind of exploration—exploration of the world far beyond our planet. ◇

Robert Smalls
An Unlikely Hero
(born 1839 • died 1915)

Robert Smalls started life as a slave. Then a daring decision gave him his freedom and changed his life.

Life as a Slave

Robert Smalls was born in Beaufort, South Carolina, in 1839. His parents were slaves, so Robert began his life as a slave, too. Little is known about his childhood. It probably was spent working on his master's property in Beaufort.

When Robert was 12 years old, his owner hired him out to work in the shipyards of Charleston, South Carolina. There, Robert learned how to navigate ships—a skill that later proved very useful.

By 1862, 23-year-old Smalls was the wheelman of a steam-powered ship named the *Planter*, which was mostly used to transport cotton. When the Civil War broke out in 1861, the *Planter* had become part of the Confederate navy. The ship was armed with four cannon and plenty of ammunition.

A Daring Escape

On May 12, 1862, the *Planter*'s white captain and white crew went ashore for the evening. At 3 o'clock the next morning, Smalls, his wife and two children, and the 12 slave crewmen and their families took over the ship. They sailed it out of the harbor. In the dark, Smalls was able to fool the watchmen: He pretended that he was the captain by wearing the captain's hat and imitating the way he walked. Smalls knew the signals, so he was able to sail past the Southern forces at Fort Sumter. Then he ran up a white flag of surrender and delivered the ship to the Union Navy. "I thought the *Planter* might be of some use to Uncle Abe," he said, referring to President Lincoln.

> "My race needs no special defense, for the past history of them in this country proves them to be the equal of any people anywhere. All they need is an equal chance in the battle of life."
>
> —Robert Smalls

The Union was pleased to get the *Planter* with its cannon and ammunition. Even more important was Smalls's knowledge about Confederate defenses and the tricky waters of Charleston Harbor. The U.S. government appointed Smalls as pilot of the *Planter* and sent the ship into service as a gunboat.

On December 1, 1863, the *Planter* was caught by heavy shelling from Confederate guns. The captain panicked and abandoned the ship. Smalls calmly took command, returned fire, then sailed the ship to safety. For his heroic actions, he was named captain of the ship until 1866, after the war. Smalls was the highest-ranking black officer in the Union Navy during the Civil War.

A New Life

After the war, Smalls returned to Beaufort. He bought his former master's home, and soon became one of the city's most respected citizens. He also served in the state militia until 1877.

In 1868, Smalls entered politics. For a short time after the Civil War, African Americans were allowed to vote and hold office in the South. Smalls was elected as a delegate to South Carolina's constitutional convention, where he drafted a resolution for

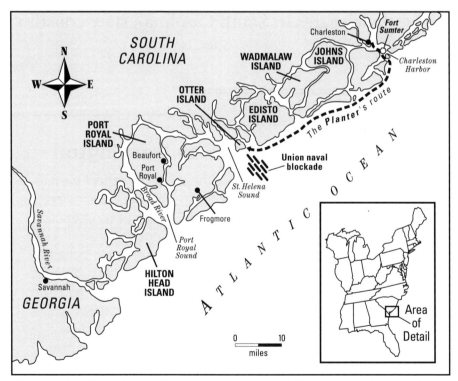

The dotted line shows the route that Robert Smalls took to freedom, sailing the *Planter* out of Charleston Harbor on May 13, 1862.

the state's first free educational system. Also in 1868, he was elected to the South Carolina legislature. Two years later, he became a state senator.

In 1875, Smalls was elected to the U.S. House of Representatives. During his five terms, he introduced or supported several pieces of civil-rights law. Those bills gave former slaves the right to own property, sign contracts, and receive equal protection under the law.

Smalls left Congress in 1887. In 1889, he was appointed customs collector for the port of Beaufort. He remained active in politics. In 1895, he was one of six black delegates to South Carolina's state constitu-

TOPICAL TIDBIT

Black Americans Go to Washington

After the Civil War ended in 1865, the U.S. government tried to reform laws and customs in the South. This period is called Reconstruction, which means "to rebuild." During Reconstruction, Southern states began sending black politicians to Washington for the first time. The first African American representative in the U.S. House was Jefferson F. Long of Georgia, in 1869. Hiram Rhoades Revels was elected to fill the Mississippi Senate seat of Jefferson Davis, who had been president of the Confederate states. Revels was followed by Blanche K. Bruce, an ex-slave who had gone to Oberlin College. In all, 22 blacks were elected from Southern states. After Reconstruction ended in 1877, however, it was many decades before Southern blacks again served in Congress.

tional convention. There he tried, unsuccessfully, to pass laws to assure voting rights for black citizens.

A Hero Once Again

In 1913, at age 74, Smalls heard that a white mob planned to kill two black men who had been jailed for the murder of a white man. To prevent the attack, Smalls announced that if the mob was not stopped, Beaufort's black citizens would burn white homes in revenge. The sheriff believed him and convinced the mob to leave peacefully.

Smalls spent the last years of his life working with children at Beaufort's black school. He died in February 1915. Late in life, Smalls saw many rights taken away from African Americans as restrictive laws were passed throughout the South. However, he always believed that the U.S. would one day live up to its ideals of "life, liberty, and the pursuit of happiness" for all citizens. ◇

LIFE EVENTS

1839
Robert Smalls is born in Beaufort, South Carolina.

1862
Smalls sails the Confederate ship *Planter* out of Charleston Harbor.

1863
Smalls is made captain of the *Planter*.

1875
Smalls is elected to the U.S. House of Representatives.

1889
Smalls is appointed customs collector for the port of Beaufort. He dies in 1915.

Elizabeth Cady Stanton
Social Reformer
(born 1815 • died 1902)

When Elizabeth Cady Stanton was alive, women and African Americans were not treated the same by law as white men. Stanton dedicated her life to winning equal rights for *all* Americans, regardless of their gender or the color of their skin.

"You Should Have Been a Boy"

Elizabeth Cady was born on November 12, 1815, in Johnstown, New York. When she was growing up, boys had many more opportunities than girls. Boys received better educations and could work at more interesting and well-paying jobs. Elizabeth's curious and intelligent personality was unusual at a time when girls were expected to be quiet and stay in the background.

When Elizabeth was young, her brother Eleazur

was killed in an accident. Elizabeth's father loved all six of his children, but his son was clearly his favorite. After Eleazur's death, Elizabeth decided to take her brother's place. To do so, she received special permission to study Greek, Latin, mathematics, and other "boys' subjects." She also asked her father to enroll her in a boys' school that had just started admitting girls. When Elizabeth won a special school award for her Greek studies, Mr. Cady was proud—and sad. "You should have been a boy," he told her. However, Elizabeth didn't want to be a boy. She liked being a girl—but she also wanted to be treated the same way boys were.

> "Women are already the equals of men in the whole of realm of thought, in art, science, literature, and government."
> —Elizabeth Cady Stanton

Elizabeth also spent a lot of time in her father's law office. As she read her father's law books, she became angry at how unfairly women were treated. She vowed that she would never get married, because married women had no right to own property.

Fighting Inequality

However, Elizabeth Cady did get married. She met a journalist named Henry Brewer Stanton, who was an abolitionist—someone opposed to slavery. Henry didn't just believe in equal rights for African Americans. He believed that women should be treated equally, too. Elizabeth and Henry married in 1840, and she became known as Elizabeth Cady Stanton.

Together, the Stantons worked to end slavery. Soon after their marriage, they traveled to London,

England, to attend the World Antislavery Convention. There, Stanton met another abolitionist, Lucretia Mott. Like the other women at the convention, Mott and Stanton had to sit behind a curtain. They could listen to the convention, but were not allowed to take part, make speeches, or even be seen. Stanton and Mott decided that someday they would hold their own convention to fight for women's rights. A few years later, they made that dream a reality.

In 1848, Stanton and Mott organized the first women's rights convention in the U.S. It was held in Seneca Falls, New York, where the Stantons lived. Three hundred people attended the convention. They heard Stanton say that "all men and women

TOPICAL TIDBIT

Mom and the Nineteenth Amendment

The Nineteenth Amendment was hotly debated until the very end. Amendments (changes) to the Constitution must be approved by three fourths of the state legislatures. In 1920, it all came down to Tennessee's legislature. Actually, it all came down to Harry Burn. Burn, a young new representative, did not want to vote Yes. It looked as if the amendment would be defeated—by one vote. Then Burn received a telegram from his mother, a strong suffragist, saying: "I have been watching to see how you stood. . . . Don't forget to be a good boy [and vote yes]." Burn switched his vote from No to Yes, and the Nineteenth Amendment passed—by one vote.

are created equal." (It was a change from the Declaration of Independence, which says that "all men are created equal.") Stanton also said that women should have suffrage—the right to vote. This idea was so shocking that even Lucretia Mott and Henry Stanton were against it.

A New Partnership

In 1851, Elizabeth Cady Stanton teamed up with Susan B. Anthony. Unlike many other people, Anthony agreed that women should have the right to vote. The two women made a dynamic team. Stanton—who usually stayed at home, caring for her seven children—wrote inspiring speeches calling for women's suffrage. Then Anthony delivered the speeches at meetings all over the country. Together, Stanton's husband said, they "stirred up the world."

LIFE EVENTS

1815
Elizabeth Cady is born in Johnstown, New York.

1848
Elizabeth Cady Stanton and Lucretia Mott organize the world's first women's rights convention.

1851
Stanton meets Susan B. Anthony.

1869
Stanton and Anthony found the National Woman Suffrage Association.

1878
Stanton drafts an amendment to the Constitution that would grant the vote to women. She dies in 1902.

1920
The Nineteenth Amendment, granting women the vote, is ratified.

In 1869, Stanton and Anthony founded the National Woman Suffrage Association (NWSA). Stanton served as the organization's president until 1892. In 1878, Stanton's efforts led to the introduction of a constitutional amendment for women's suffrage. In 1920—18 years after Stanton's death—this amendment finally became law, giving women the right to vote at last.

Although conditions for women did not change until after her death, Elizabeth Cady Stanton's hard work and dedication was aimed at ensuring that one day, men and women would indeed be treated as they were created—equal. ◇

Anne Sullivan
Teacher and Friend
(born 1866 • died 1936)

Many people have heard the story of Helen Keller, who overcame multiple handicaps to become one of the most inspiring women in the world. However, less is known about Keller's companion, Anne Sullivan. Sullivan dedicated her life to Keller, and overcame her own hardships to become a hero in her own right.

A Dark Childhood

Joanna Mansfield Sullivan—known as Anne or Annie—was born in Feeding Hills, Massachusetts, on April 14, 1866. Her parents were poor Irish immigrants who had three children. Annie's childhood was full of sorrow. When she was very young, she caught an infection called trachoma, which damaged her eyes. Her mother and brother Jimmie suffered from a terrible disease called tuberculosis, which killed her mother when Annie was eight. After her death, Annie's brother and sister were taken in

Anne Sullivan *(right)* poses with her student and friend, Helen Keller.

by relatives, while Annie stayed with her father.

By 1876, Annie's father could no longer care for her, and the family who had taken Jimmie in also had to give him up. The two Sullivan children were sent to the poorhouse in Tewksbury, Massachusetts, where Jimmie died of tuberculosis.

In 1880, Annie asked a group of visitors from the

State Board of Charities if she could leave the poorhouse and go to school. They agreed. On October 7, 1880, she enrolled at the Perkins Institution for the Blind in Boston, Massachusetts.

At Perkins, Annie met a woman named Laura Bridgman. Bridgman was the first deaf and blind person to be educated in the U.S. She communicated through a manual alphabet—a system of signs made on the palm of the hand, so the person could feel them. Anne learned the manual alphabet in order to "speak" with Bridgman. That skill became very important later in Anne Sullivan's life.

> "The most important day I remember in all my life is the one on which my teacher came to me."
>
> —Helen Keller

Helen Keller

In 1886, Sullivan graduated first in her class at Perkins. The following year, she traveled to Tuscumbia, Alabama, to teach a young girl named Helen Keller. Helen, who was six, had lost her sight and hearing when she was 19 months old. Her family had overprotected and spoiled her, and the child had become uncontrollable and frustrated by her inability to communicate with anyone.

Sullivan and Helen moved into a cottage on the Keller estate so they could work together constantly. It took Sullivan months of hard work to overcome Helen's wildness, stubbornness, and fear. Sullivan refused to give up, though. She taught Helen the manual alphabet by constantly spelling words into her hand. Learning this alphabet freed the child from her isolation and allowed her to communicate with others, completely changing her life. Helen called Sullivan "Teacher." The two became an inseparable team. They lived and worked together until Sullivan's death.

In 1900, Keller enrolled at Radcliffe College in Massachusetts, one of the best women's colleges in the country. Sullivan attended all of Keller's classes with her, spelling the lectures into her hand, helping her take notes, and assisting her in submitting

TOPICAL TIDBIT

Louis Braille

During the winters of 1888 to 1890, Helen Keller attended the Perkins Institution to learn the reading system called braille. Braille is a series of raised dots on a surface that spell out letters so that blind people can "read" them with their fingers. It is named for Louis Braille, a Frenchman who was blinded by an accident as a boy. At age 15, he was attending a school for the blind when he encountered an early version of the system. Braille perfected it, working out a code of six dots in a different form for each letter. The reading method called braille continues to give the joy of words to blind people the world over.

exams. When Keller graduated with honors in 1904, the degree belonged as much to Sullivan as it did to Keller.

In 1902, Keller published a best-selling book called *The Story of My Life*. A man named John Macy was hired to edit the book. He and Sullivan fell in love, and married in 1905. The marriage failed, however, and John Macy moved away to Europe in 1913.

By the early 1900s, Helen Keller was a popular celebrity. She and Anne Sullivan traveled around the country together, attending meetings and making public appearances. In 1924, the two women began working as fund-raisers for the American Foundation for the Blind. Sullivan made sure that Keller was rewarded and recognized for her hard work. Her dedication to her pupil and friend won a great deal of admiration for Sullivan. However, even though she worked just as hard as Keller did, she never asked for any recognition for herself.

LIFE EVENTS

1866
Joanna (Anne) Mansfield Sullivan is born in Feeding Hills, Massachusetts.

1880
Sullivan enters Perkins Institution for the Blind.

1887
Sullivan becomes the teacher of Helen Keller.

1905
Sullivan marries John Macy, editor of Keller's autobiography.

1933
Nella Braddy's biography of Sullivan is published.

1936
Sullivan dies.

The Last Years

Throughout her life, Sullivan had trouble seeing because of the eye infection that she had suffered as a child. She was legally blind and had many operations to save what little vision she had. Despite these difficulties, Sullivan remained by Keller's side. She also worked with author Nella Braddy on a biography called *Anne Sullivan Macy: The Story Behind Helen Keller*, which was published in 1933. On October 20, 1936, Anne Sullivan died at the age of 70.

Helen Keller died in 1968. After Sullivan's death, another friend, Polly Thompson, had become Keller's companion. However, Keller and the world realized that no one could ever really take the place of Anne Sullivan, her "Teacher." ◇

Tecumseh
Uniting the Tribes
(born 1768 • died 1813)

As settlers moved westward across the U.S., Native American tribes were usually too small and unprepared to defend themselves against the U.S. government. One Native American leader, Tecumseh, realized that uniting different tribes would give them a better chance to hold onto their lands and culture.

Born a Warrior

Tecumseh was a member of the Shawnee, an Eastern Woodland tribe. He was born in 1768 in what is now the state of Ohio. Tecumseh's father was a Shawnee war chief who was killed fighting white settlers in 1774. When they found his father's body, Tecumseh's mother told her six-year-old son to be a warrior like his father, "a fire spreading over the hill and valley, consuming the race of dark souls."

After his father's death, Tecumseh was adopted by another Shawnee chief, Blackfish. He spent his childhood traveling among different Shawnee settlements.

As he grew, he trained to be a warrior. In time, he developed a reputation as an outstanding leader.

Tecumseh had his first taste of war in 1783, in a battle against a group of white settlers. The young man—15 at the time—was terrified by the fighting and ran away. He was ashamed of his cowardice, and vowed that he would never again run away from a fight.

Fighting for Unity

By the time Tecumseh was 20 years old, he had led many war parties against the American settlers. Then, in 1788, his leg was badly broken when he was thrown from his horse during a buffalo hunt. It healed, but badly. From then on, Tecumseh had one leg shorter than the other. Though he walked with a limp, he refused to let his disability stop him from riding or fighting.

> "Brothers—My people wish for peace. The red men all wish for peace. But where the white people are, there is no peace for them."
>
> —Tecumseh

In 1795, the Shawnee and other Native American tribes were forced to give 25,000 acres of their land to the U.S. in the Treaty of Greenville. The area included most of present-day Ohio, part of Indiana, and what is now Chicago, Illinois, and Detroit, Michigan. Tecumseh was furious about the loss of Shawnee land. He realized that, while individual tribes might win battles, they could never hope to defeat the U.S. Army by themselves. The only way to do that would be to unite all the Eastern Woodland tribes into one group, or confederation.

Tecumseh began visiting different tribes, trying to convince them to join together to defeat the white Americans and save Indian lands. He insisted that no single tribe had the right to sell its land to white settlers, because all Native American land should be held in common. He also spoke against adopting any part of the Americans' way of life. Tecumseh would not use American weapons or tools, wear American clothes, or drink alcohol.

By 1810, Tecumseh had visited every tribe between the Great Lakes and Florida. Returning from one journey, he found that Major General William Henry Harrison had forced a group of chiefs to sell the U.S. 3 million acres of land. Tecumseh was furious. In August 1810, he met with Harrison. He told Harrison, "Sell a country! Why not sell the air, the clouds, and the great sea as well as the earth? Did not the Great Spirit make them all for the use of his children?"

TOPICAL TIDBIT

The Battle of Tippecanoe

In 1811, Tecumseh was away on one of his long journeys when William Henry Harrison moved his troops up the Wabash River in Indiana Territory. Harrison intended to threaten the settlement led by Tecumseh and his brother Tenskwatawa on the Tippecanoe River. Tenskwatawa attacked first, but was badly defeated and had to escape to Canada. Harrison's men burned down the settlement. In 1840, Harrison successfully ran for president of the U.S. using the slogan "Tippecanoe and Tyler too"—referring to his most famous battle and his running mate, John Tyler.

Over the next few years, Tecumseh made many more trips throughout the Eastern Woodland tribes. Many tribes did join Tecumseh's confederation, but Major General Harrison and other army leaders took advantage of Tecumseh's long absences to attack Native American settlements. Tecumseh's brother, Tenskwatawa, was soundly defeated at the Battle of Tippecanoe and forced to flee to Canada. Some tribes responded to the Army's attacks by raiding American settlements, which weakened Tecumseh's confederation.

The War of 1812

On June 18, 1812, the U.S. declared war on Great Britain. Tecumseh quickly swore allegiance to the British. Led by his example, many Eastern Woodland tribes also joined the British in fighting against the Americans during the War of 1812.

Tecumseh was made a brigadier general in the British army and given command of all the Indian forces. In August 1812, Tecumseh won a stunning victory when his forces captured Detroit.

The following year, Tecumseh followed the British army up the Thames River into Ontario, Canada. On October 5, 1813, he was killed in the Battle of the Thames, fighting against his old enemy, William Henry Harrison. His body was taken away by his warriors and buried in a place that has never been discovered.

Tecumseh's death ended the movement to unite the Eastern Woodland tribes. When the Americans won the War of 1812, they refused British demands to set up a separate state for Native Americans. Instead, the Shawnee, along with most of the other Eastern Woodland tribes, were sent to reservations in Oklahoma. No one knows what might have happened if Tecumseh had lived long enough to make his dream of a united Native confederation come true. ◇

LIFE EVENTS

1768
Tecumseh is born to the Shawnee tribe near present-day Springfield, Ohio.

1795
Tecumseh refuses to recognize the Treaty of Greenville, which gives away Indian land to the U.S.

1811
Tenskwatawa, Tecumseh's brother, is defeated in the Battle of Tippecanoe.

1812
During the War of 1812, Tecumseh joins the British against U.S. forces at the Battle of Detroit.

1813
Tecumseh is killed at the Battle of Thames River in Ontario, Canada.

Sojourner Truth
"Ain't I a Woman?"
(born 1797? • died 1883)

During the fights to end slavery and win equal rights for women, few voices were as powerful as Sojourner Truth's. This hard-working former slave inspired people all over the country to rethink their views on equality.

A Northern Slave

Slavery was legal in New York State when a black child named Isabella was born sometime around 1797 in Ulster County, New York. In 1808, Isabella's master died and all his slaves were sold. Isabella's new master beat her and didn't provide warm clothing or shoes for her to wear. When Isabella's father found out what was happening, he persuaded a couple named the Schryvers to buy his daughter. The Schryvers treated Isabella more kindly, but later they sold her to John Dumont, a farmer from New Paltz, New York. Isabella worked for the Dumonts from 1810 until 1826, when she left to live with another

family, who were members of the Quaker religion.

When Isabella was 14, she married another slave named Thomas, who also belonged to John Dumont. Thomas was much older than Isabella, but they had a good marriage and five children together.

Legal Battles

In 1826, Isabella's six-year-old son, Peter, was sold to a man in Alabama, even though it was illegal in New York to sell a slave to someone in another state. Isabella was determined to get her child back. Her Quaker friends agreed to help. They took Isabella to the court-house in Kingston, New York, where she filed a complaint.

The court agreed with Isabella, but Peter's new owner refused to return him. Isabella went back to court and, after many delays, finally got her son back. She was one of the first black women in the country to ever win a court case.

> "The Lord gave me *Truth*, because I was to declare truth unto people."
> —Sojourner Truth, on receiving her name

A New Life

In 1827, New York passed a law freeing all slaves in the state. However, it was difficult for the freed slaves to find work. Isabella could not afford to care for all of her children. While her four daughters lived with their father, Isabella and Peter traveled to New York City, where there were more jobs.

Shortly after their arrival in New York, Isabella joined the Methodist church. There she had a powerful religious experience in which, she later said, God revealed himself to her and she realized "that there was no place where God was not."

In 1843, Isabella changed her name to Sojourner Truth, saying that God had chosen the name for her. She began preaching at religious meetings in New York, Connecticut, and Massachusetts. At first, Sojourner Truth's speeches focused on religious matters, but she soon spoke out for social reform, too. She insisted that blacks and women be included in any fight for equality.

In 1851, Truth spoke at a women's rights convention in Akron, Ohio. In her speech, she mocked people who thought that women were too weak and fool-

TOPICAL TIDBIT

The First Freedom Rider

Sojourner Truth desegregated public transportation a century before the civil-rights movement. One day in 1864, as she tried to board a Washington, D.C., streetcar with a white friend, the conductor told her to leave. When Truth refused, the conductor pulled at her with such force that he sprained her shoulder. "Does she belong to you?" the conductor angrily asked Truth's friend. "She does not belong to me, but she belongs to Humanity," the friend replied. Truth and her friend reported the conductor, who was fired and arrested. "It is hard for the old slave-holding spirit to die," Truth said, "but die it must."

ish to be given the same rights as men. "Look at me! Look at my arm!" she said, rolling up her sleeve to show how muscular it was. "I have plowed, and planted, and gathered [crops] into barns, and no man could head me. And ain't I a woman? I could work as much and eat as much as a man— when I could get it—and bear the lash [whip] as well! And ain't I a woman?"

Truth's speech electrified the crowd. Her now-famous words showed that expecting a person to be inferior because of his or her sex or skin color was ridiculous.

For the next six years, Truth was a popular speaker throughout the U.S. During the Civil War, she gathered supplies for black volunteer regiments, and was also invited to the White House to meet President Abraham Lincoln.

After the war, Truth worked with the National Freedmen's

LIFE EVENTS

About 1797
Isabella is born a slave in Ulster County, New York.

1827
New York State outlaws slavery.

1843
Isabella changes her name to Sojourner Truth and dedicates her life to preaching.

1851
Sojourner Truth makes her famous "Ain't I a Woman" speech to a women's rights convention in Akron, Ohio.

1864
Truth is received by President Lincoln at the White House.

1875
Truth retires to Battle Creek, Michigan. She dies in 1883.

Relief Association and the Freedmen's Bureau, helping newly freed slaves find jobs and places to live. She also took part in the American Woman Suffrage Association, which fought to give women the right to vote.

Sojourner Truth finally retired in 1880, at the age of 83. She moved to Battle Creek, Michigan, where she lived with two of her daughters until her death on November 26, 1883. When she died, a Battle Creek newspaper said, "This country has lost one of its most remarkable personages." However, Truth's dedication to the causes of equality and justice still lives on today. ◇

Harriet Tubman
A Passage to Freedom
(born 1820 • died 1913)

Harriet Tubman was a slave who never learned to read or write. However, her courage and determination won her freedom, and the freedom of countless other slaves as well. She helped open the nation's eyes to the injustice of slavery.

A Harsh Childhood

Harriet Ross was born near Buckstown, Maryland, in 1820. She was one of 11 children in a family of slaves who belonged to a man named Edward Brodas. Harriet and her family worked on Brodas's plantation, planting and harvesting crops. After a long day of backbreaking work, they slept on rags on the dirt floor of a one-room shack.

Harriet started working when she was only three, delivering messages to other plantations. By the time she was nine, she was cleaning her master's house, taking care of his children, and working in the fields.

When Harriet was 15, she went into a shop where a

This statue, called *Step on Board*, honors Harriet Tubman *(front left)* leading slaves to freedom. It stands in Boston, Massachusetts.

man and his slave were fighting. Suddenly, the master threw a heavy iron weight at his slave. The weight accidentally hit Harriet in the forehead and almost killed her. For the rest of her life, she had a horrible scar and suffered terrible headaches and blackouts.

Escape!

By 1849, Harriet was married to a man named John Tubman. That year, she heard that her master was going to sell many of his slaves. Harriet didn't want to be sold, so she decided to escape. Her husband refused to go with her, so she left without him.

Harriet Tubman traveled north with the help of the Underground Railroad. The Underground Railroad was not a system of trains. It was a network of black and white people who led slaves north, where slavery was illegal. These "conductors" gave directions or rides, or provided safe places for escaping slaves to sleep. The system was called a railroad because it used specific routes, and stops along the way were called stations. "Underground" meant that it was secret.

> "I looked at my hands to see if I was the same person, now that I was free."
>
> —Harriet Tubman, on first reaching freedom

With the railroad's help, Harriet Tubman made the long, frightening journey and finally reached Philadelphia, Pennsylvania. At last, she was free!

Tubman got a job in a hotel kitchen. However, even though she was free, she couldn't stop thinking about all the slaves she had left behind. So, risking her life and her freedom, she traveled back into the South to lead other slaves to freedom—again and again.

The Underground Railroad had never seen a conductor like Tubman. She carefully planned every detail of her trips. She knew how to find her way through the woods at night, and where to find food and shelter. She even provided sleeping pills to babies so they wouldn't cry during the journey.

The arrows show Underground Railroad routes that slaves took from slave states to freedom in the northern U.S. and Canada.

When one man panicked and wanted to go back, Tubman refused to let him leave. She pointed a gun at him and said, "Move or die." The man kept going.

Tubman made 19 trips on the Underground Railroad and led more than 300 slaves to freedom. She became known as Moses, after the biblical figure who set his people free from slavery in Egypt. Soon Tubman was a hero among slaves—and hated by slave owners. The owners put up a reward of $40,000 for Tubman's capture—a huge sum of money in those days. However, Harriet Tubman was never caught, and neither was anyone who traveled with her.

Harriet the Spy

When the Civil War began between the North and South in 1861, Tubman took on another dangerous

TOPICAL TIDBIT

The Underground Railroad

When Harriet Tubman made her escape to freedom, she was given a piece of paper with two names and directions to a house. At the house, she was hidden in a wagon, covered with a sack, and driven to another house. In this way, she eventually reached Philadelphia. Many people were required to make the Underground Railroad work, and all of them put themselves in great danger. Historians estimate that 40,000 to 100,000 slaves made their way to freedom by way of the Underground Railroad.

assignment. She spent three years as a spy for the Union army. Tubman's knowledge of the woods and countryside was a huge help to Union leaders as they planned attacks on Southern forts and cities. Tubman also served as a nurse, and even led troops into battle.

When the war finally ended in 1865, Tubman moved to New York State. She took orphans and elderly people into her house and enjoyed sharing stories of her life with anyone who stopped by. Tubman also spoke out for women's rights, urging women to "stand together" in their fight for equality.

Tubman died of pneumonia in 1913, at the age of 93, and was given the honor of a military funeral by the government. In 1998, First Lady Hillary Rodham Clinton called her "a symbol of the enduring spirit of this nation." ◇

LIFE EVENTS

1820
Harriet Ross is born into slavery near Buckstown, Maryland.

1849
Now Harriet Tubman, she escapes from slavery.

1850
Tubman begins her work on the Underground Railroad by smuggling her family out of Maryland.

1862
Tubman serves as a spy and scout for the Union army in South Carolina.

1869
Tubman marries Nelson Davis in Auburn, New York.

1908
Tubman opens her home for the aged and poor in Auburn, New York. She dies in 1913.

Mary Edwards Walker

Army Doctor

(born 1832 • died 1919)

Only recently have women been accepted into the armed forces and given the same opportunities as men. During the Civil War, however, Mary Edwards Walker served on battlefields and became the only woman ever to earn a Congressional Medal of Honor.

Strong Opinions

Mary Edwards Walker was born in Oswego, New York, on November 26, 1832. Her father was a doctor who believed strongly in education and equality for women. Following his example, Mary grew up believing in women's rights. She also became a follower of Amelia Bloomer, who called for more comfortable and practical clothes for women. As an adult, Mary Edwards Walker followed Bloomer's example of wearing loose-fitting pants (which became known as "bloomers") instead of the tight-fitting, bulky, and

uncomfortable dresses women were expected to wear.

In 1855, Walker graduated from Syracuse Medical College. She was the only woman in her class and only the second woman to graduate from a U.S. medical school. The following year, she married another doctor, Albert Miller. Walker broke with tradition by keeping her own name instead of taking her husband's. The couple set up a medical practice together, but the business failed because most people would not accept a female doctor. Walker and Miller separated several years later, and were divorced in 1869.

On the Battlefield

In 1861, the U.S. Civil War broke out between the North and South. Walker traveled to Washington, D.C., and tried to join the Union Army. When she was refused a commission as a medical officer, Walker volunteered as an acting assistant surgeon at the U.S. Patent Office Hospital in Washington. She was the first female surgeon in the United States Army.

> "Dr. Mary lost the medal simply because she was a hundred years ahead of her time."
>
> —a relative of Mary Edwards Walker, to *The New York Times*

In 1863, General George H. Thomas appointed Walker assistant surgeon in the Army of the Cumberland. This finally placed her on the battlefield. Walker served near the front lines for almost two years. She cared for hundreds of sick, injured, and dying soldiers, despite shortages of medicines and supplies. She also served as a spy, and crossed Confederate lines to treat civilians.

Walker was captured by Confederate forces in 1864. She spent four months in a prison in Richmond, Virginia, before being exchanged for a Confederate officer held prisoner by the Union army. Between her release and the war's end in April 1865, Walker worked at a prison for women in Louisville, Kentucky.

The Medal of Honor

On November 11, 1865, President Andrew Johnson awarded the Congressional Medal of Honor to Walker for her contributions to the war effort. She was the only woman to ever receive the Medal,

TOPICAL TIDBIT

Walt Whitman

One of the most famous volunteers of the Civil War is also one of America's greatest poets—Walt Whitman. When his brother George was wounded in the Battle of Fredericksburg, Virginia, in December 1862, Whitman rushed from his home in Brooklyn, New York, to the field hospital. After George recovered, Whitman took a job in nearby Washington, D.C. In his spare time, he volunteered his services to the wounded soldiers in the Army hospital. He read to the men, wrote letters for them, and spent what little money he had on small comforts for them. The poet stayed in Washington through the end of the war.

which is the country's highest military award.

After the war ended, Walker was elected president of the National Dress Reform Association, a group that campaigned for more comfortable and sensible clothes for women. She often dressed as a man, including a top hat, bow tie, and long coat. Several times, she was arrested for masquerading as a man, a charge that she found ridiculous.

Meanwhile, Walker's war work was publicized by several women's rights organizations, making her a hero to feminists. Walker worked for a variety of social reforms, including the campaign for women's right to vote. Walker attended political meetings and conventions, although she wasn't always allowed to speak. She also wrote several books.

In 1917, Walker received stunning news. Congress had changed the rules for award-

LIFE EVENTS

1832
Mary Edwards Walker is born in Oswego, New York.

1855
Walker graduates from Syracuse Medical College—the second woman to graduate from a U.S. medical school.

1861
The Civil War begins. Walker volunteers and becomes the first female surgeon in the U.S. Army.

1864
Confederate forces capture Walker and hold her prisoner for four months.

1865
Walker is awarded the Congressional Medal of Honor.

1871
Walker publishes the autobiographical book *Hit*. She dies in 1919.

ing the Medal of Honor and would now recognize only people who had been in "actual combat with an enemy." Walker, along with 910 other people, was asked to return her Medal. She refused to return hers, and continued to wear it every day until her death. In 1977, President Jimmy Carter reinstated Walker's medal, citing her "self-sacrifice, patriotism, dedication, and unflinching loyalty to her country, despite the apparent discrimination because of her sex."

Dr. Mary Edwards Walker died in Oswego, New York, on February 21, 1919—just a few months before women were finally awarded the right to vote. In 1982, the U.S. issued a stamp to honor Walker as the first woman to be awarded the Congressional Medal of Honor. ◇

George Washington
Father of the United States
(born 1732 • died 1799)

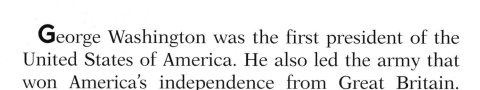

George Washington was the first president of the United States of America. He also led the army that won America's independence from Great Britain. Without him, the country might not even exist today.

Longing for Adventure

George Washington was born in the British colony of Virginia on February 22, 1732, and grew up on the family's estate, Ferry Farm. There, he learned to shoot and hunt. He also went to school and learned reading, writing, and arithmetic.

When George was 11 years old, his father died suddenly. For the next few years, he lived at home with his mother and younger siblings. However, by the time he was a teenager, George was getting restless. His older half-brother, Lawrence, suggested that he join the British Royal Navy, but George's mother refused to let him go. The boy was stuck at home, longing for adventure.

George Leaves Home

George spent a lot of time at Lawrence's estate, Mount Vernon. There, he heard about land in western Virginia that was being given to people by the government. When George was 16, he joined a party to survey (take and record measurements) those new lands.

George loved being a surveyor. The job gave him the chance to explore the wilderness. He rode his horse through thick woods and over streams. He saw Native American tribes and slept under the stars. He used some of his surveyor's pay to buy land in Virginia's Shenandoah Valley.

When George Washington was 20, his half-brother Lawrence died of tuberculosis. Lawrence left his estate of Mount Vernon to George, and it became his new home. George Washington also applied for Lawrence's position in the Virginia militia, or army. As a member of the militia, he fought with the British against Native Americans and French soldiers in the French and Indian War (1754-1763).

Commander in Chief

During the 1750s, Washington left the militia and settled down to farm his plantation at Mount Vernon. He also won election to Virginia's House of Burgesses. For the next 15 years, Washington lived quietly with his wife, Martha, and two stepchildren. Then, in 1775, the American Revolution broke out—and forever changed his life.

When the American colonies began calling for independence from Great Britain, Congress knew that the new country needed a strong military leader to command its army against the much more powerful British forces. Congress asked George Washington to take the job. Washington did not want to leave his comfortable life at Mount Vernon, but he believed in American independence, so he said yes.

Washington won early victories in Boston, Massachusetts, and New York City. However, he was forced to give up New York to the British, and he and his men struggled through a bitterly cold winter at Valley Forge, Pennsylvania, in 1777-1778.

Many of the American soldiers, who were poorly paid and ill-supplied, wanted to leave the army during those difficult times. However, Washington asked them to stay. His deep belief in American independence inspired his men, and most of them stayed with him and continued to fight.

> "The fate of unborn millions will now depend, under God, on the courage and conduct of this army. We have, therefore, to resolve to conquer or die."
>
> —George Washington, before the Battle of Long Island, 1776

The Nation's First President

The war finally came to an end in 1783, and the newly independent nation needed a leader. Once again, Washington's name came up. Did he want to be king of the new United States?

Washington refused that honor. He had fought a war to get away from the British king, and he was not about to become king himself. Instead, he went home to Mount Vernon.

Despite his wishes, his service to the U.S. wasn't over yet. When electors in each state cast ballots for America's first president, every single vote went to Washington. This time, he accepted the call to leadership. On April 30, 1789, he was sworn in as the first president of the United States of America in New York City, which was then the nation's capital.

Washington served two terms as president. During that time, he faced many decisions about whether the new country should have a strong central gov-

TOPICAL TIDBIT

Washington Crosses the Delaware

The war was going very badly for the colonists in December 1776. General Washington had just been driven out of New York, and the English were counting on an easy victory. Then Washington decided on a bold stroke. On Christmas Eve, he took 2,400 men across the icy Delaware River and launched a surprise attack against the enemy at Trenton, New Jersey. It was a shocking success, and gave the colonists a priceless boost of morale at a dismal time. The heroic painting *Washington Crossing the Delaware* by Emanuel Leutze, painted in 1851, is one of the most famous images in American history.

ernment or if individual states should have more power. Washington helped set up the central government we have today. He was considered a wise and fair leader.

During his presidency, the country's leaders decided to create a Federal City to be the nation's permanent capital. In time, the city was named Washington, D.C., after him.

George Washington refused to run for a third term as president and returned to Mount Vernon in 1797. On December 14, 1799, he died at his beloved home. Today, he is still honored in the names of many cities, towns, mountains, lakes, and schools around the country, as well as on countless monuments, including Mount Rushmore in South Dakota. His contributions to America will never be forgotten. ◇

LIFE EVENTS

1732
George Washington is born in Westmoreland County, Virginia.

1775
Washington is appointed head of the Continental Army.

1777
Washington and his men begin the long winter at Valley Forge.

1781
Washington accepts the surrender of British General Charles Cornwallis at Yorktown, Maryland.

1789
Washington becomes the first president of the United States.

1797
Washington retires to Mount Vernon. He dies in 1799.

Roger Williams
A Home for Freedom
(born 1603? • died 1683)

Today, Americans take it for granted that we can practice whatever religion we want. We owe much of that freedom to a brave man named Roger Williams. He was the first religious leader in America to declare that everyone should be free to worship as he or she chooses.

London Born and Bred

No one is sure exactly when Roger Williams was born, but historians generally agree that it was around 1603. He was born in London, England, the center of Great Britain's government and cultural life.

Roger's father was a merchant and tailor. The Williams family lived in a comfortable home near the Thames River. Like most other boys of his economic class, young Roger went to school. He also spent a great deal of time studying the Bible.

In 1621, Roger Williams met a judge named Sir Edward Coke. Coke was impressed with the young

man and hired Williams as his secretary. He also arranged for Williams to attend one of England's best schools. In 1627, Williams graduated from Cambridge University. Two years later, he was ordained as a minister.

Roger Williams had strong religious beliefs that went against the teachings of the Church of England. After he found himself in trouble with church leaders, he decided to sail for America on December 1, 1630.

Trouble in Massachusetts

When Williams arrived in the Massachusetts colony, he was quickly offered the position of minister to the Boston congregation. However, he turned it down because he thought that that the Boston church was too similar to the Church of England. Instead, he moved to Plymouth, Massachusetts, where he farmed and preached. Later, he became a minister in Salem, Massachusetts, even though the colony's Puritan leaders opposed his appointment.

> "I acknowledge that to molest any person, Jew or Gentile, for . . . practicing worship merely religious or spiritual, it is to persecute him."
>
> —Roger Williams

The more Williams spoke out for freedom of religion, the more the leaders disliked him. He also made enemies when he said that there should be a complete separation of church and government. This meant that the government could not punish somebody who broke a church law. Only the church should handle such matters, Williams said.

Another belief that got him in trouble was that Native Americans should be treated fairly. While in Plymouth, Williams had become friends with the Narragansett Indians. In Salem, he declared that no one in Massachusetts had the right to take any land unless they bought it fairly from the Native Americans, because the Native Americans had been here and lived on the land first.

By October 1635, the Massachusetts colony's leaders had had enough of Roger Williams and his dangerous ideas. In a trial in the Massachusetts General Court, Williams was called an "offensive rebel" and an "evil-worker," and was exiled (sent away) from the colony. However, since winter was coming and Williams's wife was expecting a baby, he was allowed to stay until spring, as long as he stopped preaching.

Williams did not stop preaching. Instead, he gathered about 20 followers and planned to form a new colony. When Massachusetts leaders found out

TOPICAL TIDBIT

The Narragansett Indians

Roger Williams and his followers owed their survival in the wilderness to the peaceful Narrangansett Indians of present-day Rhode Island. In time, however, new white settlers claimed more and more territory from the New England Indian tribes. In 1675, warriors of the Wampanoag tribe fought back. Other tribes, including the Narragansett, joined them in a series of bloody battles that became known as King Philip's War. (King Philip was the English name for Metacom, the Wampanoag chief.) The war was a tragedy for the Indians. When they lost, they split up and abandoned the area to the settlers.

what Williams was planning, they sent troops to arrest him. However, Williams had been warned of the plan. He and his followers escaped into the wilderness.

A New Colony

The Native Americans cared for Williams and his friends and helped them survive the winter. In the spring of 1636, Williams founded the settlement of Providence, on land that he purchased from the Narragansett Indians. Providence's government was based on complete religious freedom and the separation of church and state. Every household had a voice in the government and received an equal share of the land. Soon the colony became a welcoming home for people who didn't agree with the strict rules of other colonies.

Williams also continued working with the Narragan-

LIFE EVENTS

About 1603
Roger Williams is born in London, England.

1631
Williams arrives in Boston, in the Massachusetts Bay Colony.

1635
Williams is banished from Massachusetts for preaching heresy (ideas opposed by church leaders).

1636
Williams founds the settlement of Providence in what today is Rhode Island.

1654
Williams becomes president of the colony of Rhode Island. He serves three terms. He dies in 1683.

sett Indians. He negotiated peace treaties between the Narragansett and other tribes, and helped settle or avoid conflicts between Native Americans and English settlers.

In 1643, Williams traveled to England to obtain a charter (written legal document) from the king. The charter made the settlements of Rhode Island and "the Providence Plantations in Narragansett Bay" into a new colony. In 1654, he was elected to the first of three terms as the first president of the colony.

Roger Williams remained active in his colony's political life until his death early in 1683. He lived his life as an honest, generous, open-minded man who respected everyone, no matter what they believed in or whether they were European or Native American. His ideas helped shape the ideals and laws of the United States, a nation born nearly a century after his death. ◇

Chuck Yeager
Breaking the Sound Barrier
(born 1923)

In 1947, pilot Chuck Yeager did something that many people thought was not only dangerous, but physically impossible: He flew a plane faster than the speed of sound.

A Loner

Charles Elwood Yeager was born near Myra, West Virginia, on February 13, 1923. When he was four, his family moved to the nearby town of Hamlin. Chuck was good at math, but not very interested in school. He preferred to be out in the woods, exploring, hunting, or fishing. The boy was well-liked, but had a reputation as a loner who did things his own way.

Chuck's father owned a drilling business, and Chuck was fascinated by the machinery. He also enjoyed working on cars. After he graduated from high school in 1941, several people suggested that Chuck join the Army. After an Army recruiter told him that he could be a pilot, Chuck was ready to go.

Earning His Wings

Chuck Yeager was studying aircraft mechanics in California on December 7, 1941, when the Japanese bombed Pearl Harbor. That attack prompted the U.S. to join World War II. Yeager was eager to learn how to fly in combat. Even though he became airsick during his first few flights, he soon won his pilot's wings. On March 10, 1943, Yeager was named a flight officer. By 1944, he was stationed in England and flying in combat missions over Europe.

During the war, Yeager flew 64 missions and shot

down 13 German planes. His most frightening moment came on March 5, 1944, when he was shot down over German-occupied France. Yeager made his way across the border into Spain and, finally, back to his unit in England. During the journey, he and a companion were almost captured by

> "Somehow I always managed to live to fly another day."
> —Chuck Yeager

German soldiers, and Yeager's companion was seriously injured. Yeager saved the man's life and received the Bronze Star for his "complete disregard for his personal safety."

When the war ended in 1945, the Army assigned Yeager to be a flight instructor at an airfield in Texas. For Yeager, this job was boring after the excitement of combat flying. In 1945, Yeager became a test pilot at Wright Air Field in Dayton, Ohio. His job was to check out planes after they had been repaired and to inspect new planes being put into service.

The Mysterious Sound Barrier

By the mid-1940s, pilots could fly faster than ever before. However, something unusual happened when pilots flew very fast. The plane would shake and rock, and the controls would go wild. Some pilots couldn't control their planes, and were killed in crashes. The problem was something called the sound barrier.

When planes fly, they push waves of air in front of them. As they approach the speed of sound, called Mach 1—about 760 miles per hour—the air in front of the planes has less time to move out of the way, making something like a wall of air that must be pushed through. This puts dangerous strains on the plane. At the time, many people believed that if a plane ever actually did reach Mach 1, it would crash into the built-up waves of air and be destroyed.

There was only one way to find out what might happen if a pilot flew faster than the speed of sound: Do it. A rocket-powered plane, called the Bell X-1, was designed to "break the sound barrier." Chuck

TOPICAL TIDBIT

The Right Stuff

Being a test pilot is a life of constant danger. In 1953, Chuck Yeager reached Mach 2.4 in his jet, only to spin out of control at 80,000 feet. He plunged down 51,000 feet in 51 seconds (1,000 feet per second!) before regaining control. In 1963, Yeager again lost control and became the first pilot to eject himself from a jet in a pressurized suit used for high altitudes. The suit then caught fire from burning debris that was tangled up in the parachute. Yeager's coolness under pressure was the very definition of the kind of bravery that writer Tom Wolfe called *The Right Stuff.*

Yeager was chosen to be the pilot of that plane. He named it the *Glamorous Glennis*, after his wife.

On October 14, 1947, a B-29 bomber carried the X-1 up to 25,000 feet. Then Yeager climbed into the X-1 and released it from the B-29. His jet's rockets roared into life and Yeager zoomed up to 42,000 feet. He picked up speed, watching as the indicator moved to 1.07 Mach—just past the speed of sound. Meanwhile, on the ground, scientists heard a distant bang. Yeager had safely broken the sound barrier—and caused the first sonic boom.

After the Flight

For security reasons, Yeager's remarkable achievement was kept secret for eight months. When the news was finally released, he became a national hero.

LIFE EVENTS

1923
Chuck Yeager is born in Myra, West Virginia.

1944
Fighter pilot Yeager is shot down over France during World War II.

1945
Yeager earns the title of "ace" with five confirmed "kills" of German aircraft in one day.

1947
Test pilot Yeager breaks the sound barrier in a Bell X-1 jet.

1976
President Gerald R. Ford awards Yeager the Congressional Medal for bravery.

1985
Yeager's auto-biography, *Yeager*, is published.

Yeager remained in the supersonic (faster than sound) flight program until 1954. He set several new records, including a world speed record of 1,650 miles per hour in 1953. Later, he commanded a fighter-jet squadron in West Germany and served as a wing commander in Korea and Vietnam.

By the time Chuck Yeager retired in 1975, he was a brigadier general. He wrote an autobiography, *Yeager*, published in 1985, and was a subject of *The Right Stuff*, a popular book and movie. His fearlessness, dedication, and competitive spirit helped shatter a much-feared barrier. ◇

Alvin York
Patriotic Soldier
(born 1887 • died 1964)

Alvin York placed his dedication to his country above his personal beliefs and left home to fight in World War I. He became one of the most heroic and admired soldiers in American history.

A Wild Young Man

Alvin Cullum York was born in Pall Mall, Tennessee, on December 13, 1887. He was the third of eleven children. Alvin's father, William, was a farmer and a blacksmith. He was so well-respected by his neighbors that he was often asked to settle arguments among them. William York passed his sense of honesty and fair dealing on to his children.

The York family was poor, and young Alvin learned to hunt as a way of putting food on the table. He became an excellent shot and was very much at home in the forest. When he was a little older, he left school to go to work in his father's blacksmith shop.

When Alvin York was 24, his father died, and the

young man took on the responsibility of supporting his mother and younger siblings. However, the loss of his father and the pressure of his new obligations made York wild. He worked hard during the week, but spent the weekends drinking, gambling, and fighting. In time, though, he was able to turn his life around. A religious conversion and the efforts of his mother and the woman he later married persuaded York to stop drinking.

A Conscientious Objector Goes to War

In 1917, the U.S. entered World War I. Because of York's religious faith, he believed that it was wrong to go to war. People who did not want to go to war for religious or other personal beliefs were called conscientious objectors. They were sometimes excused from military service.

Even though York believed that war was wrong, he also believed that he had a duty to his country. After much soul-searching, he decided

> "Sir, it is not man power. A higher power than man guided and watched over me and told me what to do."
>
> —Alvin York to a general, about his bravery in the Argonne

that he had to put his country first. He reported for military duty on November 14, 1917, and left immediately for basic training. On May 1, 1918, he sailed for England. By the end of June, he was on the battlefield in France.

York's first few months in France were relatively quiet. Then, on October 8, he took part in the fierce fighting of the Battle of the Argonne. He and 16 other U.S. soldiers were ordered to capture a German machine-gun unit. York and his comrades surprised the Germans while they were having breakfast, and captured them. But another German machine-gun emplacement on a nearby hill had the Americans in full view. The Germans began pouring fire down on them. Half of York's patrol was killed, including the officer in charge. York was caught, by himself, out in the open.

"I didn't have time to dodge behind a tree or dive into the brush, I didn't even have time to kneel or lie down," he said later. Instead, he stood his ground and, with deadly accuracy, quickly shot down 25

TOPICAL TIDBIT

Sergeant York, the Movie

In May 1919, a movie producer named Jesse Lasky leaned out of his eighth-floor window in New York to watch Alvin York pass by in his ticker-tape parade. For years, Lasky tried to make a movie of York's adventures, but York refused to cooperate. Not only did he hate war, he believed that movies were sinful. In time, Adolf Hitler changed York's mind. In 1940, Hitler was conquering Europe, and America had to do something. York finally said yes to Lasky, hoping that his story would inspire others. The movie *Sergeant York*, starring Gary Cooper, reached theaters in July 1941. It was only one way Alvin York insisted that America had to stop Adolf Hitler.

enemy gunners, one by one. Finally, the rest of the Germans surrendered. On the way back to their lines, Corporal York and his seven remaining companions took a total of 132 prisoners.

When they turned over their prisoners, York received a tremendous amount of attention. Even though he downplayed his efforts, he received a field promotion to sergeant and was honored as "having a far-reaching effect in relieving the enemy pressure against American forces in the heart of the Argonne Forest."

Sergeant York remained on the front lines until November 1. The war ended ten days later. He spent the next six months traveling in France, speaking to French soldiers. He also received America's Distinguished Service Cross and the Congressional Medal of Honor, as well as the French Croix de Guerre (Cross of War).

Back Home

York discovered that he was a huge celebrity in America when he arrived in New Jersey on May 22, 1919. After a ticker-tape parade in New York City, Sergeant York was honored in Washington, D.C. Finally, on May 29, he arrived back home in Pall Mall.

Even though he was back in Tennessee, life was not quiet for Alvin York. He was offered a lot of money to promote products and write books. He refused all those offers, deciding instead to help the people in his hometown. He established the York Foundation and founded a school to educate poor children living in the Tennessee mountains. York accepted donations for his project. He also funded it by making speeches and other public appearances. The school, the Alvin C. York Institute, is still in operation today.

Later in life, York was disabled by illness and was bedridden for the last 10 years of his life. Alvin York died on September 2, 1964, at the Veterans' Hospital in Nashville, Tennessee. He was 76 years old. About 8,000 people attended his military funeral, including representatives from the U.S. government as well as his friends and neighbors. All were there to pay tribute to an American hero. ◇

LIFE EVENTS

1887
Alvin York is born in Pall Mall, Tennessee.

1917
York is drafted for World War I.

1918
Corporal York's day of bravery in the Argonne forest wins him the Congressional Medal of Honor.

1926
York founds the Alvin C. York Institute in Fentress County, Tennessee.

1928
York's autobiography, *Sergeant York, His Own Life Story and War Diary*, is published.

1941
Sergeant York, a movie based on his adventures, is released. Alvin York dies in 1964.

ony • Neil Armstrong • Crispus Attucks • James Baldwin • Clara
ey • John Brown • Ralph Bunche • Richard Byrd • Kit Carson • Ra
Davy Crockett • Benjamin O. Davis Jr. • Thomas A. Dooley • Fred
in Franklin • Varian Fry • Geronimo • John Glenn • Ulysses S. Gra
trick Henry • Wild Bill Hickok • Samuel Houston • Anne Hutchin
ef Joseph • John F. Kennedy • Bob Kerrey • Billie Jean King • Ma
vis and William Clark • Abraham Lincoln • Charles Lindbergh • De
ll • John McCain • John Muir • Audie Murphy • Thomas Paine • R
• Oliver Hazard Perry • John J. Pershing • Molly Pitcher • Pocah
Ride • Matthew B. Ridgway • Jackie Robinson • Eleanor Roosev
Shepard • Robert Smalls • Elizabeth Cady Stanton • Anne Sulli
ge Washington • Roger Williams • Chuck Yeager • Alvin York • Sa
eil Armstrong • Crispus Attucks • James Baldwin • Clara Barton •
n Brown • Ralph Bunche • Richard Byrd • Kit Carson • Rachel Cars
ett • Benjamin O. Davis Jr. • Thomas A. Dooley • Frederick Doug
n • Varian Fry • Geronimo • John Glenn • Ulysses S. Grant • Woo
nry • Wild Bill Hickok • Samuel Houston • Anne Hutchinson • A
• John F. Kennedy • Bob Kerrey • Billie Jean King • Martin Luthe
iam Clark • Abraham Lincoln • Charles Lindbergh • Douglas MacA
McCain • John Muir • Audie Murphy • Thomas Paine • Rosa Parks
r Hazard Perry • John J. Pershing • Molly Pitcher • Pocahontas •
Matthew B. Ridgway • Jackie Robinson • Eleanor Roosevelt • Fra
• Robert Smalls • Elizabeth Cady Stanton • Anne Sullivan • Tecu
gton • Roger Williams • Chuck Yeager • Alvin York • Samuel Ada
rong • Crispus Attucks • James Baldwin • Clara Barton • Daisy Ba
n • Ralph Bunche • Richard Byrd • Kit Carson • Rachel Carson • J
t • Benjamin O. Davis Jr. • Thomas A. Dooley • Frederick Douglas
n • Varian Fry • Geronimo • John Glenn • Ulysses S. Grant • Woo
nry • Wild Bill Hickok • Samuel Houston • Anne Hutchinson • A
• John F. Kennedy • Bob Kerrey • Billie Jean King • Martin Luthe
iam Clark • Abraham Lincoln • Charles Lindbergh • Douglas MacA
McCain • John Muir • Audie Murphy • Thomas Paine • Rosa Parks